ARTHUR MACHEN

SELECTED LETTERS

The private writings of the Master of the Macabre

Edited by
Roger Dobson, Godfrey Brangham
and R. A. Gilbert

THE AQUARIAN PRESS

First published 1988

British Library Cataloguing in Publication Data

Machen, Arthur, *1863–1947*
Selected letters
1. Fiction in English. Machen, Arthur,
1863–1947
I. Title   II   Dobson, Roger.
III.   Brangham, Godfrey   IV.   Gilbert, R.A.
823'.8

ISBN 0–85030–782–1

*The Aquarian Press is part of the Thorsons Publishing Group,
Wellingborough, Northamptonshire, NN8 2RQ, England*

Printed in Great Britain by MacKays of Chatham, Kent

1   3   5   7   9   10   8   6   4   2

ARTHUR MACHEN SELECTED LETTERS

Frontispiece: Arthur Machen in 1909 (photograph by E. O. Hoppé).

PREFACE

Since Arthur Machen's death in 1947 his reputation has risen to new heights. He has once more attained cult status, not only in Britain and the United States but all over the world. His fiction, translated into a number of languages including French, Italian and Japanese, is read and admired more extensively than at any time during his own day. His mystical Celtic romances *The Hill of Dreams* and *The Secret Glory* continue to intoxicate fresh devotees through their incomparable evocations of landscape. The best of his influential and disquieting works of supernatural horror, while possessing many imperfections, transcend the confines of their sensationalistic tradition by reflecting a genuine spiritual philosophy, the keynote of which is that 'man is made a mystery for mysteries and visions'. Machen's memoirs, *Far Off Things* and *Things Near and Far*, figure among the greatest autobiographical writing of our time, while *Hieroglyphics*, that challenging exposition of his artistic credo, is revered as a minor classic. Critical and biographical studies of Machen have been published, and a succession of enthusiasts have issued a wealth of ephemera by and about him since John Gawsworth began the tradition in the 1930s. Poets have hymned Machen in verse, musicians have woven melodies under the spell of his works, and artists have delighted in capturing his features. Over the years his writings have drawn applause from such diverse figures as John Betjeman, Jorge Luis Borges, Walter de la Mare, John Dos Passos, Jerome K. Jerome, Joseph Wood Krutch, H. P. Lovecraft, John Masefield, and Henry Miller. First editions of his books inevitably command impressive sums. And more than 70 years on, the legend of the Angels of Mons, which sprang from Machen's minor fantasy 'The Bowmen', still survives as an old soldier's tale.

The Machen cult has waxed and waned, and renewed its power in keeping with the vagaries of literary tastes, since its birth in America after the end of the First World War. After spending almost 40 years writing in obscurity, producing some of the most extraordinary stories in the English language—for which he earned pitiful amounts—Machen was dispiritedly employed as a

journalist on the London *Evening News* when a number of American authors
hailed him as an unsung genius. On the strength of his best work from the 1890s
he was extravagantly proclaimed a mystagogue of the secrets of existence, a
Titan fit to stand beside Poe, Hawthorne and De Quincey. He was seen as a
Blakean prophet whose supernal style and rich symbolism celebrated the
sacramental nature of the world; a consummate exponent of the divine and
diabolic; a mystic who held that art's true purpose was to penetrate the prosaic
veil of outward appearances to reveal the celestial splendour latent in the
commonest things.

His new-found followers, exalted by his transcendental philosophy and his
accomplished prose, lauded Machen with such ornate titles as 'a novelist of
ecstasy and sin' and 'the flower-tunicked priest of nightmare'. His leading
advocates, Vincent Starrett, James Branch Cabell, Carl Van Vechten and Paul
Jordan-Smith, drew the attention of the nation's literati to Machen's uncom-
promising dedication to his craft and his battles against penury, critical disdain
and the philistinism of publishers. Starrett warned that 'posterity is going to
demand of us, why when the opportunity was ours, we did not open our hearts
to Arthur Machen and name him among the very great'. Martin Secker and
Alfred A. Knopf began publishing Machen's long-out-of-print titles and his
new or previously rejected manuscripts. *The Hill of Dreams*, his poetic
re-creation of his early life in his beloved Monmouthshire or Gwent, was
proclaimed by Van Vechten in his novel *Peter Whiffle* as the most beautiful book
in the world. Lovecraft called it a 'memorable epic of the sensitive aesthetic
mind', while to Henry Miller the book ranked with Spengler's *The Decline of the
West* and Joyce's *Ulysses*. The critic Madeleine Cazamian, writing in the 1930s,
would pronounce it 'without doubt the most decadent book in all of English
literature'. *Hieroglyphics*, in which Machen eloquently argued that 'the master
word—Ecstasy' rather than 'fidelity to life' was the indispensable ingredient of
all great writing, was reassessed and found to be a *tour de force*.

This belated surge of worship led to Machen enjoying a decade or so as a
literary celebrity. It became fashionable for American writers to visit his home
in St John's Wood and drink with the sage in his favourite taverns. By the end of
the 1920s, however, Machen had fallen victim to the caprices of fame; the vogue
for his 'Silurian Mysteries' disappeared—for a time at least—and his royalties
dwindled to minute sums. The revival had come too late. Believing that his
creative fire had expired, and feeling incapable of producing further imaginative
work, Machen had earlier taken refuge in autobiography. He recounted the
story of his rapturous youth in Gwent, to which his lonely years as a struggling
author in Victorian Grub Street acted as a poignant counterpoint. In several
ways his memoirs proved to be his greatest triumph: he succeeded in shaping
the material of his often tortured career into visionary art. But by 1924, when

his reminiscences were completed, Machen considered that he had said all that lay within his power. Despite being at the apotheosis of his renown, he realized sorrowfully that his aspiration of composing 'a Great Romance', the book first envisaged in the 1880s, would remain forever unfulfilled. 'Always, or almost always, I have had the horror of beginning a new book,' he wrote. 'I have burnt my fingers to the bone again and again in the last forty years and I dread the fire of literature.' He had 'toiled and despaired over the impossible alchemy of letters' and found only ashes in his crucible. Convinced that he was unable to transform the visions which glowed in his imagination into words, his faith in himself as a writer ebbed away: 'it is one thing to dream dreams; and quite another to interpret them' was his mournful verdict on his work.

In the 1930s dire need of funds compelled Machen to return to fiction, and he surprised even himself by weaving a few last fantasies. Although *The Green Round* and the stories in *The Children of the Pool* are not devoid of merit, and no Machen *aficionado* would be without them, they are essentially recastings of his earlier themes and concepts. Yet if Machen's inventive faculty had diminished, writing remained an obsession to the end, and was expressed in his passion for corresponding prodigiously with friends and readers in Britain and across the Atlantic. Indeed, of the large quantity of his letters which survive (most are held by American libraries and universities) the finest date from his advanced old age. They became, in effect, a substitute for artistic utterance.

This book, the first major collection of his correspondence to be published—a small amount of material has appeared in limited editions in America—stands as a testament to a career which spanned the Victorian era to the atomic age. Here Machen is revealed in all his aspects: as literary man of the *fin de siècle*, philosopher, mystic, occultist in the fraternity of the Golden Dawn, High Churchman, actor and journalist.

His letters are replete with seraphic wisdom and nobility of spirit; and even in the face of poverty, adversity and twentieth-century alienation he affirms his great love of life. Marked by a forthright style, his correspondence is suffused by references and allusions to Christian theology, faith and ritual, illuminating his perennial preoccupation with matters of the soul. He chiefly dwells on these themes in writing to his kindred spirits—the scholar and mystic A. E. Waite and the journalist and publisher Colin Summerford. With the poet John Gawsworth and other 'Macheniacs' he courteously responds to enquiries about his work and acts as an oracle on that realm defined in *Hieroglyphics* as 'the eternal world of ideas'. Throughout the 60-year period from which this selection of letters is taken Machen maintains a remarkably consistent vision: he is without peer as the indomitable champion of individuality, beauty, faith, tradition, humanity and romance.

Those early American devotees were perhaps misguided in elevating

Machen to the rarefied heights of a literary Parnassus; but the incontestable fact remains that his writings constitute an unparalleled homage to man's spiritual nature in celebrating life in all its mystery and ecstasy. To enter his world, through his books and his letters, is an enriching experience.

ROGER DOBSON

ACKNOWLEDGEMENTS

For the generous help provided during the preparation of this book we are indebted to the late Mr Hilary Machen, Mrs Janet Pollock, the daughter of Arthur Machen, Mr Michael Goth, Mr Colin Summerford, Mr Mark Valentine, and Mr Christopher Watkins.

Our thanks are also due to Dr Gail-Nina Anderson, Mrs Kathleen Baker, Mr Ben Bass, Mr William Charlton, Mr Rupert Cook, Mr Claudio De Nardi, Mr Tim Earnshaw, Mr Steve Eng, Mr Kenneth W. Faig, jnr, Mr Nigel Jarrett, Mr S. T. Joshi, Mr Frank Kibblewhite, Mr T. E. D. Klein, Miss Pat Lister, the late Mr Michael Murphy, Dr Kathleen Raine, Mr Aidan Reynolds, Miss Joan Rodker, Mr Anthony Rota, the Revd Brocard Sewell, Dr Julie Speedie, Mr Edwin Steffe, Mrs Mollie Stoner, the late Mr Oliver Stonor, Professor Wesley D. Sweetser, Mrs Rita Tait, Mr J. C. Trewin, Mr Jon Wynne-Tyson and the members of staff at the Bodleian Library, Oxford, and at Newport Central Library, Gwent, and the officers of the John Ireland Trust.

For the benefit of those readers new to Machen a chronology and bibliography of his life and works have been included. Page references in the text refer to first editions of his books.

CONTENTS

Preface   *Page 5*
Acknowledgements   *Page 9*
Foreword by Hilary Machen   *Page 13*

Arthur Machen: Chronology   *Page 19*

A. E. WAITE
Introduction   *Page 25*
Letters to A. E. Waite, 1902–1942   *Page 31*

COLIN SUMMERFORD
Introduction   *Page 83*
Letters to Colin Summerford, 1924–1947   *Page 89*

JOHN GAWSWORTH
Introduction   *Page 169*
Letters to John Gawsworth, 1929–1947   *Page 173*

MISCELLANEOUS CORRESPONDENCE
Miscellaneous Correspondence, 1887–1946   *Page 211*

Select Bibliography   *Page 253*

FOREWORD

The door in the garden wall had been painted green, but many years before, so that the original grass colour had faded, with the suns and the rains, to a gentle turquoise. The lilac tree which looked over the wall had pushed, gently but inexorably, year by year, and the wall had yielded into a gentle curve. And many of the garden walls in Melina Place, in St John's Wood, were so curved and misshapen, and few of the houses behind the walls could be seen for the gardens and the greenery, so that each family lived in its own world, and for the small boy there was security against outside affairs, which even then seemed to consist, generally speaking, of what Arthur called 'grit'. I asked him once what 'grit' was, and he said, 'The pomps and vanities of a world designed by Newspaper Proprietors.'

It was, in a sense, to mark the emancipation from Carmelite House★ — it is, perhaps, not without meaning that the Reformers expelled the friars and got Lord Northcliffe in their place — that my father moved to this house. That was forty years ago, and the annual rent was £37. And forty years back, I can still remember the grim sadness with which my father set out each morning to his highly paid journalism: as is the way with all good families, his sadness affected both my mother and myself, and is not yet forgotten, and has bequeathed to me a valuable asset: an overwhelming hatred and contempt for the popular press. The last words of his autobiography describe his feelings on leaving the employment of the *Evening News*. '*Eduxit me de lacu miseriæ, et de luto fæcis. Et statuit super petram pedes meos: et direxit gressus meos.*'

With those words, unknown then to me, yet certainly experienced, we came to the house with the green shutters and the regency verandah, behind the garden wall. I have chosen to write about my father at this time for various reasons. It seems probable that the impressions of childhood are unwarped: and

★   Arthur Machen left the *Evening News* in the autumn of 1918 to work for the *Daily Express* for a short time.

I think it likely that the eight or nine years in that house were among the happiest of his life. After that time, when the charm of that part of London began to attract Musical Comedy stars and their attendant swains, and the house was sold over my father's head, the material adversity which was never far off struck at him savagely, and it was not until the last years of his life, and by the efforts of good friends, that he attained a sufficiency for happiness and tranquillity. He was never tired of quoting Micawber on finance and happiness; and I can remember none of his opinions that my own life's experience has not shown to be true. He had little sympathy with the spirituality of Léon Bloy, who discovered 'with a kind of joy, that we have neither food in the house nor money to buy it'. Indeed, I think I remember him referring to that author as 'Wonnie the Weeper', a character in one of the early American gangster novels. Contrary to popular rumour at the time of his death, he was never anything but a High Church Tory.

His whole attitude to the Catholic Church was curious. When we went on our holiday each year to a beautiful and remote part of Pembrokeshire it was found that the only celebration of Holy Communion in the village was at eight, an hour at which he did not care to be about at any time: least of all on his holidays. But hear Mass he must: and so each Sunday we walked a long mile-and-a-half to the Catholic church at Tenby, where he joined devoutly in the post-Mass Hail Marys, and was on terms of the greatest friendship with the parish priest, and where I heard for the first time the masses of Fr Turner, OSB, which have haunted me, as an organist, almost to the present day. At that time I loved them: they were so very different from the Sarum plainchant of our London church.

He always encouraged me to discuss theological subjects with him: giving to my childish enquiries a thoughtful and courteous consideration, as one adult to another. Only once did I know him speak shortly on these subjects. Having a schoolfriend who was a Catholic, I once asked him about the Sacred Heart. 'Their appetite,' he said, 'for obscuring their treasures of eternal Truth with semi-literate pieties of Italian or French origin is extraordinary — and insatiable.' I had early learned when it was unwise to press a subject: and asked no more.

Almost completely unmusical, except for *Adeste Fideles* and *Divini Mysterium*, he had a great love of plainchant. It was our organist, Francis Burgess, who told him that the Chant was done beautifully at Westminster Cathedral. That was, of course, in the days of Terry. He decided, therefore, to hear the then midday office of Holy Saturday there. He got back a little late for lunch, and I saw at once that all was not well: but my mother was sewing and without looking up said, 'Hullo, dear: was the chant good?' 'Chant!' roared Arthur, 'Devil a bit of chant! Glees and madrigals! Impudent scoundrels!' The story got back to Terry and we were told that he laughed till the tears ran.

But he had his own particular pieties. St Thomas Aquinas was one: King Charles I was another. We once passed the statue of that king, and I asked him why he took his hat off. He was taking me to the Café Royal for the first time: and at the end of my second grenadine syrup he was still telling me about the Royal Martyr: and it has taken a deal of reading and thought to get that one out of my head. My mother once told me that Arthur never began to write without a prayer to Samuel Johnson for intercession: and I suppose that is the reason why his son, a tenth-rate organist, never opens an organ console without the same sort of prayer to Johann Sebastian Bach.

But the house. It had been built in the early part of the nineteenth century, and was everything that a house should be, except for the kitchen range, which moved my mother, and Elsie, the *bonne*, to antiphonal strong language. In the front was a room lined with books, and against the only bare wall a Broadwood piano, another mark of prosperity in that it had replaced at last the Victorian fretwork piano belonging to my grandmother. My mother was a pianist of parts, fiery and inaccurate, and she played Bach organ fugues, and sometimes stopped with a hearty 'Damn' at a missed pedal entry: at which Arthur would look up from Copperfield or Quixote and say, mildly, 'Why don't you dash away like Burney?' to which my mother would reply, heartily, 'Old Idiot!' and Arthur would chuckle, and twist his feet together, and blow huge clouds of tobacco smoke before returning to his own. Surely no child was ever better brought up to despise the world. There was a dining room behind, with a desk and many more books, where my mother served rare and delicious meals, and where my father sat down to write in the evenings, with a muttered lamentation: 'Mutton chops, mutton chops.' So that even now I see all the curse of Adam in that joint. Overhead were three small bedrooms and an oak panelled bathroom: and nearly all the windows, above and below, looked out on to the garden in which my mother showed as much skill and success as she did in the kitchen; and behind, to corners of other small houses, hidden among the fruit trees, which were the survivors of the eighteenth-century market-gardening wood.

It was in that room that my father coached me in Latin and Greek, in the hope, which my own laziness did not fulfil, that I might get a scholarship at Merchant Taylors. He used an eighteenth-century Ambrosian Breviary, and the letters of the younger Pliny. Belshazzar's Feast I remember with pleasure and the planning of Pliny's vineyards.

From the Breviary also I learned *Creator alme siderum*, and my mother taught me the beautiful music that goes with it. *Si jeunesse savait*! If only I had realized how lucky I was!

It was on a Saturday night that the house really came into its own, especially in the summer. After dinner, before the first ring at the bell, my father and I got out the ingredients for the punch: a two gallon earthenware jar, Gin, Burgundy and Sauterne, in due and large proportion, bottles of the stuff; and the glasses were large, thick and bellshaped.

I could, I suppose, reel off a list of the names of those who used to come to Melina Place on Saturday night; some names would be well known, others less, many more forgotten. Many of the Benson company came, H. O. Nicholson, Frank Pittar, and sometimes Sir Frank or Lady Benson, but not, alas, together: J. C. Squire, Augustus John, John Ireland, and E. J. Moeran. Christopher Wilson, the musical director of the Benson company, who carried and played on the slightest encouragement, an oboe d'amore. I sat in a corner out of the way, and got drunk on a small allowance of punch and the unlimited and glorious conversation; a world which even now has considerable powers against the beastliness of the present times. This article would be ten times longer if I tried, and inevitably failed, to convey the glory of their talk, led and guided by Arthur. But Christopher's story of the Bedford Temperance Hotel is too good to miss. In the 'la-ounge' was a set of pictures, a sort of debased Victorian Rake's Progress, illustrating the degradation of those who like a pint of bitter. The last and dreadful scene was missing, and had been replaced by another picture. 'Poor fellow,' said Christopher, wagging his head sorrowfully, 'the end of it was that he turned into a bloodhound bitch with six puppies.'

All this was in the time of the American boom in my father's work; and indeed I think it was that which largely made the Melina Place life possible. Many Americans came to the house on those Saturday nights; nearly all of them were men of charm, wit, and learning. But there was one archetypal bore, who had the particularly American gift of monopolizing the conversation, and 'holding forth' interminably about Schopenhauer, or else Nietzsche. As he went on and on, the silence of despair would settle on the company until, on one such occasion, the bull-dog, which had been groaning and writhing for some time, leaped up with an hysterical yelp, and bit the poor man in the leg. He was never seen again; and on Monday morning, in spite of my mother's protests, Arthur went out and bought a pound of prime steak for the dog.

A few years ago I found myself in the area, and, inevitably, outside the garden door. The lilac tree was down, and the wall straight and forbiddingly high, with broken glass on the top. The door was new, red, and ever so contemporary, and above it hung an Olde Englysshe lantern. Fool that I was, I rang the bell and found myself explaining to a suspicious manservant that I once lived there. 'There used to be a big pear tree,' I ended weakly. 'There still is, sir,' he said; and shut the door in my face. And I walked away, and said my customary *requiem aeternam* for my father, and thought, as I have thought many times, that he had indeed earned his rest: for this modern world will give little rest to those who despise it unaffectedly; and I thought of his favourite biblical text, '*Fratres, nolite mirari, si odit vos mundum*', and yet again, I thought of his beginning and end: of the youth waiting by the stile for the postman, and the old man who 'increasingly loved me', and of the one thing, above all, that he taught me: *Omnia exeunt in mysterium.*

HILARY MACHEN

Hilary Machen died at the age of seventy-five at his home in Berkshire on 18 December 1987, a few days after the fortieth anniversary of his father's death. His Foreword originally appeared under the title 'In My Father's House' in the Aylesford Review, *Vol. V, No. 2, Spring 1963.*

ARTHUR MACHEN
Chronology

1863   Arthur Machen is born (as Arthur Llewelyn Jones) on 3 March at 33 High Street, Caerleon-on-Usk, Gwent.

1864   The Revd John Edward Jones, the Rector of St David's Church, Llanddewi Fach, his wife Janet and their son move to Llanddewi Rectory, four miles north of Caerleon.

1874   Arthur Jones enters Hereford Cathedral School in January. The Rector adds his wife's maiden name of Machen to the family.

1880   Jones-Machen leaves school in April because his impoverished father can no longer afford the fees. First visit to London in June. Fails the preliminary examination of the Royal College of Surgeons. Returns to Llanddewi in the autumn. Begins *Eleusinia* in the winter.

1881   *Eleusinia* published in 100 copies by a Hereford printer in March. Machen returns to London in the summer to prepare for a career in journalism. Boards with a journalist at Turnham Green, studies shorthand, and spends much time writing verse.

1883   Works for a month for publishers Marcus Ward, called 'Chandos and Co.' in *Far Off Things*. Leaves to tutor journalist's children at Turnham Green. Explores north and west London and begins *The Anatomy of Tobacco* in the spring while living in poverty at 23 Clarendon Road, Notting Hill Gate.

1884   Returns to Llanddewi in the summer. George Redway publishes *The Anatomy of Tobacco* in the autumn and commissions Machen to translate *The Heptameron* of Margaret of Navarre for £20.

1885   Returns to London in June to perform cataloguing tasks for Redway. *The Literature of Occultism and Archaeology* published. Begins *The*

Chronicle of Clemendy in the autumn. Summoned home to Llanddewi, as his mother, an invalid for fifteen years, is dying.

1886   Finishes *The Chronicle of Clemendy* at Llanddewi in August. *The Heptameron* published.

1887   Meets A. E. Waite at the British Museum Reading Room in January. Writes for *Walford's Antiquarian*. *Don Quijote de la Mancha* published in the summer. Marries Amelia (Amy) Hogg at Worthing on 31 August. Father dies in September.

1888   Works as a cataloguer for booksellers Robson & Kerslake in Coventry Street. Begins translating François Béroalde de Verville's *Le Moyen de Parvenir* and *The Memoirs of Jacques Casanova*. *The Chronicle of Clemendy* published in spring, *Thesaurus Incantatus* in the winter.

1889   A fragment of *Le Moyen de Parvenir* produced as *The Way to Attain*. Begins contributing to *The Globe* and *The St James's Gazette*.

1890   *Le Moyen de Parvenir* published as *Fantastic Tales* in the spring. Meets and dines with Oscar Wilde. First chapter of *The Great God Pan* appears in *The Whirlwind* in December.

1891   Rents a cottage on the Chiltern Hills until the winter of 1893. Writes two books during this period, but destroys them, save for the 'Novel of the Dark Valley' incorporated into *The Three Impostors*.

1893   Returns to London in November and lives at 36 Great Russell Street, Bloomsbury. Begins exploring the hidden regions of the metropolis.

1894   *The Memoirs of Jacques Casanova* published in the spring. Begins *The Three Impostors*. John Lane publishes *The Great God Pan* in December.

1895   Moves to 4 Verulam Buildings, Gray's Inn, in the autumn. John Lane publishes *The Three Impostors* in November. 'The Shining Pyramid' appears in *The Unknown World*.

1896   Begins *The Hill of Dreams* in February.

1897   Finishes *The Hill of Dreams* in the spring. Writes *Ornaments in Jade*.

1898   Works as an assistant editor and reviewer for *Literature*.

1899   Leaves *Literature* in March. Writes 'The White People' and *Hieroglyphics*. Begins *A Fragment of Life*. Amy dies of cancer on 31 July. Joins the Hermetic Order of the Golden Dawn as Frater Avallaunius on 21 November.

1900   Encounters the strange individuals who appear in *Things Near and Far* (Chapter X).

1901   Joins Frank Benson's stage company in January and plays minor Shakespearian roles. Tours with Bensonians in pastorals. Appears in music hall, melodrama and comedy in London and on tour.

1902   *Hieroglyphics* published in March. Appears in *Paolo and Francesca* at the St James's Theatre from February, and in *If I Were King* from the autumn.

1903   Continues at the St James's. Marries Dorothie Purefoy Hudleston at St Marylebone Parish Church on 25 June. Lives at 5 Stafford Street (later Cosway Street), NW1. Tours with George Alexander in the autumn. Returns to the St James's in *Old Heidelberg*.

1904   Takes part in the Benson company tour of public schools. 'The White People', *A Fragment of Life* and *The Garden of Avallaunius (The Hill of Dreams)* appear in *Horlick's Magazine*. *The House of the Hidden Light*, a collaboration with Waite, published. Tours with Herbert Beerbohm Tree in the autumn.

1906   Begins researching the Grail legends. Joins the New Bohemians in May. *The House of Souls* published in June, *Dr Stiggins* in November.

1907   Begins *The Secret Glory*. *The Hill of Dreams* published in February. Begins contributing to *The Academy*. Moves to 6 Cosway Street, NW1. Final tour in *His House in Order*.

1908   Begins contributing to *T.P.'s Weekly*.

1909   Begins contributing to the *Daily Mail*. Final stage performance in Benson's production of *Henry VI, Part II*.

1910   Moves to Edward House, 7 Lisson Grove, NW1, in the spring. Begins working for the London *Evening News* in April.

1912   Hilary Machen is born on 3 February.

1914   'The Bowmen' appears in the *Evening News* on 29 September.

1915   The Angels of Mons rumours grow in the spring. *The Confessions of a Literary Man (Far Off Things)* appears in the *Evening News* from March to July. Begins corresponding with Vincent Starrett in August. *The Bowmen and Other Legends of the War* published in August, *The Great Return* in December.

1917   *The Terror* published in February. Janet Machen is born on 26 February. Starrett's essay on Machen appears in *Reedy's Mirror* in October.

1918   *War and the Christian Faith* published in June. Works for the *Daily Express* from September to November. Starrett's *Arthur Machen: A Novelist of Ecstasy and Sin* published.

1919   Returns to the *Evening News*. The family move to 12 Melina Place, St John's Wood, in March. Begins contributing to *The Lyons Mail*.

1921   Sacked by the *Evening News* in November after Lord Alfred Douglas sues over a premature and critical obituary written by Machen.

1922   *The Secret Glory* published in February. Plays Dr Johnson in a film about old and new London in May. *Far Off Things* published in August. Alfred A. Knopf begins issuing Machen's works. *Casanova* reprinted.

1923   *Things Near and Far* published in January, *The Grande Trouvaille* in March, Starrett's *The Shining Pyramid* in May, *Strange Roads* and *The Collector's Craft* in November.

1924   *Dog and Duck* published in February. Meets Colin Summerford in the early spring. *The London Adventure* published in March, *The Glorious Mystery* in April, *Precious Balms* in July, *Ornaments in Jade* in September, *The Shining Pyramid* (Martin Secker) in December.

1925   Begins contributing to *The London Graphic*. *The Canning Wonder* published in October.

1926   Meets Oliver Stonor. Begins contributing to *The Observer*. *Dreads and Drolls* published in October, *Notes and Queries* in November.

1927   The family lose their home at Melina Place in December and move to nearby 28 Loudoun Road.

1928   Writes on cookery for the *Sunday Express*.

1929   Begins corresponding with John Gawsworth. The family move to 'Lynwood', Old Amersham, Buckinghamshire, in June.

1930   *Tom O'Bedlam and His Song* published in December.

1931   Gawsworth publishes *Beneath the Barley* in June and *In the 'Eighties* in August.

1932   *A Few Letters from Arthur Machen* published in March. Writes *The Green*

Round. Receives a Civil List pension of £100 a year. *The Glitter of the Brook* published in October.

1933   Reading for Ernest Benn ceases and *The Green Round* published in June. Gawsworth begins assembling material for a biography of Machen. Begins contributing to *The Independent*.

1936   *The Cosy Room and Other Stories* published in March, *The Children of the Pool and Other Stories* in September.

1937   A civic luncheon to mark Machen's seventy-fourth birthday held at Newport, Gwent. Broadcasts on the Welsh Home Service in March. He and Purefoy visit Paris with Edwin and Mollie Greenwood in April and holiday in Gwent in the summer.

1938   Review of Waite's autobiography, *Shadows of Life and Thought*, appears in May.

1941   *A Handy Dickens* published in December.

1942   Waite dies, aged eighty-four, on 19 May.

1943   Celebrates his eightieth birthday with many friends and admirers at the Hungaria Restaurant in London on 3 March. Taken ill with double pneumonia at Christmas and is removed to hospital at Chesham, where it is feared he will die.

1944   Recovers from his illness and convalesces at the home of Oliver Stonor's sister Barbara Pickup at Gerrards Cross early in the year.

1946   *Holy Terrors* published in February.

1947   Purefoy dies on 30 March. Machen becomes a patient at St Joseph's Nursing Home, Beaconsfield, in the winter. Dies, aged eighty-four, on 15 December and is buried next to Purefoy in the cemetery at Amersham.

A. E. Waite.

A. E. WAITE
Introduction

When the first part of his autobiography, *Far Off Things*, was published in autumn 1922 Machen immediately sent a copy, as an advance birthday present, to his friend A. E. Waite; not, as might have been expected, one of the sumptuous signed, limited edition, but the ordinary trade issue, for Machen knew that Waite (unlike the avaricious collectors for whom one-and-a-half guineas worth of extra-large margins was all-important) would *read* the book. And read it he did; en route from Ramsgate to London on 27 September, the day it arrived.

In an ideal world he would have been on his way to visit Machen, but after 1920, when Waite moved out of London, they rarely met, and the purpose of Waite's journey was to preside over the ceremonies of the Fellowship of the Rosy Cross — the mystical Order he had founded in 1915 upon the wreckage of the old Golden Dawn. The Fellowship, which gave practical expression to the ideas and ideals that he propagated in his books, was the focus of Waite's life, but to Machen it was incomprehensible. He had, many years before, joined the original Golden Dawn but it did little for him — 'it shed no ray of any kind on my path', he commented in *Things Near and Far* — and Waite's creed remained a mystery to him: 'I have known my very dear friend A. E. Waite for 38 years', he told Colin Summerford in 1925, 'and I have not the faintest notion as to his real beliefs.' What then was the bond between them? A bond broken only by Waite's death, 55 years after it had been forged.

They had met in January of 1887 'under the great dome of the Museum', at the instigation of Machen's first wife, Amy Hogg, whom Waite had met the previous summer while staying at Worthing. Waite was then 29 years old and Machen six years his junior. Each was just beginning to find his place in the world after a long period of anguished introspection, and despite their being 'utterly at variance over fundamental things' (as Machen told Oliver Stonor many years later), there was between them 'a strong underlying sympathy'. They enjoyed equally exploring the byways of London and the byways of religion and occultism — celebrating their discoveries and their disputes alike with strong drink, as is recalled in more than one of Machen's letters.

Their literary careers while utterly different in content, yet ran in curious parallel: both were launched by George Redway, both maintained a prodigious output, and neither could quite succeed in converting critical acclaim into financial success. And there were other ties. In 1899 it was Waite who pulled Machen back from the brink of self-destructive despair after Amy's death, while three years later Machen was instrumental in enabling Waite to come to terms with his complex and unconventional relationship with Dora Stuart-Menteath. This last episode, which is hinted at in the letters, led in 1904 to their most important literary collaboration, when — as a kind of catharsis — the story was told more fully, albeit more cryptically, in *The House of the Hidden Light*.

But as their literary careers advanced, so one significant difference emerged: Machen was known in the world of letters while Waite was not. Machen's writing gained for him, both in Britain and in America, an ever-growing band of admirers and enthusiasts, eager to publicize his work, but Waite remained — and remains — largely unknown, recognized, if at all, only for his translations of Eliphas Lévi and for the Tarot pack that bears his name. Even admirers of his work are generally ignorant of his life, seeing him as a reclusive scholar and as the epitome of the conservative Englishman of independent means.

In fact Waite was American, having been born at Brooklyn on 2 October 1857, although he was brought to England with his infant sister, Frederica, some two years later following the death at sea of his father, a Connecticut ship's captain. His mother's return to her family was far from welcome — they had disapproved of her irregular relationship with Captain Waite — and she was left to bring up her children alone and in near poverty.

For reasons unknown she became a convert to Roman Catholicism, so that Arthur Waite and his sister were raised in an atmosphere of fervent piety. This, coupled with frequent unsettling moves around the northern and western suburbs of London, erratic schooling and effective isolation from his wider family led him into a painfully introverted adolescence. And in 1874 the weight of grief was added to this burden of self-doubt when Frederica died. Her death alienated Waite from his mother — 'there was nothing in common between us and there was no sympathy' he recalled at the end of his life — and brought about a loss of faith: a loss that is reflected in the verse he had begun to compose and would soon begin to publish.

To combat his religious doubts he turned from the Catholic faith to Spiritualism, attending séances, reading avidly, but eventually finding the spirits wanting — although he did not return to the Church, much as he loved its ritual. He moved on to Theosophy, and thence to alchemy and to magic in the person of Eliphas Lévi whose extraordinary books fascinated him. And as he wandered down these byways of occultism he developed a fine critical sense in respect of its vast and doubtful literature, set this sense to work, and in 1886 produced the first of his many books on what he termed 'The Secret Tradition'. This was *The Mysteries of Magic*, a 'digest' of the writings of Eliphas Lévi that appeared coincidentally with his falling in love with Dora Lakeman, a young woman of startling beauty who put common-sense before sentiment and married the Revd Granville Stuart-Menteath, an elderly but wealthy clergyman who could, at the least, provide all the creature comforts that would have been unattainable to the wife of a penniless poet.

Waite's reaction was pragmatic: in January 1888 he married Ada Lakeman, Dora's far from attractive sister; set about his literary career in earnest; and celebrated the anniversary of his first meeting with Arthur Machen. He had much in common with Machen: not only were they both aspiring writers associated with the same devious publisher, but both of them had, in Machen's words, 'the great and absorbing desire of going the other way', and neither of them had any money. They also enjoyed each other's company hugely, and as Waite poured out an increasing flood of works on alchemy, magic and mysticism, so Machen found a niche as a nineties novelist, and their friendship deepened.

By 1891 Waite's enthusiasm for the occult had led him into the Hermetic Order of the Golden Dawn, a magical society made famous as much by the membership of W. B. Yeats as by its spectacular rituals, and it was here that he learned the practicalities of occultism. But it was not until eight years later that he persuaded Machen to join the Order — thereby saving him from the total moral and psychic collapse towards which grief at Amy's death was hurrying him. Magic was not, however, to Machen's taste — for all that he later brought his second wife, Purefoy, into the Golden Dawn — but his gratitude to Waite was real and in 1900 he encouraged Waite to take up again their old revelling, although with one significant difference. This time they were accompanied by Dora, as dissatisfied with her marriage as Waite was with his, and their adventures were to make it an *Annus mirabilis*, albeit one that led paradoxically to the making of Machen's second marriage and to the salvation of Waite's first.

And as this wonderful year ended both men began new careers: Machen on the stage and Waite as manager of Horlicks, the Malted Milk company. Still they continued to meet and to collaborate in writing. (*The House of the Hidden Light* was followed by Waite's *Strange Houses of Sleep* in 1906 and *The Hidden Church of the Holy Graal* in 1909, to both of which Machen contributed), but an inevitable staidness was setting in. Machen might still be a Bohemian, but Waite was now established as a competent, scholarly and eminently respectable writer on alchemy, the Kabbalah, the Holy Grail, the Tarot and all other branches of the Hermetic tradition; he also controlled the Independent and Rectified Rite, a branch of the Golden Dawn (which had split in 1903) that reflected his own mystical philosophy.

This was founded on Waite's beliefs, which were extremely complex and which Machen could never understand. Essentially they comprised a non-denominational variety of sacramental Christianity in which personal experience of God took precedence over theological dogma, but Waite's creed was difficult to comprehend and Machen was not alone in finding it confusing; partly from doctrinal confusion and partly from other causes dissension arose within the Independent and Rectified Rite, growing to such a pitch that in 1914 Waite closed it down.

There was, of course, a successor, but the Fellowship of the Rosy Cross was just as much of a mystery to Machen, although it was to prove far more satisfying to Waite. He had long ceased to work for Horlick & Co. and in 1920 he moved away from London to live at Ramsgate on the Kent coast, where he continued to write, to suffer agonies of guilt when the much-neglected Ada died in 1924, and to construct the remarkable rituals of his Order. This now absorbed most of his energy, and as it grew so it drew to itself such unlikely members as the photographer Alvin Langdon Coburn, and the poet and novelist Charles Williams. But in spite of the pressures upon him Waite maintained his correspondence with Machen, visiting him as and when he could, to dine, to drink, to argue joyously — and to suffer short shrift from Purefoy Machen: 'Get up, you old fool,' she ordered him once, 'you're drunk!'

Their arguments were always constructive, and however much he might reject Machen's opinions — on the Grail, on freemasonry, or on mystical experience — Waite yet needed them to sharpen and refine his own ideas as he revised and extended his earlier works into new and definitive editions. But it all slowly came to an end. Machen moved to Amersham and their meetings became rare events as Waite's health declined — a decline accelerated after 1933 by the domestic stresses consequent upon his daughter's virtual hatred for his second wife, Mary Schofield.

In 1938 Waite's autobiography, *Shadows of Life and Thought*, appeared, a diffuse and difficult work, but among his most important for it contains the essence of his philosophy of mysticism. Machen was delighted with the book, partly because it records his friendship with Waite, but the more so because it paints a self-portrait of both the outer and the inner man: a picture that only Machen among all of Waite's surviving friends could fully appreciate. When Waite died, in May 1942, it was that closeness to him, so clearly visible in the letters, that led Machen to express his grief in 'a silence and a sadness'; he grieved not only for the loss of his oldest friend, but also for the death of a true, if unsung, mystic.

R. A. GILBERT

LETTERS TO A. E. WAITE
1902 – 1942

S∴C∴D∴.[1]
13 Rupert Street, W.
Monday

My Dear Waite,

Be not forgetful of the summons for tomorrow (Tuesday). You must go into the *Wine Bar* at Stone's, & if you see no one there, ask for Mr Ayrton,[2] and then you shall be taken into the appointed place. But be there by two, without fail, if you would see long days in the land of the living.

There is still silence over all the mystic territory. It is true I have received a letter, but rather, I believe, from the terrestrial & inferior Shepherdess than from the Supernal Lilith.[3] However, I have made an appointment with her, which I shall keep alone, that I may more thoroughly discover whether she have any Rite to administer. Otherwise, as I have said, there is silence & dimness over all things. 'In the good time the torches shall be lighted, and there shall be the voice of singing in the Syon.'

Yours fraternally,

Arthur Machen

Wine Bar: Stones: Panton Street: Haymarket: 2 p.m.: Tuesday.

[1]   The initials of Machen's 'Rabelaisian Order of Tosspots' under its Welsh name of 'Sasiwn Cwrw Dda' (i.e. 'The Society of Good Beer Drinkers'). The Order was a drinking society founded by Machen at Stratford in April 1901, with his fellow Bensonians as members. Waite joined the Order, at Machen's invitation, on 6 October 1902; the letter was thus written on the 5th which was, in fact, a Sunday.

[2]   Frederick Randle Ayrton was one of the 'Lords Maltworm' of the Society (i.e. a founder member) and a distinguished Benson player.

[3]   The Shepherdess was the actress Vivienne Pierpont, who in 1902 married Frederick Rosse. She was known as Lilith in her role as a participant — with Machen, Waite and Waite's sister-in-law, Dora Stuart-Menteath — in the nocturnal junketings that were solemnly recorded in *The House of the Hidden Light*: an extraordinary book written jointly by Machen and Waite and printed in 1904 in an edition of three copies.

13 Rupert Street, W.
Sunday

My Dear Waite,

I think the Fairy Melusine[1] gave you to understand in the course of your impressive conversation yesterday that I could not see you on Wednesday, on account of the matinée. Will Thursday do instead? And if so, could not Melusine also be present, that we might discuss the very grave affair of your reformation, which dates, I think, from tomorrow? It seems to me a 3 bottle problem, if any true light is to be cast on the matter.

I believe I am deeply pledged, *sub conditione*, to submit to the Latin church. Here also there is need of a conference; and indeed there seems to be to be enough matter between us to authorize a session without end. We have done amiss in the past, my dear brother, in neglecting one another, and it seems to me that we should repair our errors by a more constant association. For the day of the great battle Armageddon assuredly draws nigh, and the time is short.

Will Thursday at 4, Café de l'Europe, suit you? Let me know.

Yours fraternally,

Arthur Machen

---

[1] Melusine was one of many pet names that Waite gave to Dora Stuart-Menteath. His 'reformation' apparently concerned his somewhat irregular relationship with Dora, whom he had met in 1886 at a séance in the home of the Revd Granville Stuart-Menteath. To Waite's dismay she subsequently married Stuart-Menteath, leaving him to marry her rather plain sister, Ada. Dora seems to have regretted her somewhat hasty marriage and by 1900 she had turned to Waite for consolation. The letter probably dates from October 1902.

13 Rupert Street, W.
Saturday

My Dear Waite,

In the first place let me ask you to visit me here on Wednesday next at 5.30 for tea and conversation. Let it be done punctually and without fail. Secondly, let me tell you of my interview with the Shepherdess on Friday last. It has filled me with alarm, after much the same fashion as I was filled with alarm to see that Christopher[1] was unable to eat his luncheon some fortnight ago. What did I find? A pleasant, pretty woman who did not much interest me, whom I greeted without joy and left without a sense of loss. And I remembered the acute and exquisite delight that her mere presence had once afforded me; the romances, the wonders, the fascinations that she had once dispensed as from an inexhaustible house of treasure; and my anguish was great, not because I had desired and lost her, but because I knew that if she were to be given to me now, she would be but little to me. And my anguish was great *because I desired desire*. I remembered something I had written about one 'who, as it were, shivered in the eternal ice, and yet was insensible to the heat of fire, even if it were given him'.

It is clear that I ought to go to a spiritual Derby, call in a ghostly doctor, and live on spiritual milk and soda for many days — following the analogy of Christopher & the beefsteak.

But I do not know how this can be done, and shall be glad of your profound consideration and advice. I only know that Mrs Rosse, late Lilith, does not interest me at all: I confess and deplore it, because a great sacrament is taken away, and none other given to replace it.

We wonder and adore while we tremble; being assured that Life is to come, that Love is to be plenteously bestowed, that we shall see the good things of the Lord in *terra viventium*. *Immo vere, frater Dilecta*, even now the *Mensa dulcissimi convivii* is prepared. Write to us concerning these latter things.

Yours fraternally,

Arthur Machen

[1]   Hugh Christopher Wilson was the musical director of the Benson company. He came from Derby — hence Machen's reference to the town. The letter was probably written in November 1902.

13 Rupert Street, W.
Wednesday

My Dear Waite,

I saw Dorothy Purefoy[1] yesterday, and asked her if she would meet you on Friday at the Café. She would have been overjoyed, bur she has folk coming to tea.

Do you, nevertheless, call here at 4 on that day, and we will proceed to the Café or delay here as you feel inclined. Let it be done without fail, since (to use a phrase altogether mundane), the times are 'ticklish' and require great consultations.

The Page's[2] Pageant seems to advance with rapid steps, and the Page appears inclined to preconise a Feast of Eight Torches with Ruling of the Choir. Her mother, with an asperity unworthy of a mother in Yisroal, has acquired a habit of raining blows on her head, charging her with whoredom the while; the which amenities have caused Berthelda to declare that she will have 'peace'.

Yours fraternally,

A. M.

[1] Machen told Waite of his forthcoming marriage in December 1902, but he did not introduce Waite to his future wife, Dorothie Purefoy Hudleston, until 14 March 1903. The letter was thus, presumably, written early in 1903.

[2] 'The Page Berthelda' was Leah Hanman, a Jewish actress who was Christopher Wilson's lady friend. Machen had met her at the Hoxton 'Empire'.

5 Cosway Street
In Vigilie Nat. Dni
1905

Dilectissime Frater,

In return for your card, take from us both all good wishes to you & to yours, now & always. In the great Names, & by the great Names may you always be defended from persons who, in themselves harmless idiots, are yet symbols & omens of danger & distraction & perturbation within & without. *Dissipentur inimici tui: ab homine iniquo et doloro Dni eruat te.* I am sorry you did not join us the other day: there was a defection, from one cause or another, well nigh universal; & this much hinders our working.[1] But I fear you have hardly penetrated the peculiar veils which we use in this special Order, & the said veils are certainly very remote from those which experience has led you to expect. May I hint to you that very curious circumstances in the way of grades & the fashion in which they are taken are latent in the society? I mean that it is possible that the grades as they are commonly known do not always coincide with certain other grades interior & more secret. Do not think that I am making pretensions of that kind which, (I am sure), must be to you most familiar & accursed in your dealings & parleyings with secret Orders. But — to say as much as it is convenient or possible to say — you know, do you not, that this world in all things, & above all in interior things, is a world of paradox. To take an example of what I mean: Florence Farr[2] & Blackden[3] are, I believe & suppose, learned in all the 'Wisdom of the Egyptians', in all 'occult' knowledge. But — for all essential purposes — they are about as complete a pair of 'rotters' as I have ever seen. This is a paradox; not without suggestive application. And: another point: the average secret society presupposes, as you yourself have said, that the initiator is, in a certain sense, superior to the initiated, superior, that is, because he possesses certain information which he imparts to the neophyte; who is, by this process, admitted into a circle of knowledge outside which, (by the hypothesis) he stood, before his initiation. Now, imagine if you will, a society which makes no pretence of knowing anything which the outsider, the neophyte, does not know; which has no temple or circle to which admittance is given; which bids its members look within, & uncover, & remove, & Behold, & Make the Great Interior Entrance — from Within to Within, instead of from Without to Somebody Else's notion of Within. I hasten to say that these are hints & suggestions & not by any means Scientific Information. And let me add: *it is all secret from Miss B!*[4]

We have been most wonderfully fortunate in worldly things this Xmas. A fortnight ago we really & literally had not nearly enough to eat. And then came presents: two £5 notes; two pheasants, a dozen of wine, a fowl, two plum puddings, a great box of chocolates, & minor gifts. To cap all this Grant Richards writes to say that he will buy the copyright of those books of mine[5] for the £50 which I demanded. I shall believe this, though, when I get his cheque. He also repeats, more or less, his proposals for a new book.[6] I wish I thought I could do it; but I fear there is little hope. However; if he becomes definite I shall try what I can do.

I wish I could report to you as handsome things of the Supersubstantial

Bread.[7] Alas! there is still dryness, dryness, dryness; there is darkness within, the doors are closed, the ears are deaf & the sound of the incantation is not heard in the streets. I know of no help but in the homely maxim of 'patience & perseverance'. After all; what have I deserved else? what do I deserve else?

Have you ever remarked the fact that a bodily benefit is put forward by the church as the result of a good Communion? Such benefit is noted, I find, in the 'Imitation', & is prayed for in the mass. Curiously enough, in the Anglican Rite the phrase 'preserve thy *body* & soul to everlasting life' is used. I have reason to believe that the claim is no vain one. I think, too, that there are facts which some have noted that make it most improbable that such corporeal effects are the results of 'imagination'. If I give you a glass of plain water, & tell you, as soon as you have swallowed it, that it contains a powerful though tasteless cathartic drug, you will, likely enough, be violently ill on the spot; though the water is absolutely pure. But if I give you a glass of water in a ritual, saying: Drink this; it is the Communion of Death: & you go away expecting that nothing very much will happen to you — certainly nothing bodily — & yet fall dead in four or five hours time when you have forgotten all about the Ritual — then, I think, we may fairly conclude that 'there is something in it'.

Did I show you that curious story of Jondar in the *Arabian Nights*? If I did, you will remember that Jondar, searching after an Enchanted Treasure, (symbolizing, from its description, Wisdom & Power), has to *knock* / // /// on a gate & then has to pass through Seven Trials. He is required to *submit*: to stretch forth his neck to the swordsman, to bare his breast to the Archers &c till at last his mother appears, & her he must curse & revile & make to take off her clothes! Is not all this very suggestive of a Ritual? Do you know of any mention of *masonic knocking* as early as this? (10th or 11th century isn't it?) Oddly enough Jondar is a widow's son, who is persecuted & finally killed by his two wicked Brothers. And oddly enough he is given an Enchanted Saddle Bag from which every kind of food can be produced — the Graal, is it not, in its earlier form? It seems to me we have here some odd points, which ought to lead to something.

I wish you could send me the collections you have made on the Graal.[8] In the first place I should very much like to read them; & secondly, coming fresh to the subject points might strike me which might prove useful in the investigation. But, I think we ought to know more about the survival of the Gnostic Sects; & I am inclined to doubt whether the Manichaean sect is the only possible origin. There were other Gnostic heresies which might easily have lingered in the Syrian hills — which, perhaps, are there now.

Forgive all this discursion & discussion: but you know Mahomet must in certain circumstances go to the mountain.

I remain, very dear Brother,
Yours ever fraternally

A. M.

[1] Presumably this is a reference to 'The Sodality of the Shadows' — 'another unorthodox little club' as St John Adcock called it in *The Glory that was Grub Street* (p. 218) — that Machen had dreamed up for the benefit of his drinking friends.

[2] Florence Farr (Mrs Edward Emery, 1860-1917), Bernard Shaw's 'New Woman', was an actress, author, and, later, an educationalist. She was an active member of the Hermetic Order of the Golden Dawn although not involved in Waite's Independent and Rectified Rite.

[3] Marcus Worsley Blackden, artist, Egyptologist and occultist, was a friend of Waite who was actively involved in setting up the Independent & Rectified Rite. Later, in 1914, he was equally active in bringing about its demise.

[4] It has not proved possible to identify 'Miss B'.

[5] i.e. *The House of Souls* (1906).

[6] The new book was presumably the sequel to *The Three Impostors* that Grant Richards continually, but vainly, urged Machen to write. It never was written.

[7] This probably refers to Machen's inability to produce further imaginative works.

[8] Waite and Machen were both enthusiasts of the Grail legends and their symbolism. At this time Waite was beginning to assemble material for his study of the legends, *The Hidden Church of the Holy Graal* (1909).

---

5 Cosway St., N.W.
21 Feb. 1906

Dilectissime,

Very many thanks for your good epistle. Firstly: as to the practical matter. Nutt's[1] epitomes *are* epitomes and nothing more: absolutely dry enumerations of the events: like this something: 'Percival, the son of a widow (1) brought up in ignorance of the world (2) sees three Knights (3) and asks his mother what they are (4) &c &c.' This is not what I mean: I suggest *extracts*, nicely translated, eked out by full *summaries*, where and if the text threatens to become of undue length. I do not think, though, you need be afraid of the length: one can get a lot of matter into an average-sized book, and if needful you could have two volumes without any difficulty from the publisher's point of view, or the selling point. Next, as to our working together, I hardly see how this can be, except indirectly.[2] You know that all my notes are at your disposition in the fullest sense, for any purpose you may have: but if I understand you aright, they are not likely to be of much service to you; since they tend to support a hypothesis which it would not interest you to work out. When I began this investigation I had three main points before me: (1) The Celtic Church (2) The Templars (3) The Albigenses, or some other possibly existing society. It is by a process of exhaustion that (2) and (3) have vanished; as I have been convinced that the Graal has no more to do with either one or the other than it has with the Particular Baptists. But you must not think that I believe the 'Theory' I sent you exhausts the whole case: it merely posits the probable Celtic *prima materies* from which the Graal Legend as we have it, was shaped. This is not to say that the Romancers have not introduced much new matter into their recasting.

Now, I gather that your position with respect to the proposed work — say rather with respect to any work on the subject — is somewhat difficult. You have a theory, but you can get no convincing evidence in support of it. This is a position which you must consider with yourself: but I again repeat you must think of all my notes as absolutely your own — if they are of service to you.

I must tell you that I read Sebastian Evans's book[3] yesterday, and found it most entertaining. Here are his solutions:

Percival = S. Dominic
Galahad = S. Francis of Assisi
Gawain = Archbp. Fulk
Lancelot = Simon de Montfort senior
The Rich Fisher = Innocent III
Percival's Silence = The failure of Dominic to discuss the Universal
    Exemption of the Cistercians from Interdict with Pope Innocent.
Gawain's Silence = The failure of Fulk in the same way.
The 'blasting' that befell Lloegrwys = The Interdict on England 1208 –
    1214.
The Recovery of the Graal = The Removal of the Interdict.
The Graal = Celebration of the Eucharist.

All this is most ingeniously and elaborately supported. Two points strike me

(1) How does this theory explain the final withdrawal of the Graal? (2) Can it not be absolutely shewn that the 'Silence of Percival' was known and written down before 1208–1214?

I think there are three ways of explaining the 'Withdrawal of the Graal'; which as you say is most important, since it signifies that True Masses have ceased from the world. Firstly, we may take this as a remanent from the Folk Lore, which is always ready to assume that 'once upon a time' there were great marvels and happenings, which have ceased to be. It is the 'long, long ago' feeling, which admits there are no marvels and miracles now, but believes there were such things of old time.

Secondly, it may be the expression of some Celts' opinion that the Mass, without the Epiclesis, is a maimed mass.

And again; it may be the union and commixture of these two feelings: and this is my *personal* explanation of the matter and also the disappearance of the actual relic. Was there not a tacit convention that we should avoid mere argument? If this still stands: good: if not: have at you for *all* your opinions as to the Church and the Heresies! From them all, so far as I understand them, I wholly and heartily dissent: in the hypothesis of the Holy Assembly I do not believe: in the Popish Church as the *Sole* Custodian of the Faith or Sacraments I utterly disbelieve! I am ready if necessary to maintain theses on all these points, when and where you will.

I expect you on Saturday at the Museum, somewhere on the A range of desks *before* 4:30.

I remain
Yours ever fraternally,

Arthur Machen

---

[1]   i.e. Alfred Nutt, *Studies on the Legend of the Holy Grail with especial reference to the hypothesis of its Celtic Origin* (Folk-lore Society, 1888).

[2]   In fact they did collaborate: Waite acknowledged Machen's help over 'the presentation of the hypothesis concerning the Graal and the Celtic Church' in *The Hidden Church of the Holy Graal* (p. 461).

[3]   Sebastian Evans, *In Quest of the Holy Graal: An Introduction to the Study of the Legend* (Dent, 1898).

5 Cosway Street,
N.W.
Tuesday

Dilectissime,

Herewith I send you the titles of Werner: you will see that the plays you are interested in are included in the 'Theater'.[1]

Also find herewith a brief acknowledgement from Benson. I shall be curious to learn what use he proposes to make of our masterpiece.[2] You see he calls it *my* play: of course I told him that it was our joint labour. In any case, I feel certain that he will not give an order to his wardrobe master for the making of seven dalmatics of red silk — to say nothing of a set of red episcopal vestments. It would be *possible* of course to dress the seven as Eastern Deacons — albs and red stoles — but I should prefer dalmatics.

With respect to the Dove in H[oly] G[rail] symbolism — you know that the Blessed Sacrament was reserved in England (and I think everywhere) in the Middle Ages in a vessel shaped like a Dove. 'Dove-House', Columbarium was synonymous with Tabernacle. The sculpture I told you of — a Dove holding a wafer over a vessel shaped thus — ⊻ — alludes, perhaps, to this custom; or rather the custom and the sculpture both allude to the working of the Holy Spirit in the Eucharist; a matter which became and remains somewhat obscured in the west. I have written to the author of the *Church Times* article on the Healing Cup,[3] asking if there is any kind of documentary evidence. In my opinion it is probable that the relic is much earlier than the crusades — wooden chalices date back to centuries IV and V. I propose also to take steps to find out the meaning of those curious statements about the chalice in the 'High History' and the 'Panegyric' of S. Columba.

Yours ever fraternally,

Arthur Machen

We shall meet on Saturday; and after the Rites you will come home with us. Purefoy will be at M.M.H. at 1.30 for examination.[4]

---

[1] Waite was interested in the two plays of Werner that concerned the Knights Templar: *The Brethren of the Cross*, and *The Sons of the Valley*. The latter was translated into English for him by Maud Cracknell, a member of the Hermetic Order of the Golden Dawn.

2   i.e. *The Hidden Sacrament of the Holy Graal*, the 'Mystery Play' written jointly by
    Waite and Machen. It was published in 1906 in *Strange Houses of Sleep*, a collection
    of Waite's poetry.

3   The Healing Cup of Nant Eos, in mid-Wales, is a wooden dish of uncertain date
    (but probably medieval); before the Reformation it had been kept at the Abbey of
    Valle Crucis. The article, which appeared in *The Church Times* of 16 February 1906,
    has been preserved in one of Machen's notebooks devoted to his Grail
    investigations. The letter thus probably dates from early 1906.

4   Machen was already a member of the Golden Dawn — he had entered it on 21
    November 1899 — and in 1904 he persuaded Purefoy to join. She entered Waite's
    branch of the G.D. (the Independent and Rectified Rite) on 24 September 1904, but
    was never a very active member. 'M.M.H.' is Mark Masons' Hall, then in Great
    Queen Street, where the Order held its meetings.

---

5 Cosway Street,
N.W.
Tuesday

Dilectissime,

I see that we shall meet on Saturday next: mind you set your house in order
so that you can come home with us for the evening. I must again urge on you
the weekly meeting at the Garrick Tavern, on Fridays, at 2 p.m.

Proposition (after reading morsels of strange, outlandish, dubious Liturgies
— Coptic, Jacobite, Nestorian, Abyssinian &c).

The torn and soiled hem of the Raiment of Holy Church compared with
the whole Sacristy of 'Occultism' is as Fair Rubies and Orient Pearls
compared with Mud and Dung.

Proposition. The most holy and interior Truths or Mysteries, being uttered
or formulated, *ipso facto*, become foolish and soul-poisoning Heresies. So
'Protestantism' itself was once a holy, everburning Lamp. The Doors were
opened, and it was instantly made and remains a Black Smoke of Perdition,
and a Pestiferous and Stinking Vapour.

You will be interested to hear that I have found an Albigensian Ritual,[1]
containing the Rites of Admission, Consolation, and Consolation of the Sick.
Date about 1250-1260. 'Dissenting' in tone: no hint of Eucharist:
'Consolation' (administered by laying on of a Book and of Hands and by the
Kiss) described as the Baptism of the Holy Ghost and of Fire. Ministers the
ancien and the *bons hommes*. But, oddly enough, the chief, one might say the
only, ornament of the MS is the *Fish*; which is repeated again and again! —

sometimes it is an initial letter, sometimes a Fish in the margin is caught by a line attached to a letter in the text.

I have found out some curious coincidences about an early British person I have been investigating lately. We will call him X, or rather St. X,[2] as he was much reputed for holiness, and for the planting of Xty. in Britain.

Firstly, then, his birth was prophesied by the catching of a Fish.

2. He was famous under a Welsh nickname which is said to mean *Vir Aquaticus*.
3. He was of the Lineage of King David.
4. He had ancestors of the name of 'Avallach'.
5. He is described as providing the Xtians with the Sacred Vessels for the Eucharist.
6. The first church he built was at Glastonbury.
7. He obtained his Order from Jerusalem where he was given a mysterious Altar in which the Lord's Body had lain. This altar, the matter of which no man could comprehend, was transported to him through the air from Jerusalem, and vanished after his death. William of Malmesbury says it was 'lost' for a long time, and identifies it with the Glastonbury Altar stone, called *Sapphirus*. It is called *altare anceps* by an earlier writer (*c*.1090 A.D.), *anceps* meaning both 'uncertain' and 'perilous'.
8. Cadwaladr the Blessed after whose death in 664 the whole British Church for some unknown reason drooped and pined away, was of Saint X's Lineage, and was called the Last King of Britain. Cadwaladr is said to have gone on some kind of holy errand to some far land; and it was believed that with the return of his bones (or of himself, reincarnate), with the return also of certain lost relics all things would be restored and the Golden Age be renewed.

It makes the foundation of a pretty hypothesis, which may or may not be strengthened. Let us always remember Prof. Saintsbury's caution, and decline to say *nous savons* unless we *do* know.

I have looked up the Bollandists on S. Joseph of Arimathea. They scoff at the 'Apostle of Britain' Story, and say, more or less rudely, that it was invented by the Liar who wrote about King Arthur.

By the way, I see that Nutt, in his little book,[3] is of the opinion that the G. Romances 'reveal attempts to claim for the Knightly priesthood a position and sanction equal if not superior to those of the regular priesthood'. He is speaking, of course, of the Templars, and he thinks that Henry II 'backed up' this movement.

Yours ever fraternally,

Arthur Machen

1 L. Clédat, *Le Nouveau Testament traduit au XIIIe siècle en langue provençale, suivi d'un rituel cathare* (Paris, 1887).

2 i.e. St David. Machen is drawing parallels with the legends surrounding Joseph of Arimathea. See 'The Secret of the Sangraal', in *The Shining Pyramid* (1925), pp.100-106.

3 Alfred Nutt, *The Legends of the Holy Grail*, 1902 (Popular Studies in Mythology, Romance & Folklore, No. 14), p. 49.

---

6 Cosway Street,
N.W.
Thursday

Dilectissime,

We hope to turn up to Tea & Equinox[1] next Saturday: you will come back with us, I hope.

I know the possibility of keeping anything secret interests you; & I think that the case of 'Shelta' is probably unique. About 30 years ago, I suppose, Leland[2] heard two men jabbering a strange lingo in the Euston Road. This lingo turned out to be a secret Gaelic language: a mixture of primitive Gaelic, rhyming slang, back slang, Latin, Greek, & Hebrew invented by Irish monks *c.* 900 A.D., & transmitted by them, through the ecclesiastical metal workers of Ireland to the tinkers of today. The secret was kept, say, from 900 to 1875!

Yours ever fraternally,

Arthur Machen

1 i.e. The Ceremony of the Equinox of the Independent and Rectified Rite of the Golden Dawn. The letter was thus, probably, written on 21 March or 19 September 1907.

2 Charles Godfrey Leland (1824-1903) was the American essayist and folklorist who discovered Shelta, the secret language of the tinkers. His book *The English Gypsies and their Language* was published in 1872.

6 Cosway Street,
St. Marylebone N.W.
Tuesday

Dilectissime,

What has befallen you? You go out into the confusion of the night, and are seen no more. I have been expecting more proofs of the Graal.

We went down for ten days into the country in August and had a very pleasant time. I trust you are keeping well and that 'things' — meaning worldly matters — are tolerable, or more than tolerable.

I am dwelling in the midst of alarms. On receiving my last *Academy* cheque I was startled by its appalling minuteness, and on reckoning up my contributions found that, without any intimation to me, they had reduced my rate by 10% per thousand! Alas for the word of an English noble! I regard the scutcheon of the proud Douglases as stained. I have written a very civil letter to Douglas,[1] pointing out the demerits of the case, and suggesting that it must be a clerical error in the office. But I fear me that my *Academy* days are done. In the meanwhile I have got an apology for a job on a lousy sheet called 'T.P.s Weekly'. Of course it is all the doing of the extraordinary Crosland,[2] who acts, I think, from some obscure and mysterious centre of purposeless malignity, without any true Act of the Will, properly so called. I do not know to what he would be 'referred' cabalistically but he seems to me to approximate to those Ghosts who are always breaking crockery, and throwing saucepans about, without any very clear idea of why they do it, or what they want. As a student of things deep, obscure, and hidden beneath the earth, I am sure you will be interested in a remark that I heard Crosland make. After proclaiming (with oaths) his entire devotion to the Holy Roman Catholic and Apostolic Church; he declared (also with oaths) that there was more holiness to the square yard in the Primitive Methodist denomination than in any other sect or assembly of Christians. On the whole I am inclined to think that a Paper should be read on him at Oliver's.

I received a brief note from England[3] this morning informing me that he has just been received into the Roman Fold. I trust it will be to his soul's health.

Woolley, the curate, has got a 'job' on the phrase 'a Watcher and a Holy One' from the Prophet Daniel. He intends to prove that 'a Watcher' is an emissary of Satan; and I believe he will devote his life to this great task. Is purposeless mania to be the chief feature of the days before the last great battle called Armageddon?

When shall we see you?

Yours ever fraternally,

Arthur Machen

[1]   Lord Alfred Douglas (1870-1945) gave Machen a regular job with *The Academy* in 1907; Machen's last contribution — a piece entitled 'Paganism' — was published on 29 August 1908. Two weeks earlier he had begun contributing to *T.P.'s Weekly*; the letter can thus be dated to the early days of September 1908.

[2]   T. W. H. Crosland (1868-1924), the minor poet and essayist of the 1890s and the Edwardian era, was assistant editor of *The Academy* from 1908-11. He disliked Machen, referring to him as 'MacHen', and wrote a parody of 'The Bowmen', entitled *The Showmen,* in 1915.

[3]   Paul England (1865-1932) was an actor and singing teacher. He was a friend of Frank Hudleston and the two of them brought Machen into theatrical circles.

---

6 Cosway Street,
N.W.
Monday
['after Sept. 21, 1908'
added in pencil]

Dilectissime,

We were sorry not to see you on Saturday night. I think Purefoy had said something to our vicar[1] about the possibility of your coming round, as the said priest called and hoped you would come, since he wanted you to give him some tips about the angels!

I gather that the Dr Cobb[2] of whom you have spoken is not exactly a *persona grata* in Catholic Anglican circles. He is regarded as a renegade, a Hensley Henson[3] (= a rationalist) under a feeble disguise of mysticism, and finally as a 'blasphemous madman!'

Is what I call the 'Bristol Graal'[4] stirring at all?

When are you coming round?

Yours ever fraternally,

Arthur Machen

[1]   The Revd James Newland-Smith was the Vicar of St Mark's, Marylebone Road, from 1904–29.

[2]   The Revd W. F. Geikie Cobb was the Vicar of St Ethelburga's in the City of London. His interest in occultism is apparent in his book *Mysticism and the Creed* (1914). He was also one of the founders of the androgynous 'Order of Antient Masonry'.

[3]   The Revd Herbert Hensley Henson was, at the time Machen wrote this letter, Rector of St Margaret's, Westminster. In 1920 he was appointed Bishop of Durham after having been, successively, Dean of Durham and Bishop of Hereford.

[4]   This was the glass vessel, allegedly found at Glastonbury, which was being publicized by W. Tudor Pole of Bristol.

---

6 Cosway Street,
N.W.
Omn. Anim. 1908
[2 November]

Dilectissime,

I should have written to you before to say that I cannot be with you on Wednesday, since Hudleston[1] has a fortnight's engagement to dine with me on that night. I am sorry. When can you come here? I ask particularly because I have a drink that might 'do you some good'. One of the Stingo[2] people mixed absinthe and Italian vermouth in one bottle by mistake. They were going to throw it down the sink, but Mr Brown said 'Mr Machen may like it!' I tasted it, and called on the rocks to cover me.

I wish I had your power of recuperating by the way of Rites. Yesterday I heard Mass, went to evensong, and then sang the Vespers of the Dead. This morning I 'assisted' at High Mass at 7 *a.m.*! We are both tired to death; in spite of the fact that these high rites were performed with great liturgical exactness.

Perhaps it would be as well — in the event of the remaining proofs not being forthcoming in a day or two — if you would send me your great and marvellous conclusions in the whole matter of the Graal in numbered and summarized form, so that I could present your case in your own words to my intelligent readers of *T.P.'s Weekly*.[3] And since they are so intelligent: You had better not go beyond words of two syllables! I have not heard yet from

Rebman about my book;[4] and I scarcely know what I want to hear. Great is my need of money indeed; but strong is my conviction that, in my case, they would do no good.

Yours ever fraternally,

Arthur Machen

[1]   Frank Hudleston, Machen's brother-in-law.

[2]   'The Yorkshire Stingo' was a public-house in the Marylebone Road, frequented by Machen and Waite.

[3]   Machen's review of *The Hidden Church of the Holy Graal* appeared on 12 February 1909, as 'The Holy Graal: A New Theory.'

[4]   This was presumably *The Secret Glory*. It was eventually published in 1922.

---

12 Melina Place,
London, N.W. 8
Dec. 13. '26

Dilectissime Frater,

Very many thanks for your kind reply to Summerford[1] (Exeter College) who wanted to know about the Grail Romances. He is a very promising lad. I believe that he is going into a publishing business with a friend older than himself.[2] It is a small liturgical publishing firm that they have acquired; & I gather that they want to make it more general. I know not what they will make of it.

Herewith a brief note on an old topic. There is something very pleasing in the operations of a Magic Stone being ended by the Board of Agriculture. [The enclosure has not survived.]

With every good wish
Yours ever fraternally,

Arthur Machen

It is very nearly 40 years since we first met!

And, by the way, Gow[3] told me that you had come to regard the Universe as a joke of the Eternal; & from what I could infer, not a very good joke at that. I perceive you will end by symbolizing with 'Rosicrucian' Jennings. *Send for Father Murphy: quick!*

[1]   For Colin John Summerford, see pp. 83–6. Waite had written to him on 5 December.

[2]   Lance Fairtlough, see pp. 108–109.

[3]   David Gow (1866–1939), the Scottish poet and journalist and a long-standing friend of Waite. At this time he was editor of the Spiritualist journal, *Light*.

---

12 Melina Place,
London, N.W. 8
Feby. 8. 1927

Frater Dilectissime,

I am so glad you found some minor treasures in the ashes.[1] Dustmen, they say, are sometimes gladdened by the rare discovery of a silver spoon! By the way, I believe my Arthurian story is the only version that makes Lancelot 'Bishop of Canterbury'!

I am sorry; but I have only single copies of 'Precious Balms', & 'Strange Roads'. 'P.B.' is simply a collection of all the bad reviews of my books from 1895–1924. 'S.R.' is a small thing: two articles of mine made into a little book.[2] They are not bad articles; but nothing to write home about. It never struck me that either book would signify anything to you.

I think you will be glad to hear that Hilary[3] (aged 15) is clamouring to learn Hebrew in place of Physics (what *is* that nonsense?) &, he hopes, Mathematics. Of course he shall learn Hebrew, & read the *Greater Holy Assembly*[4] in the original, and Hebrew always comes in useful for incantations.

Are you still thinking of that book I told you to write: your Confession of Faith & Doctrine without the veil of symbolism? Why don't you combine it with a loose autobiography?[5] I can answer for it that it would be of vital interest & high value.

With all good wishes, vows, & prayers
Yours ever fraternally,

Arthur Machen

(Have you read anything about the Revised Common Prayer? I regard it as a miracle; it is so much better than I had expected.)

---

[1]   Waite was then working on his great kabbalistic study, *The Holy Kabbalah*; much of his research he saw as a 'raking around among the ash-heaps'. Machen had sent a copy of his book *Notes and Queries*, published in November 1926, containing the story 'Guinevere and Lancelot'.

[2]   *Precious Balms* was published in 1924, and *Strange Roads* in 1923. The two articles that comprise the latter, 'Strange Roads' and 'With the Gods in Spring', first appeared in Vol. I of *Out and Away* in 1919 and 1920.

[3]   Arthur Hilary Blaize Machen was born on 3 February 1912, St Blaize's Day. He died, aged seventy-five, on 18 December 1987.

[4]   i.e. the *Idra Rabba*, that part of the *Zohar* that was best known (in translation) to would-be Western kabbalists.

[5]   Waite published his autobiography, *Shadows of Life and Thought*, in 1938. It can fairly be said to incorporate his 'Confession of Faith & Doctrine'.

Lynwood:
Amersham: Bucks.
Aug. 20. 1929

Frater Dilectissime,

All my thanks: just what I wanted.

As for the end of a literary life; there is a picturesque way, & a plain way of putting it. You may say that it is a very sad thing that a life of strenuous work, conscientiously performed, should be rewarded with penury & all the miseries and terrors that come in its train. Or, again, you may say that if a man brings goods to the market, whether they be books or cheeses, they must, above all, be marketable. The man may urge that his cheeses were the best he could make, & that it is not his fault if they failed to please. It will be answered — in the words of the judge in 'Erewhon' — 'It may not be your fault, but it is a fault in you.'

Do you remember the case? The prisoner was charged with Pulmonary Consumption, a felony. His defence was that he had counterfeited the disease for purposes of fraud; a perfect defence, if he could have sustained it.

I don't remember the title I suggested for your book.[1] Has 'Behind the Veil' (of symbolism) been used? I was very much struck by a sentence I saw somewhere in Hugh Benson: to the effect that he held the Catholic Faith 'by analogy'. He meant, I suppose, that while he believed in 'the foot of the mountain', he did not expect to find mountains based on gigantic human feet, with toes and toenails. I thought the point a remarkable one.

Yours ever fraternally,

Arthur Machen

[1]   i.e. Waite's autobiography.

Lynwood,
Amersham,
Bucks.
April 28. '30

Dilectissime Frater,

It was a very great pleasure to receive your letter: you did a good action in writing it.

First as to Williams[1] & his *War in Heaven*: I am afraid the book is of little value. It is largely spoilt by its corrupt following of Chesterton: the Archdeacon, full of craft & piety, with his refrain of 'For His mercy endureth for ever', is pure Chesterton. The Latin, of course, is just wild, & your postcard satisfied me that Williams was wrong in thinking that Black Magicians' Latin has rules peculiar to itself. Gollancz,[2] the publisher, is a most amiable Jew, but I am afraid he lacks discretion. More than a year ago he announced that he was reprinting the complete works of M. P. Shiel.[3] Three or four were issued; & then silence. I often wondered what happened, but I fear I shall never know. A prospectus was issued, giving a short life of Shiel, written by himself: a mass of the most infernal & extraordinary lies. I don't know whether you remember, but in Gray's Inn, I used to have a sort of parlour game of asking people to what race they supposed Shiel belonged, & each one guessed a different nation. And Jew Gollancz told me that he was quite sure that S. was a Jew, till he read a bit of Hebrew in one of his own books, & pronounced Tetragrammaton 'Jehovah'.

As to the Grail: I know of no other example of the incident of the omitted question — which is made odder, if I remember, by the fact that Percival had been strictly instructed that it is bad manners to ask questions. (A curious survival, by the way, of this ancient rule of politeness is found in court circles: you must not ask royalty even whether it has enjoyed the shooting, or whether it admires the scenery.) But I am inclined to think that the question is a matter for the folklorists, that it belongs to the pre-Christian element, & that it has no real concern with the root matter of the Grail. I place it, in fact, in the same class as the Wounded Keeper, who belongs, as I hold, to a remote antiquity. But is there no *Folk Lore Journal*, or some such paper, in which you could appeal for skilled information on this point?

I have no belief in 'heretical sects' as a source of any Grail doctrine. Whatever the Grail may be, it is written in exaltation of the Sacrament at the Altar; & whatever heretical sect you choose, you will find, I believe, that its doctrine of the Sacrament is null, dull, and Protestant. You remember that Albigensian Ritual I found? I could hear something very like it any Sunday; in any meeting house.

Hutchinsons[4] are scoundrels, & always have been. Their conduct to you is entirely blackguardly, & just what I should expect from them. I hope you will recover.

You say nothing of your health or Sybil's?[5] I hope you are both well. I forget whether I told you that Hilary has been building organs for the last four months. He seems to like it.

Now, remember: when you write to me, you do a good work.

Yours ever fraternally,

Arthur Machen

[1]   Charles Walter Stansby Williams (1886-1945) had been an active member of Waite's Fellowship of the Rosy Cross from 1917-28. There is no evidence, however, that Waite read any of his novels, of which *War in Heaven* (1930) was the first to be published.

[2]   Victor Gollancz (1893-1967), the publisher and political idealist, founded his own firm in 1928 after working for Ernest Benn. He admired Machen's works but did not publish any of his books.

[3]   Matthew Phipps Shiel (1865-1947) was a prolific author of fantastic and adventurous tales. The five novels reprinted by Gollancz in 1929 were *The Purple Cloud* (in which Machen appears as a poet), *The Lord of the Sea, Cold Steel, The Last Miracle* and *The Yellow Peril*. See p. 142.

[4]   Hutchinson had acquired the publishing firm of William Rider & Son in 1927 — and

with it the periodical *The Occult Review*. In March 1930 the editor told Waite that they were looking for someone else to write the regular feature 'Periodical Literature' that he had contributed since 1911.

[5]   Sybil Waite (1888–1980) was Waite's only child, with whom he lived.

Lynwood,
High St.,
Amersham, Bucks.
March 30. 1932

Dilectissime Frater,

Now you, of all people are the last to ask, 'Why'. The *ratio essendi* (scholastic Gerund) of the enclosed [the enclosure is missing] may be dark to you, but you know well that we are surrounded by mysteries; that it is of the definition of man that he can ask many questions which he can never answer.

How are you, & how is Sybil? I hope that you are making grand progress in your terrific task.[1]

Paul England is dead. I have not yet heard fully how & of what; but I gather that he had fallen into a sad condition of mind & body: neurasthenia, I think they call it.

With all good wishes
Yours ever fraternally,

Arthur Machen

---

[1]   At this time Waite was working on a revision of his Grail study. The revised work, *The Holy Grail*, was published in 1933.

Lynwood,
Amersham, Bucks.
March 6th, 1933

Frater Dilectissime,

What a present![1] I cannot thank you enough for it, & for the inscription to old friendship, to many adventures of body and spirit undertaken together in the gardens & the halls of Camelot in the days that were. And, by a happy chance, the book came on the day after my seventieth birthday: a good omen for such days as are to come.

Do you know what was the first thing I looked up, as soon as string & brown paper were abolished from the book? Why, that matter of the Albigenses & Simon de Montfort, which has been a weight on my mind for months. *Now*, I understand why St Louis loved the story; & am much relieved. You cannot extract the odours of the sanctuary from the matter of the muckheap. It was, certainly, horrible to slaughter & massacre & burn those poor wretches: but I like them none the better for the violence & cruelty of their punishment — though I like the authority, civil & ecclesiastical, worse.

It is a grand book; & I find it well produced; the page is admirably clear, a comfort to dim eyes.

Shortly, I shall begin to write to you about it.

Yours ever fraternally,

Arthur Machen

I am drinking Noble Square Face this very day to the prosperity of the *magnum*. I was too late with *John O'London*; I feared it would be so.

---

[1]   i.e. *The Holy Grail*, which Machen saw as Waite's *magnum opus*. It was published on 1 February 1933. The review in *John O'London's Weekly*, by 'W.G.', appeared on 11 March.

Lynwood,
High St.,
Amersham, Bucks.
Dec. 19. '35

Frater Dilectissime,

The hour draws on; the Clerks are singing the Great Oes; I give you the greeting of Christmas: *induamus arma Lucis.*

Did I ever tell you, how, going to Mass on a Christmas morning, when we lived in Melina Place, I saw, down in Lisson Grove, the milkman going his rounds. He knew nothing of me, but I knew, somehow, that he was a Welshman. So I shouted across the street: *Nadólig Llawen*★ (★pronounce: *lthlówen*: the *th* to be insinuated between the two *lls*, as if a man said *Elthl* for *Ethel*) — Merry Christmas. He leapt into the air, & answered with a torrent of his native tongue, with tremendous joy.

I have just been glancing over the current *Light*: they still send it to me, as I suppose they do to you. I find there the true significance of Xmas, that Myers has gone a bit reincarnationist, & all about St Paul, as delivered by the Cummins — who, I think, was Bligh Bond's typist till she discovered that she could do it on her own, without the bother of Bligh Bond. It is all rather Melancholy.[1]

I remember speaking of Bligh Bond & his Glastonbury nonsense to the learned Oswald Barron, the antiquary. 'No doubt.' said he, 'they think that the early mediaeval Latin for William was *Gulielmus*. They're wrong: it was *Willelmus.*'

And your news? What work finished: what on hand? Let us hear of it. You are like *Sylvanus Urban* in Johnson's Latin Ode: *Urbane, nullis fesse laboribus.* What would an editor of today say, if a contributor addressed him in smooth Alcaics? Anyhow, I am sure he would not print them in the next issue of the magazine. I enclose a cutting that may or may not have an interest for you.

Our news begins with Janet,[2] who has made a promising enough beginning to the precarious career of the stage. We have seen her as the Apparition of the Crown'd Child in *Macbeth*, also as the Parlour maid (with dreadful screams) in *Jekyll and Hyde*. She has been re-engaged for *Faust* after Xmas. What little she has to do, she does well. Hilary, in a small farm near Northampton, has begun to write to some purpose. He has a beautiful little Xmas story, 'Caspar on the Dole' in a recent no. of 'G.K.'s Weekly'. For myself: Armstrong[3] (he wrote to you once) went grubbing in my dustbins for 45 years, & got together a collection of short stories, which will be published in the coming spring. It is a strange and — to me, at all events — an appalling thing to be confronted with the casual, temporary stuff of 1890. But there is a little money in this shady transaction. What about the old French saying: *dégoûté de fame, et affamé d'argent*? And, another small matter: Hutchinson has asked me to write a Preface to a book Philip Sergeant is getting together: 'Witches and Warlocks',[4] I think it is to be called.

To you and your family, & your wife[5] and Sybil, all our love and Christmas wishes.

Yours ever fraternally,

Arthur Machen

Faust. Do you remember how we had beer at the old, vanished Bell in Holborn, and went to see *Faust* at the Lyceum[6] — nearly 49 years ago?

---

[1] Geraldine Cummins (1890-1969) produced automatic writing allegedly inspired variously by Philip the Evangelist, Cleophas and F. W. H. Myers. She was involved in a bitter dispute with F. Bligh Bond over the 'Cleophas' scripts.

[2] Janet Frances Machen (b. 1917). See also p. 69 and pp. 147-8.

[3] T. I. Fytton Armstrong (1912-70), who wrote under the name of 'John Gawsworth'. See pp. 169-70 ff. The short story collection which he compiled was *The Cosy Room* (1936).

[4] *Witches and Warlocks* was published in 1936.

[5] i.e. Waite's second wife, Mary Broadbent Schofield, whom he had married in August 1933.

[6] Probably *Faust and Loose*, a burlesque by F. C. Burnand, first performed in 1886.

Lynwood,
High St.,
Amersham, Bucks.
April 11. '36

Dilectissime Frater,

In the first place: I would say that the Autobiography, so happily commissioned, is, in effect, the book which I urged you to write some time ago — your unofficial, 'unvestimented' views of life as you have led it and seen it. You will put down everything which strikes you as significant, & leave out everything which seems void of consequence or meaning — and the result will be rich reading. Selwyn & Blount are reputable publishers, a firm of good name.

Fytton Armstrong earned that dedication. If it had not been for him, there would have been no such book. He dug and scraped in old literary dustbins, got the stuff typed, discovered the agent, who found the publisher. I believe the 'Life' at which, as you know, he made an attempt is now abandoned. And very well too, since, externally, there is nothing to write about, and internally, I have done it all already in 2 books called, 'Far Off Things' & 'Things Near & Far'.

'All so good together': I remember your comment on that text — 'Does she[1] mean that time when we sat up all night drinking port, with Menteith locked in his bedroom, till at 8 o'clock in the morning, the housemaid came into the room, just as she fell on my neck, & I said, "You drunken little cat!"' I hope she fares well, or tolerably well. I think you said she had made money by speculating — which seems strange — *Medio de fonte jocorum Surgit amandi aliquid.*

They are pleasant & diverting memories. You remember your interior doctrine that, on a somewhat scandalous morning of Coronation, Dora, though she visibly and phenomenally got into a cab in Holborn, *never got home*. There is something of what the blasted Reformers called 'most comfortable' in this teaching.

And since we are discoursing of interior things: tell me if I am right in declaring that the Serpent did not ascend beyond Daath (the logical understanding) in the Tree of Life? And furthermore; that being so, we may speak of the world of Kether, & the works of it as uncorrupted? Or, in terms of literature, may it justly be said that Pope's Character of Addison is of Daath, while Coleridge's *Kubla Khan* is of Kether?

All this, let me tell you, relates to a mystical painter of mine[2] in a 50,000 word collection of stories, commissioned by your old pal Hutchinson. Which reminds me. The original editor of *The Evening News* liked pulling the leg of Dick, the sporting editor. So he would go to him and ask what was to be the football news of the day. 'Well', Dick might reply, 'the Pensioners & Bromley United ought to show good sport.' (You know football people called the Chelsea team 'the Pensioners'?) Whereupon Evans, in simulated horror: 'What! do you mean to tell me that you make those poor old b—s, with half their arms & legs missing, turn out & play football on a day like this?' Whereupon Dick turns purple with rage.

But; *de me fabula*.

And finally; most hearty congratulations on your report of yourself, that in spite of hard & weary & all night toiling in the masonic boat[3] with 12 hours sleep, you would be as good a man as ever.

Who could say better of himself?

With all our good wishes to Sybil, your wife & yourself

Yours ever fraternally,

Arthur Machen

P.S. It has suddenly struck me that you used to suffer badly from your feet. Do you still? If so, & if the trouble is on the soles, write to

Mr J. W. Simpson, Aldwych House, The Strand, London W.C. 2 — and say Please send me a pair of Iodine Socks Mans size? — enclosing 1/3.

Purefoy and I have worn them for the last eight months. They have entirely cured most damnably painful callouses. The pain ceases in about 6 weeks.

A.M.

[1] i.e. Dora Stuart-Menteath, for whom see p. 32.

[2] i.e. In the story 'Out of the Picture', published in *The Children of the Pool* (1936).

[3] Waite was then working on a revision of his *The Secret Tradition in Freemasonry*; it was published in 1937.

High St.,
Amersham, Bucks.
May 18. '36

Dilectissime Frater,

In the first place: I think it is the general rule that in imaginative literature, as distinct from mechanical, though often highly valuable, bookmaking, no man can help another.

But, in exception to this rule, I remember that you gave me very important help in the matter of 'The Garden of Aval[launiu]s',[1] described as rather a disease than a book. You did this by urging me to 'cut the cackle and come to the 'osses' — though you did not use the Circus Master's idiom.

By the way: Jekyll was the mixed, natural man, good predominating. Hyde was pure Evil.

Now for your Memoirs. What you are looking for, I suspect, is the point of view, the key, from which & in which they are to be written. Since a man can only illustrate usefully from his own experience: I may say that I experienced your difficulty, in writing my memoirs (called, 'Far Off Things' & 'Things Near & Far'). Referring to them now, I seem to have solved the problem by writing a book which might have been called 'Pictures, Memories, Impressions, & Digressions'. Nothing in the least systematic, no tinge of: 'I was born on March 3rd 1863, at Caerleon-on-Usk, in Monmouthshire. My father, & etc.'

Now, of course, since you are A.E.W. & not A.M. *your* problem is, no doubt, entirely different from mine; & my vein of solution cannot be yours. But I gather that you also are not going to have any truck with systematic autobiography. Think then of topics & not dates, & of topics in which you have a vivid interest. For example: in the course of many years study & investigation, you had found no evidence that such an art as Magic had any existence. Moreover, you went on to say that you had found no evidence of that lower form of Magic which is said to induce delusion. In other words: 'Not only have I no proof that spirits can be evoked: I have no proof that the magician can make the other man (the spectator) think spirits have been evoked.'

Well; 'I come from my vineyard, I know nothing' (Sancho Panza); but here is a topic which should make interesting discussion?

Another possible point. You wrote to the effect that you had seen certain rituals, the mere existence of which was known to very few people. Good: now ask yourself whether the matter of these rituals contains any truth or doctrine, of high consequence to the soul of man, not already known & acknowledged by the masters of the interior life.

To give an example of what I mean; I would cite masonry, & its doctrine of a Loss. I admit the picturesque & novel *manner* in which the doctrine is presented: but the matter of it is all in Genesis. — or: what do *you* say?

Many thanks for your *Daath* information. Now; shall we call this doctrine — whatever its origin — new? I am not sure.

I hope your spouse is better by now.

With our best wishes to you both

Yours ever fraternally,

Arthur Machen

---

[1]   *The Hill of Dreams* was serialized, in an abridged form, under the title of *The Garden of Avallaunius* in *Horlick's Magazine*, edited by Waite, from July–December 1904.

High St.,
Amersham, Bucks.
Nov. 16. '36

Frater Dilectissime,

So many thanks for your letter of Oct. 18, which I have left unanswered for all these shameful weeks. I believe you are right in thinking that there are hints or indications of new paths in 'The Children of the Pool': — but it is getting very late & dark for treading of strange ways.

Now, here is a proposition. Fortify yourself.

The next time you are in town: will you come down here, dine, & spend the night (in a pub hardby)? I will meet you at the station, & take you down the hill in a 'bus. Your train would be from Marylebone Station at 3.25.

Don't say no: I repeat: *vesperascit.*

Is the *magnum* finished & passed for press? Writing the other day to Summerford who was enquiring after you, I said: 'When they take in Walter Hutchinson's[1] tea of an afternoon, they find him sobbing quietly to himself. They think they hear the words "600 pages in quarto" amidst his tears. He is impotent in the grasp of the mighty Old One.'[2].

In case you do not see the *Observer:* mark the enclosed [now missing]. It looks to me a most interesting attack on this bewildered question. The Reviewer does not seem fully aware that the latest science justifies the main proposition of the alchemists: the transmutability of matter, or elements, so-called.

Never bother about the *S. Wales Argus* cuttings. The minor prophet who is unknown in his own country is generally lucky, if he knew it.

I have had an interesting newspaper controversy with one Lord Raglan[3] as to tradition & Mithraism, & a very old man in Hampshire, who said his father had told him there was a Golden Calf somewhere in the 'buried church' of the parish. Lord Raglan says he has come across 3 or 4 similar traditions, 'but', he adds, 'of course no Golden Calf has ever been found in any of these places; so that shows what tradition is worth.' I don't think he fully appreciates the bearings of the case.

Do you know that one of these tales has contrived to get into the Roman Breviary under the Feast of the Apparition of St Michael?

I should think Mead[4] was quite wrong in his attribution of that Ritual. I don't think he was a solid man.

Now: let me have a favourable answer to my question and invitation.

Yours ever fraternally,

Arthur Machen

You note, in the Review, the allusion to Flamel. I was rapt and fascinated by Flamel's story as given in a vol. of Dickens's *Household Words*: I read it more than 60 years ago![5]

[1]   Walter Victor Hutchinson (1887-1950), the chairman and managing director of Hutchinson & Co.

[2]   See pp. 150-51.

[3]   This refers, presumably, to Machen's piece, 'Can We Trust Tradition?', which appeared in *John O'London's Weekly*, 12 September 1936.

[4]   G.R.S. Mead (1863-1933) was a pioneer of the study of Gnosticism. Machen's doubt as to his reliability as a scholar probably stemmed from Mead having been a prominent figure in the Theosophical Society from 1890 to 1909. The 'Ritual' was probably *A Mithraic Ritual* (1907), edited by Mead as Vol. VI of his series *Echoes from the Gnosis*.

[5]   See *Far Off Things* (pp. 38-9).

High St.,
Old Amersham,
Bucks.
April 14. '37

Dilectissime Frater,

This is sad news & bad news, too. We are extremely sorry to hear of your wife's illness. Pray express to her our sympathy & wishes for a speedy and thorough recovery.

We will try again towards the end of May.

Was it at the King's Arms you spent your day with Bailey Weaver?[1] I thought he stayed at the Griffin. What a splendid liar he was when he was in the bonds of sin & brandy & morphia and good dinners. When he purged and lived theosophically I found him mouldy & deplorable. Years afterwards I came upon a storied inventor of fables, a sometime Roman Priest, named Moritz Weston. Did he ever come your way? I found, to my sorrow, that I had lost my relish of mighty lies; & when Weston told me how he had disguised himself as a woman in order to steal a document from the French Foreign Office; I was simply bored.

He ought to have been good enough for anybody. He had been a Rosicrucian, a silver miner in Nevada, a whaler in the arctic; he was a graduate of Heidelberg & Oxford; he was a Licentiate of Valladolid. He held the Xtian Gospels to be an Adonis Ritual. And I was merely bored!

Yours ever fraternally,

Arthur Machen

---

[1] Harold Baillie-Weaver (d. 1926) was a lawyer and man-about-town of the Edwardian era. He was converted to Theosophy and from 1916 to 1921 was General Secretary of the Theosophical Society.

High St.,
Old Amersham,
Bucks.
April 28. '38

Frater Dilectissime,

I got the book[1] all right; & I have heard something of the afterthoughts as to price & wrapper, & all that nonsense.

The drivelling imbecilities of the people who call themselves men of business cannot amaze me. Did I tell you what happened to me over my last book?[2] I had sent the MS. to my agent, & I was hungrily awaiting the small sum due to me on delivery. I waited for 3 weeks, & then asked the agent to hurry Hutch up. She replied that she didn't quite know what to do, as the MS. was 20,000 words short. A couple of days later she wrote that she had made a little mistake; it wasn't 20,000 words short, or any words short.

Yours is a wonderful book; of the deepest interest to me from beginning to end. Those early chapters are most affecting; in some ways reminding me a good deal of my early days in London, when I lived in my cell in Clarendon Road & wandered out westward, & knew Acton as a little old town, & the ways of Perivale, & the worries of Brentford.

Though I was solitary, & you found friends by degrees, there again, is sad reading, some of it. I am reminded of Johnson in his old age. As he sat, musing, people would sometimes catch a low murmur: 'Poor man! And then he died'. He was thinking of old friends of the black, starving, Grub Street days.

You have really written the book that I have urged you to write, more than once. You have cast of[f] symbols, & have opened your mind plainly.

I can't review it competently: for one thing the Editor has limited me to 800 words.[3] But you have my mind on it.

Our best to Sybil. You will feel better as I shall, when it gets warmer.

Yours ever fraternally,

Arthur Machen

---

[1]   *Shadows of Life and Thought. A Retrospective Review in the Form of Memoirs.* It was published in May 1938.

[2]   *The Children of the Pool.*

[3] Machen's review, entitled 'Mysteries of Religion', appeared in *The New Statesman and Nation* on 7 May 1938. It finally ran to some 1200 words.

High St.,
Old Amersham,
Bucks.
May 29. '38

Dilectissime Frater,

You have always suffered my reviews gladly: so doing you have doubtless acquired merit.

In fact — & more particularly on this occasion — 'you remind me of a man': — I hope you have not forgotten your old formula, the formal preface to great threatenings of judgement and ruin.[1]

But this man that you remind me of was a Hindoo, & an ascetic, a man of blameless life & innocency. Unfortunately for him, we were suppressing the Indian Mutiny, & the English soldier, coming upon the holy man in his meditation, bayoneted him on general principles. As he died, the saint, looking with great composure on the soldier, observed: 'Thou also art *that*'.

You speak of heaviness and inhibitions, & I feel that too. On purely physical grounds, I put such maladies down to north east winds & the human liver. I hope we shall feel better, the pair of us, when the winds die down, & a little warmth comes to the sun. We are at least recovered here from one of the worst chills that I have ever experienced: in my case complicated by that liver I have just spoken of. A cold in the head, a violent cough, an ache in every joint, a band of iron *outside* the head, a puddle of confusion *inside* it, fever, deliriums of nights, collapse of all appetite, & a profound conviction that a little drop of drink would do me a great deal of harm. What a way to live!

I never tried Vodka, since I have never been drawn to anything Russian. Now I like the Dutch, & respect them, & all the varieties of Hollands I find admirable. And I think I told you, that an acquaintance who knows the Netherlands, informed me that the Dutch regard the watering of Schiedam as quite absurd and unthinkable.

I read the *Times Lit. Sup.* review; and it gave me the impression that the writer of it was strongly & strangely attracted by your book & would have liked to praise it. But the subject matter was so much outside his range, that he didn't know how to begin.

An odd party came down to see us the other day.

Item, a former theatrical manager who ran our last tour.
Item, a 'leading man', one De Marney
Item, a Superintendent, from 'the Yard'
Item, Jimmy Wilde, ex-fly-weight champion of the world.
There entered, I think, into this composition something of that strangeness in the proportion, which Bacon praises so highly & so justly.

And, by the way, I have always thought that this Bacon dictum is one of the profoundest & most significant things uttered.

Remember us most cordially to your wife and Sybil.

Yours ever fraternally,

Arthur Machen

Greenwood[2] read your book with very great affection.

---

[1] Waite possessed a manuscript notebook, in Machen's hand, entitled *Similis Es*,* a collection of blackly humorous aphorisms much in the style of *Steps to the Crown*, which Waite had published in 1906. Most of the aphorisms begin with the same formula, as with 'You remind me of a man who opens a trap-door leading to the Infernal Regions, and says: Come let us seek the Interior Light.' They are probably the work of both men.
    (* In full: *Similis Es that is the book of Prophecies now fairly and truly recovered from the Ancient Writings.*)

[2] Edwin Greenwood (1895-1939) was an actor, stage-manager, novelist and screen-writer who lived at Amersham. In 1937 he and his wife took the Machens to Paris for a visit that was afterwards treasured. Machen's one consolation at Greenwood's tragic death was that such a keen Francophile should not have seen the fall of France.

High St.,
Old Amersham,
Bucks.
March 19. '40

Frater Dilectissime,

A day or two ago, I was reading, as I often am, in 'Shadows of Life', & came upon a very minor mystery. It is contained in your notes on William Sharp, &

refs (p.118) to Mrs Sharp: 'She also wrote verse in her earlier days, under the name of Graham R. Tomson'.

Now, in the late 'eighties there was a lady — whose name originally I don't remember — married to a barrister. She left him for an artist, named Graham Tomson, & I think wrote verse under that name. She then abandoned Graham Tomson for one Marriott Watson, who was one of Henley's young men on the *National Observer*, wrote in the very bright *Pall Mall Gazette* of the day, wrote books, including a 'Keynote'. Thus I met 'Mr & Mrs Marriott Watson' at a 'Keynotes Dinner' given by John Lane, *c.*1895. In Lane's List of this period you find: —

Watson (Rosamund Marriott)
  Vespertilia and other Poems.
  A Summer Night and other Poems.

I have a quite vague recollection of a handsome woman: — and that is all. I think that she & he are both dead years ago. But, surely, this Rosamund couldn't have been also, Mrs. Sharp, of a somewhat later period?[1]

I disagree, profoundly, with La Rochefoucauld's dictum: that there is something not wholly displeasing to us in the misfortune of our best friends. La Rochefoucauld was doubtless *armiger auratus* & *generosus* — even *generosissimus* — but his saying is cheap, & cheapness does not become a gentleman. It is also a lie — a matter of less consequence, perhaps; since lying is sometimes a painful duty. But though the axiom as it stands is false; it is yet true that there is some small comfort in the thought — 'we are in the same boat'; in misfortune, if you like, but still companions.

On two 'Royalty Dates', then, I sent my Royalties on to a friend.[2] On each occasion, they were contained in a Postal Order for 1/4; &, before the War, 1/4 just bought a 'Double'. My Christmas Royalties, through some chance which I forget, ran to 17/6. This sum I kept, for this sum I thanked Heaven. We have nothing to complain of. If, for one reason or another, our work fails to interest large numbers of people; the result, our Royalties in shillings and pence, are inevitable.

As to your health; you will go slow and lie quiet, & I am sure you will soon be all right. And you have the advantage, that the weather is growing gentler, & the change will be good for all of us. Here, the winter has been quite hideous: 2 months of the hardest frost, with a couple of slight short thaws, so that when the frost returned, the wet ground turned to glass, & we went abroad with socks over our shoes.

I heard from Brother Vivian Summerford[3] at Christmas, & am looking for another letter soon. Novices may receive as many letters as their friends like to write them; but they are only allowed to write letters themselves at Christmas & Easter. I think his chief impression of the cloister in his first week's experience was that it was a very cold place. But they did bravely on Twelfth Night: they had Cakes & Ale — & good ale, too — and the whole Convent, from the Prior to the Lay brothers, danced Sir Roger de Coverley, & kept it up till past eleven.

P[4] Don't pass this on. Just before he went in he was discussing his brand of politics — some noisome *saloperie* of Communism-cum-Pacifism, it happened to be just then — to one of the Fathers, who responded: 'He who is not loyal to his King will never be loyal to his God.'

The Father evidently has the root of the matter in him. Look in the Book: 'He that loveth not his brother, whom he hath seen,' &.t.c.

But poor Summerford had been seeing a good deal of Compton Mackenzie in the last few years. And when that English Officer, who spied for Germany, & was known for a time to the Press as, 'the Prisoner in the Tower,' came out of gaol, he was cordially entertained by Compton.

And, by the way, it gave me the greatest pleasure, at our last meeting with Summerford, to hear from him that Compton was beginning to think that there might be a good deal to be said for the theory that we, the English, are the Lost Ten Tribes. I thought to myself: 'Lucky for you, my young friend, that the cloister gates are closing on you. Else, we should have seen you going over the Egyptian Pyramid with a graduated rule & the Table of Pyramid-Feet & Pyramid-Inches, calling out the measurements to Compton Mackenzie *in sabulo*.'*

Which, oddly, reminds me. Lee[5] is coming down here, with Lester, next week; & he will try to convert me to the Cummins (?) Scripts; & I shall try to keep my temper.

Do give our warmest regards to your wife & Sybil; & though, perhaps, you are all off 'the Drink' for the present, let me give to you all the friendly greeting of the Bar Parlour: '*Cheerio.*' Which, being interpreted, is *Leebari*.

Yours ever fraternally,

Arthur Machen

* Rather a good burden for a song here?
   'He jots it down in sabulo
     Below, below,
   'He builds a house in sabulo,
     Below.'

[1] Rosamund Marriott Watson (1860-1911) published two collections of verse under the name of 'Graham R. Tomson': *A Bird-Bride* (1889) and *A Summer Night* (1891). Waite evidently confused her with Elizabeth Sharp who seems to have edited two of

the titles in *The Canterbury Poets* series — of which William Sharp was general editor — *Border Ballads* and *Ballads of the North Country*, also under the pseudonym of 'Graham Tomson'.

2　　Oliver Stonor, for whom see p. 111.

3　　Colin Summerford had entered the Dominican Priory at Woodchester in Gloucestershire in the autumn of 1939. He took 'Vivian' as his name during his novitiate.

4　　Machen used a large capital 'P' in the margin to indicate that this piece of information was private and confidential.

5　　The Revd. A. H. E. Lee (d. 1941) had been a member, with Machen, of Waite's Independent and Rectified Rite of the Golden Dawn. He was for many years the Vicar of St Martin's, Kensal Rise, and was the editor with D. H. S. Nicholson of *The Oxford Book of English Mystical Verse* (1916).

High St.,
Old Amersham,
Bucks.
May 17. '40

Frater Dilectissime,

What cheer? Don't answer, with *Captain Bunsby*[1] in Dickens, 'Damned bad'. I do hope you are feeling much better than when you wrote last; that you, your wife, and Sybil are all relishing the sun. Are you facing out the storm at Broadstairs? I confess that I would rather be somewhere in Central Wales — Builth or Brecon — than a mere 26 miles from town. It is possible, no doubt, to find faults of many kinds in Hitler — but one cannot deny that he is a thorough man. He does not scamp his work.

When you find a *scriba velociter scribens* — in point of fact, a typist — to your hand, don't forget the minor mystery of 'Graham Tomson.' Was the 'Mrs Sharp' you knew a beautiful dark creature?

You knew Ernest Rhys,[2] I think? Or did you only encounter him in business? His autobiography is reviewed in *The Times* 'Lit. Sup.' today. I should call him fortunate in his life. He was clearly born to edit series, & he edited series: — and a very useful work, too. I once met him, & was not greatly drawn to him. But our meeting was, I believe, one of the three Unfortunate Encounters of the Isle of Britain. A most amiable man of my acquaintance asked me to meet Rhys at

Stone's. And the kind host brought a friend of his with him. Inevitably, as it seemed, a certain community of race, age, interests, & employment led Rhys & myself to talk together a good deal. Thereupon, our host in a very bitter manner, bid his friend notice that such nobodies as *themselves* could not expect to share in any conversation with such magnates as *ourselves* — Rhys & I. The evening was chilled.

Another Unfortunate Encounter of the Isle of Britain was my meeting with Masefield,[3] now Laureate Poet. That was even more unfortunate.

I had an Easter letter from Colin Summerford. The habit seems to be fitting more easily than it did at first.

You are one of the few people who knew me when I looked a little like the enclosed [the enclosure is missing]; shall we say, like a somnolent Daudet. Nimes, where he came from, is very much a Roman town; so is Caerleon-on-Usk; but Nimes is a fiercer, more fiery place. In all respects — the amiable landlady, whose hotel gave on the perfectly preserved Temple of Diana, was speaking of the Bull Fights in the Arena, and said, in a hissing manner: 'the people down here love *Blood.*' In old Caerleon we preferred *Beer.*

Did you ever read Daudet's *Les Trois Messes Basses*? They were the masses of Christmas. The Priest had seen the magnificent Réveillon Feast spread by Monseigneur, whose chaplain he was. He longed for that feast, he could only see the Truffled Turkey over the Altar. His masses went faster & faster; his Server became the Devil: & when the Priest said: — *Dom scum* the Server answered *Sputuo*.

I need not tell you that this affair had a bad end.

Again: all our good wishes to you and yours. Let us try hard to live into a better age.

Yours ever fraternally,

Arthur Machen

---

[1]   The eccentric captain of the 'Cautious Clara', in *Dombey and Son*.

[2]   Ernest Rhys (1859-1946), essayist, poet and editor of the 'Everyman' series. Waite may have met him in the company of William Sharp when Rhys was editing *The Camelot Classics*.

[3]   Machen did not explain the nature of this 'Unfortunate Encounter'. In 1943 John Masefield was one of the signatories of the letter inaugurating a national appeal on Machen's behalf.

High St.,
Old Amersham,
Bucks.
July 3. '40

Dilectissime Frater,

We were very much distressed to hear of those 'attacks' of which you speak.[1] I see a month has passed since your letter: I do hope you are all the better for its passage.

I suppose the truth is that the good & strong air of the Isle of Thanet is *too* good, & *too* strong for you. I confess I should like to hear that you have moved, for the time, into some moist & warm valley of the west & south, where the wind is too tired to blow. You remember our old Marylebone Vicar, Newland Smith? He helped you over some Greek; in *Lumen de Lumine* I think it was.[2] Well, his heart was threatening, or more than threatening, & he lived for 12 years near Torquay. A Cockney in vain; he cursed his parishes & parishioners steadfastly for all those years, & would have thrown Dartmoor on the dust-heap, if it could have been done. But the climate cured all that heart trouble in less than no time, & it has stayed cured.

As for bombs & planes & roarings on sea & land; I was talking to a man here about flying from all such things, & telling him that I had a friend older than I, a little troubled about his heart, who lived at Broadstairs & found explosives soothing. He burst into eldritch screams, & ran down an alley.

I see the Case of the two Graham Tomsons must remain a mystery.

Janet is the fortunate member of our family. I think I told you that she went out, not quite a year ago, for a six weeks visit to friends in New York. As she was about to return, there came the war; and she has been entertained by her kind hosts ever since. They have shown her Connecticut, & what remains of the New England that your mother knew.[3] They took her down south to Georgia, where she saw plantation negroes, Spanish moss, & the cardinal bird. Her last excursion has been to the Rocky Mountains, where she sat a Mexican saddle, & learnt the cowboy seat.

We were relieved, I can tell you, to hear from Hilary a week or ten days ago, back, safe and sound, from France. So far, we have had no details of his campaigning. An earlier letter, from France, expressed high appreciation of the country, the people, the omelettes, & the good little red wine at 2½d a glass. He found the Church-Latin of the country a little puzzling at first.

All our very best wishes to you, to your wife, and to Sybil.

Yours ever fraternally,

Arthur Machen

1   At this time Waite was suffering from angina, which contributed to his death in 1942.

2   For J. N. Newland-Smith, see p. 46. In 1918 he helped Waite with the Greek
    quotations in *Anima Magica Abscondita*, a part of *The Works of Thomas Vaughan* that
    Waite was then editing. It was published in 1919.

3   Waite's father came from Lyme in Connecticut, and after his death in 1858, Waite's
    mother, Emma Lovell, lived at Lyme for twelve months before returning to
    England.

High St.,
Old Amersham,
Bucks.
Aug. 17. '40

Dilectissime Frater,

Lee & Lester were down here about a month ago; and Lee said that he
understood you have moved to the Canterbury neighbourhood.

But, since I am not sure that you have returned to the old Bishopsbourne
address; I send this to Betsy,[1] hoping that it will reach you. And I trust the
report that you have gone inland is true; not chiefly on account of bombs and
bangs, but rather because inland airs are milder than seafront breezes. Three
years ago, when poor Greenwood took us to Paris, I thought the seabreezes of
the Channel crossing would do me no end of good. I was all but dead when I
was hauled into the train at Dieppe.

From an accursed print called the *New Statesman*, I have extracted the
enclosed. I have a vague notion that I once met Ladbroke Black;[2] & yet again, I
cannot remember anything about him. I judge from his obituary notice that he
was a very good fellow, but a very bad journalist. The notion that it is clever to
describe something you haven't seen is held, or was held, I believe, outside the
Reporters' Room; but not inside. That path is plainly marked: *This Way to the
Sack and Boot* — an ill tavern, where all the drinks are sour.

I wish I were a Folklorist. For this reason: the other day when I was
meditating, as I often do, on our old Grail studies, it struck me that Merlin,
National Enchanter, is a unique figure in early legend & romance. I emphasize
'national': what may be called private enchanters and wizards are, of course,
plentiful enough; but I cannot recall another instance of a magician who
stage-managed a whole people.

Can you put me right on this point?

I need not say that I hope & Purefoy hopes that you are feeling much better.

Pray commend us to your wife and Sybil; & if I say that the aromas and the savours of certain noble meats & of certain bottles of opimian Burgundy are still grateful; let me remind you that it was a great and good man[3] who said: 'I mind my belly very carefully and very studiously; and I take it that he who does not mind his belly will mind nothing else.'

Yours ever fraternally,

Arthur Machen

Do you remember how, long ago, we explored Bermondsey, & how the Bermondsey Barmaids, on our calling for Gin, would offer us: 'Two Two's'. Those twopenny drinks would be about 15s 2d each now.

---

[1]   i.e. Betsy Cottage, Broadstairs. Waite's daughter also owned a cottage at Bishops-bourne, near Bridge, outside Canterbury.

[2]   Ladbroke Lionel Day Black (1877-1940), was a novelist, short-story writer and journalist. Machen probably met him in 1904 or 1905 when both men were contributors to *Horlick's Magazine*, which Waite edited.

[3]   i.e. Dr Johnson. The quotation is from a letter to Lord Chesterfield of 5 August 1763.

High St.,
Old Amersham,
Bucks.
Sept. 16. '40

Dilectissime Frater,

Fourteen years ago or thereabouts, I met 'Egyptian' Budge.[1] I told you of the encounter, & I remember your asking me, if I met him again, to enquire of him whether the Book of the Dead was dramatically enacted in Egypt. I never saw Budge again, I am sorry to say — he was famous company — and the question was not put; but here, from an unexpected quarter, comes the answer to it. If you would like to verify; you might write to Ivor Brown, c/o *The Observer*, & ask for his sources.

Did you ever hear of Budge's Vision of Examination, when he was an undergraduate? He told me how he dreamed the same dream, three times, on the night before his examination in Cuneiform; seeing the Paper, with one question for which he was not prepared. On the third repetition, he got up, made tea, & went thoroughly into the matter of the question. The next morning, fact justified the dream in every particular, including some quite trivial and insignificant circumstances.

I hope that the change inland has done you good. Do give our most cordial remembrances to your wife & to Sybil.

I don't think we have any news. Hilary, under arms, prepares to defend us from invasion. Janet roams about the U.S. & sees the Red Man in his flaming blankets.

But; by the way, there is some news — unless you have already heard it. Colin Summerford found that he was not called to be one of the Lord's Watchdogs; and left the Priory, about a month ago, with the blessing of the fathers. I know not what he will do next; nor, I think, does he.

Yours ever fraternally,

Arthur Machen

[1]   Sir E. A. Wallis Budge (1857-1934) was one of the foremost Egyptologists of his day and a prolific author. From 1893 to 1924 he was Keeper of Egyptian and Assyrian Antiquities at the British Museum.

High St.
Old Amersham,
Bucks.
Dec. 18. '40

Excuse 'Copy Paper' and being without a Breviary, I know not which of the Great Oes is now sounding in Choirs and Places where they sing—

Dilectissime Frater,

Every good and happy wish to you, to your wife, and to Sybil from Purefoy and myself.

I hope you are much better since the summer: that the bombs do not vex any of you over much. Here, we often fall asleep to the drone of Geman planes; but so far, the old town remains undamaged and untouched. Mass in the morning is said in darkness, save for the two altar candles & the lamp before the Sacrament: there is a solemnity about the scene.

The other night: 'listening in' I heard a Welsh country postman tell of his experiences now, in the dark of the morning. There were perils in roads & lanes from lorries, cars, bicycles; but what took me & made me think forthwith of you was his tale of a lonely cottage, far from the common tracks of men. Here there lives an old woman, who has a letter once a week. There are three ways of getting to this cottage, & the Postman has tried them all. One by the marsh: (it was here that I thought of you & certain lines in 'The Soul's Comedy'[1]) but in the dark, he lost his footing, & found himself sinking in black ooze & mire. One by the dense thicket of trees & undergrowth: but the boughs caught him, & he was swung into the air, saying to himself, 'if I hang & die here, nobody will ever find my body'. The third way is by fording the river, (a shallow one I suppose); and beyond the wet & the run of the waters, that, by comparison, he found easy.

I almost think that a very Secret Doctrine must be latent in this fable.

I wrote to you before the Xmas of 1886: now I write again, 54 years after.

Yours ever fraternally,

Arthur Machen

---

[1]   *A Soul's Comedy* (1887) was one of Waite's earliest works. It is a verse drama with significant autobiographical elements.

High St.,
Old Amersham,
Bucks.
In the Great Oes, 1941
[i.e. 17-23 December;
in fact 1940]

Dilectissime Frater,

It must be just about 55 years ago since you & I corresponded; since you got letters dated 'Llanthewi Rectory'. We have lived into another world. Like the Bishop of Hippo, we heard the Barbarians thundering at the gates. May our day show a better issue than his. It is curious to read the letters of Sidonius — born at Lyons, 431; died at Clermont, 489 — He is living through it all, still a perfect Roman country gentleman, & doesn't quite understand what is happening. 'No good talking Latin in Belgium or on the Rhine, now; a censorship on letters; very odd to see a Frankish wedding the other day, everybody armed to the teeth, more Mars than Venus about it, I thought. However, I daresay we shall live long enough to laugh at our fears' — and so on. When I first read this, four or five years ago, I thought how very odd it would be to see the bridegroom & his friends at an Amersham wedding carrying their guns to the church door. But I don't know: they might well be in 'battle kit'. I suppose Franks were also in battle-kit.

As to *Casanova*: I have letters from America, asking me when it will be issued; & I can only answer, I don't know. I believe there was some trouble caused about 18 months ago, by the man who issued an edition here in the earlier twenties. He fancies the copyright belongs to him: I don't think it belongs to anybody. However that may be as regards England, it certainly doesn't apply to the U.S. But I don't worry; as I told you, I have had the money & I don't want the book. The first edition, I remember, I gave you; second, I gave to another friend; I can get on well without the third.[1] The Penguin business does really concern me, since the publication of the book[2] would bring me £50 down. I had a letter from the Penguin firm the other day, from which I gather that they are still struggling bravely against Adversity and Hutchinson, and Secker and Warburg & the rest. I wish them well in their endeavours. As to *The Handy Dickens*;[3] I infer that Constables will be publishing it in the Spring; & whenever it comes my way, it shall certainly come yours, & quickly. you know, I daresay, that there are often discussions to be heard on the BBC, discussions about everything from Mangold to Magic. The other night I was a good deal disgusted to hear one of these discussion gangs uttering what were pretty well my sentiments about 'characters' in fiction, laying down the principle — for example — that if a character in a story were really lifelike, then the book must be rotten! *Pereant illi qui ante nos nostra dixerunt*; but what about those who say things *after* us? I laid down my doctrine in the matter 40 years ago in *Hieroglyphics*; & hence my difficulty, & I fear, lack of unction in writing the Dickens Introduction. I can't say the same thing all over again with ease & relish. I was glad to hear one, but only one, of the discussion people keeping to the good old stupid way. He said that the character of Micawber was not primarily intended to be amusing; but rather to enforce the Mid-Victorian moral of careful economy.

There is one of these B.B.C. discussions which often entertains us: that is the thing horribly called 'The Brains Trust'. At it I have heard Professor Joad, reckoned, I believe, a man of science, profess his belief in the theory, at least, of

Black Magic. The 'Question' had been sent in: 'What about Black Magic?' & the Professor, replying, said that he was convinced that there were evil powers as well as good in the make up of the universe, & that it might be possible to approach those powers, and — well, there you were; there was your Black Magic for you. He added that, if you could brush aside the great mass of imposture, & penetrate to the core of the Spiritualist séance, there you would find a manifestation of the powers of evil. He weakened his case, in my opinion, by advancing the Poltergeist — which he investigated at Borley Rectory[4] — as another emissary of Satan. Can evil manifest itself through Bad Boy Monkey Tricks? It seems to me highly improbable, at the least.

Another surprise from the B.B.C. Aldous Huxley,[5] once perhaps the brightest, smartest, most contemptuous of the Bright Young Literary Scoffers of the nineteen twenties, has given his judgement of the art of acting in terms more vehement & more damnatory than those of the late Cardinal Manning. Huxley experienced a change of heart some years ago. He was at first inclined to think that salvation was to be found in Mexican Serpent Worship, as expounded by the late D. H. Lawrence, & went to New Mexico, to see how the cultus worked among the Indians there. But this, it seemed, would not do; & he is now, I gather, a High Mystic, chiefly on the Christian basis, but with support from the *Bhagavat Gita*.

Let me finish on an Annoying Note. To delay on the Paston matter for a moment: the phrase struck me as highly curious & enigmatic; but I don't think it could possibly have any reference to fifteenth century freemasonry. But what I want to say is, that in my belief the fundamental matter of the 3rd Degree was a traditional ceremony of the journeymen, the paid labourers, on a man having finished his apprenticeship, & becoming a master mason, entitled to a higher rate of pay: that the men who worked it had no notion of any high or spiritual significance in what they did or said, that the main notion of the whole thing was a mixture of jocularity & the giving of a bit of a jolt to the candidate. The notion that a young fellow should have a bit of a jolt when he ceases to be a boy & is to be accounted a man, is most ancient & most diffused. The definition of 'jolt' varies: amongst the Red Indians, the young fellow had iron hooks run through his arms & was swung round & round in the air before he could be reckoned a warrior. Among the Coopers of England, the young fellow was (quite recently) put into a cask & trundled round & round the yard. When they let him out, he stood a bottle of whiskey.

Finally: it is highly improbable that the Rite — the words accompanying the Ceremony — were ever written down.

There: put that in your pipe and smoke it.

And with all our love to you & Sybil.

Yours ever fraternally,

Arthur Machen

Nota bene, that I do not attempt to trace the admittance ceremony of the medieval journeymen masons to its ultimate origins. Possibly, these were most ancient & august, & the rites had become rude in a long transmission through the hands of illiterate labourers: I know not.

[1] *The Memoirs of Jacques Casanova* was first translated by Machen in 1888–89 and published in 1894. It was reprinted in 1922 with a new preface by Machen, and his preface was revised yet again for an edition of 1940.

[2] *Holy Terrors*, a collection of fourteen of Machen's short stories, was eventually published as Penguin Book No. 526, in 1946.

[3] *A Handy Dickens*, selections from the works of Charles Dickens made and introduced by Arthur Machen, was published in 1941. The reference to its publication 'in the Spring', together with Machen's uncertainty about the re-issue of *Casanova* would seem to imply that the letter was written in 1940, not in 1941.

[4] The village of Borley, on the borders of Essex and Suffolk, was the site of a remarkable, alleged poltergeist haunting in and around its Victorian Rectory. Before the building burned down in 1939 it had been visited by hordes of investigators and sightseers. Professor Joad carried out his investigations in 1938; they are summarized in Harry Price's *The Most Haunted House in England* (1940).

[5] For Machen's views on Huxley's *Antic Hay*, see p. 119.

High St.,
Old Amersham,
Bucks.
Sept. 17 '41

Dilectissime frater,

Many long years ago, as you sat at your board in Ealing[1] I remember your filling a small glass — a 'pony' glass I think they called it — with whiskey in its purity, which you thereupon drank. You considered the matter judicially for a short while, & then gave sentence: 'This does me no good, Machen.' And I am hoping that this summer, such as it has been, has done better for you than that glass of whiskey, drunk forty years ago or more.

Not long since, Purefoy & I, relishing a rare cup at the King's Arms, fell to talking of those old days & of you, & we wondered whether we had ever related to you the sad story of the Marquis d'Autische. On the chance that this was formerly omitted; let it now be related.

The Marquis d'Autische, then, was a French Nobleman, of ancient & distinguished race. An ancestor of his, it is said, crusaded with St. Louis, & thus derived his title. The Marquis of, say, 40 years ago, was all that he should have been, loyal to the House of the lilies, *bien pensant*, profoundly Catholic. But there were moments, rare moments, when doubts assailed him; & in one of these painful seizures he was heard to exclaim: '*Je ne croisai jamais que le bon Dieu aurait fondé son église sur un calembour!*'

He was thinking, of course, of

Σν εἰ ὁ πετρος και πετρα ταντη ὁικοδομηοαι την εκκλησιαν μου[2]

And that reminds me: do you recall what the Norman Prior called Friar Tuck in *Ivanhoe*? *Tu es petra scandali et lapis offensionis*. I suppose that the Prior in the book is not a bit like the Prior in the 12th century, nor the irregular clerk of that age: but how jolly it all is! And it has been said that jollity is joy talking in the vulgar tongue.

Let me defend Sir Walter against an accusation that some might find latent in one of the above sentences: *Ivanhoe* is quite as true a picture of England in the XIIth century as *Hamlet* is of Denmark in the tenth.

Did you ever know anything of the thinking of Bergson, brother-in-law of our old friend, S. Liddell MacGregor Mathers?[3] I never read him, being put off, I think, by his discovery that Life was to be explained by the *élan vital*. This reminded me too much of the country doctor. I had remarked to him that I understood that asparagus was only beneficial to the action of the kidneys. 'If that is so,' said he, 'the effect must be due to the presence of asparagin.' But I saw somewhere the other day that Bergson held that the faculty by which man apprehends reality is akin to the faculty of instinct in animals. This struck me as impressive.

Brief News. Hilary, who has now been in the army for more than two years, thinks that he will be ordered abroad again before long. Janet, who has been in the USA for two years, got back to Amersham last Sunday, *via* Halifax, Greenland, Iceland, Northern Ireland, Liverpool. She sailed on a small Dutch ship, & that, perhaps, may explain the happy circumstances that she brought with her 2 bottles, not of 'Noble Square Face', but of the nobler Bols. Mark the felicity of the mere name: it seems to figure the utterance of one, who having enjoyed this rare spirit, perhaps too fully, should endeavour to say 'bottles'.

I hope Sybil is well & that your wife is well. You hate letter writing I know;

but tell Sybil that a brief line from her would be gratefully received.

Yours ever fraternally,

Arthur Machen

[1]   Waite lived in Ealing, at Sidmouth Lodge, South Ealing Road, from 1901-20.

[2]   Matthew 16: 18, 'You are Peter, and on this rock I will build My church.'

[3]   Samuel Liddell [MacGregor] Mathers (1854-1918) was an eccentric and autocratic occultist who devised and developed the rituals used within the Hermetic Order of the Golden Dawn — the magical Order created in 1888 by Dr William Wynn Westcott, and of which Waite and Machen had been members. Mathers had married Moina, the sister of the philosopher Henri Bergson.

High St.,
Old Amersham,
Bucks.
April 8. '42

Dilectissime frater,

Please give my hearty thanks to Sybil for her letter. I know that with that obstinate & most distressing neuritis the business of pen and ink must be a painful one; & I almost feel a sinner when I put her to it. I hope that both you & she are feeling some degree of aid from these milder airs. What a winter it has been! Do you remember a formula in frequent use with you some 42 years ago or thereabouts, a formula prefacing remarks to my address of a highly minatory and terrific nature? The formula was: 'You remind me of a man.' Well, this last winter reminds me of the winter of 1895 — six weeks of frost, a jolly dinner at the Greyhound with you, your wife, & Mrs Menteith: Bucellas; & the story of the Black Seal which I was writing just then. It is hard to realize that in this interval of 47 years a whole world has passed away & that you and I have survived into a new age. But so it is.

Let me give you an instance, trivial & jocose.

Three or four weeks ago, the retiring Archbp. of Canterbury, Dr Lang, was addressing a meeting of the S.P.C.K. He said in the course of his remarks: 'And, now, will you excuse me for a few minutes. I have to see these . . . photographers. I won't mention the adjective.' (Howls of laughter from the S.P.C.K.)

Can you conceive an Archbp. practically blessing the expletive 'bloody' in 1895? And, by the way, Lang is probably ignorant of the fact that 'the adjective' is derived from the terrific medieval oath: 'By God's Blood'. It is curious that the corresponding 'woundy' has utterly failed to survive.[1] I wish the new Archbp., Temple, were as innocent as Lang. He was delivering serious addresses in this Holy Week. He suggested that the darkness of the Crucifixion might have been occasioned by 'a coincidental eclipse of the sun'. There is a feebleness of mind here, which seems parallel to me with the mental state of those who derived the inn sign of *The Goat and Compasses* from 'God Encompasseth Us'.

Another sign of the new age: serious & dolorous, this omen. The other night, feeling somewhat low & downcast, I said at the King's Arms that I would have a Double Gin. What do you think it cost Me? Two shillings and fourpence; & I suppose that, allowing for the watery adulteration of the distiller, I got just about the amount of spirit that you and I received in those 'twos' that we drank at Bermondsey, in the former age. This drink of the New World did me no good. I don't think it would have done me any good if there had been 2/4 to spare in my pocket. Perhaps it would be not only harsh but hasty to say of our rulers *miseriam potius quam victoriam apti evocare*. It is, doubtless, a great process that is going on. To this day, nobody knows why the Roman Empire collapsed.

I am glad you were entertained by the Dickens Preface. How odd that such a man as Plato, set up by the judgement of more than two thousand years amongst the very highest of men, should have been not merely mistaken in his opinions of art, but entirely ignorant of what art was, what it was for, what it was about. Who would believe that this supreme philosopher had attained on this matter to the critical eminence of our George II, who 'hated Boetry and Bainting'. So it is; & it is quite incredible.

I hope you noted the passage relating to the spiritual things concealed under the correspondence of a 'comfortable cup o'tea'. High doctrine here, if you will believe me.

With all our good wishes to you & to Sybil, & better health to you both.

Yours ever fraternally,

Arthur Machen

A cutting from the *Daily Telegraph* of 8 April 1942, concerning the payment of an insurance claim on an alleged case of fire-damage by poltergeist at Fife, in Scotland.

For a long time Engineering Concerns & Land Development Companies have been paying good money to Dowsers. Now, you can see, an insurance Co. pays for the damage caused by the Poltergeist. Would it be good business to continue to accept this risk? Or should the companies decline the liability to compensate for any damage worked 'by the Devil or his Imps'?

[1] In this Machen was wrong. One of the children in M. R. James's ghost story 'An Evening's Entertainment' — published in 1925 — says, in reference to his father: 'Yes, I know: he'll be woundy cross-tempered and send us off to bed.'

High St.,
Old Amersham,
Bucks.
April 12. '42

Dilectissime frater,

Here, then, is the Sweeney Todd. I am interested to see that, apparently, there is a genuine 18th century English tradition behind the fable. I had read somewhere that it was founded on a French feuilleton.

Do you know anything about Montague Summers?[1] He is, I believe, *presbyter Romanus*, & dresses as a cleric. He has written about Restoration Drama, & also on occult matters — very credulously on these latter. For some reason or another, if you mention his name, you are apt to encounter an uplifted eyebrow or a latent grin. As Sancho Panza says: 'I come from my vineyard; I know nothing.'

By the way, reading a day or two ago in your 'Shadows' — a book I love to read in — I see you make some question as to how I met the Young Man in Spectacles. It was at the G.D. I have no notion of whether he be alive or dead; I have forgotten his very name.[2] But why should one trouble? The play is over, the actors have put off their costumes, dressed in their 'street dress', & gone home. There is no sense in desiring to follow them there.

I am all the more sure of that, from the very occasional appearance of the lady who once depicted so brilliantly the role of 'the Fair Wanton'.[3] I assure you these are sad and rather ghastly occasions.

But 'street dress' awakes a cheerful ocasion of the stage. I was touring with a Tree Company from His Majesty's. We were depicting 'Julius Caesar', & Brutus & another principal, alone on the stage, were commenting on the shouts of 'Ave Caesar', proceeding from the mob 'off'. One night, no shouts were heard; consequently, the remarks of Brutus & the other conspirator must have been puzzling to the house. Just before the curtain went up on the next set, the Forum Scene, — 'Friends, Romans, Countrymen' &c — the Stage Manager, in a dark Disguise Cloak, appeared in the assembled mob, & said, addressing the Super Master, who was one of them, 'Look here! What the. . . do you mean by not giving those "Ave Caesars"? If that happens again you can put on your street dress & go back to Hell, or Jerusalem, or His Majesty's Theatre! I don't want you here. Now then (turning to the Roman mob at large) "We will be satisfied! We will be satisfied!"' Thus indicating the shouts that took up the curtain, the Stage Manager melted into the wings.

The skies & the airs seem to mend. Do you & Sybil follow this example.

Yours ever fraternally,

Arthur Machen

[1] The Revd Montague Summers (1880-1948) — although there is no certainty that he *was* ordained — was an authority on both Restoration drama (which he helped to revive) and demonology and witchcraft. His many editions and translations of early works on witchcraft undoubtedly helped to stimulate the great revival of interest in the subject from the 1930s onwards.

[2] The 'Young Man in Spectacles' figures as a character in *The Three Impostors*. Machen describes his counterpart in real life in *Things Near and Far*, he was, indeed, a member of the Golden Dawn: his name was W. B. Yeats.

[3] The 'Fair Wanton' was Mrs C. F. Leyel (1880-1957), for whom see p. 200.

This was Machen's last letter to Waite, who died at Bridge on 19 May 1942.

Colin Summerford

COLIN SUMMERFORD
Introduction

Arthur Machen's macabre works of the 1890s, such as *The Great God Pan*, 'The Inmost Light' and *The Three Impostors*, are rich in bizarre encounters between denizens of the great maze that constitutes London. Although he acknowledged his debt to Robert Louis Stevenson's *New Arabian Nights* for these chronicles of Baghdad-on-the-Thames, Machen himself experienced incidents of a similar nature while 'a dweller in the tents of London'. Consider, for example, those curious individuals, tantalizingly sketched in Chapter X of *Things Near and Far*, whose paths crossed Machen's during that strange interlude at the turn of the century when the metropolis was transmuted into Syon and Baghdad, as he vainly sought a solution to the mysteries of existence while an initiate in the Hermetic Order of the Golden Dawn.

But Machen's most remarkable 'Encounter of the Pavement' occurred when his days of occult adventure were long past. The scene was played early in the year 1924, outside that haunt of happy memory, the Café Royal. Machen, then in his early sixties, and wrapped in his venerable Inverness cape, was awaiting one of his readers, an admirer of *The Secret Glory*, the flawed yet visionary romance inspired by the Grail legends, published by Martin Secker two years earlier. Grave and learned letters from Mr Colin Summerford, evidently a master at Winchester College, enquiring into the source material of the book had kindled Machen's interest, and although knowing nothing of their author, he suggested a meeting at which they could discuss the great question of the Grail over drinks and tobacco.

Machen's correspondent arrived, but the Wykehamist was far from being some greying, bookish pedagogue. The episode was an excellent illustration of A. E. Waite's aphorism, often quoted by Machen, that the universe possesses an element of waggery; for Colin Summerford was revealed to be a fresh-faced boy, not quite sixteen — a *pupil*, not a master, at Winchester.

Many another literary man of Machen's distinction would merely have mouthed a few platitudes, murmured of an unforeseen pressing engagement, shook the youth's hand, and departed speedily in embarrassment and amusement, resolving to take greater care replying to readers' encomiums in future. But Colin Summerford had chosen well; although Machen's pen could often be caustic he was famed for his impeccable manners. A reader, plainly of some perception and intelligence, had been kind enough to exhibit an interest in his work; the question of age was immaterial. And so, after exchanging greetings, the silver-haired man of letters led the precocious schoolboy to the Café Royal, where he introduced him to the dubious delights of absinthe.

That afternoon, while Machen smoked his pipe, the two companions conversed on themes dear to their hearts; the solemn liturgy and ritual of the Church, the exalted faith and heroism of the old Celtic saints, and the unsolvable complexities of the Sangraal were considered. Despite the disparity in years, a bond formed between them. Neither knew it, but a friendship that would endure twenty-three years had begun.

Quite aside from young Colin's inherent charm and personality, Machen found him to be a fellow student of holy things and the eternal mysteries. With Waite domiciled in Kent, there had been no one with whom he could discuss such recondite matters in any depth. Now he had discovered a kindred spirit.

Machen's adoption of an adolescent as a friend may appear puzzling; but as his works reveal, he was no orthodox individual. As Oliver Stonor noted in one of his last tributes to his mentor, Machen was 'to the very end young in heart and inclined towards the society of those who in this regard resembled him, whatever their actual years'. Both Colin Summerford and the novelist and critic Anthony Lejeune, another of Machen's youthful friends, have emphasized that the writer treated them as equals, without condescension. In his memoir 'An Old Man and a Boy', published in *The Listener* in March 1956, Mr Lejeune explained that from their first meeting Machen 'talked to me as one gentleman to another, both men of the world, equal in age and understanding'.

During term breaks Colin Summerford, who lived at Harrow at this period, attended the Machens' soirées at Melina Place, St John's Wood. He was introduced to Dog and Duck Punch, that potent concoction dispensed by Machen from the famous earthenware jar with all the ceremony of an alchemist bringing forth gold from the athanor. The boy found himself part of a colourful assembly of writers, artists and stage personalities. He recalls: 'On my first occasion I was preposterously dressed in a dinner jacket, and stood out incongruously among Machen's Bohemian friends. I missed the last train back to Harrow, and so had to walk home. Arriving in the early hours of the morning I faced my mother's displeasure. "If they keep you out until this hour they can't be very nice people," she observed.' It does not appear that this reflection was reported to Machen, who would undoubtedly have been delighted at outraging middle-class notions of respectability.

Machen clearly relished Colin Summerford's company from their early days. 'It seems a long time since I have heard from you. I hope you are getting along all right. When are you coming up to town?' runs a brief salutation from him on 7 July 1924. Machen, as the letters to his friend illustrate, provided kind and fatherly instruction on matters spiritual and practical, while Colin Summerford cheered him and Purefoy with his refreshing good fellowship.

As his father's poverty denied Machen a place at Oxford in the 1880s, one would readily forgive some lingering bitterness if he had didactically reminded his young friend of the importance of applying himself to his books when at the university; but there is no necessity. 'I hope you are having a very good time,' Machen tells him on 15 November 1926. 'Remember it is your duty to enjoy yourself enormously at Oxford.'

During the 1930s, as Machen was beset by financial crises, their roles were reversed, and Colin Summerford was able to repay the now elderly writer for all his guidance and consideration by securing reviewing and editorial work for him. '. . . I am fortunate to have such a friend,' Machen writes in gratitude in July 1937.

This assistance culminated in the national appeal inaugurated by Desmond MacCarthy, with Colin Summerford acting as secretary and treasurer; an endeavour supported by a number of distinguished authors, including Max Beerbohm, Algernon Blackwood, Walter de la Mare, T. S. Eliot, John Masefield and Bernard Shaw. Despite the austerities of war donations were received from many of Machen's admirers in Britain and the United States, enabling a cheque for a substantial sum to be presented during the celebrations for his eightieth birthday at a West End restaurant on 3 March 1943.

The depth of Machen's esteem and affection for Colin Summerford can be gauged from the letters which follow, but one additional point is worthy of notice. The staunch traditionalist finally broke the practice of a lifetime and was persuaded to call his friend by his first name — 'I never use Christian names,' he would asseverate — although this radical act did not extend to correspondence, as can be seen. The love and respect were mutual, for Mr Summerford has commented: 'Machen was undoubtedly the most gifted and remarkable man I have ever known. Quite apart from his greatness as a writer, he was a conversationalist without equal and a splendid host. It was a privilege to be in his company. Yet he was basically a shy and humble man who underrated his achievements. His philosophy of life could be summed up in the words of Thomas à Kempis, which appear in his works: *Strive to be unknown, and to be thought of no account.*'

After a full life variously spent in publishing, as a literary critic for *The Observer*, novice in a Dominican priory, tutor of the Montessori system, and librarian at the Royal Mint, Mr Summerford now lives in retirement on the

Hampshire coast. He has also toiled in stockjobbing, served as a wartime fire-watcher, worked at a London hospital, broadcast on radio, written a cookery column, and composed comic song lyrics; and in April 1988 he celebrated his eightieth birthday. The Grail romances possess an abiding fascination for him, and some sixty-five years after first becoming entranced by its evocation of wonders and mysteries, he remains devoted to *The Secret Glory*, which he values above all Machen's more technically adroit works. In the autumn of 1987, through the good offices of the American publisher and literary scholar S. T. Joshi, Mr Summerford examined with pleasure a photocopy of the original conclusion to the book; the manuscript of 143 quarto pages is held by Yale University. And his verdict? 'I believe it thoroughly deserves to be published,' he said. Perhaps at some time in the future a complete edition of Machen's most ambitious fictional creation will appear in print.

More than forty years have passed since Machen's death, but Mr Summerford's reverence for the memory of his friend is an enduring aspect of his life. The reason for this is relatively simple. Besides sharing many of the qualities and characteristics of his hero Dr Johnson — erudition and love of learning, religious faith, an unapologetic dogmatism, and spellbinding oratory — Machen, like Johnson, exercised a lasting and benign effect on the lives and beliefs of the members of his circle. One need only examine the numerous eulogies devoted to him by his disciples to realize the degree of this influence. But perhaps the most perceptive comment on Machen's personality was made by Oliver Stonor, in a letter to Colin Summerford of 28 September 1986, written a few months before his death at the age of eighty-three: '. . . the essence of the whole matter has simply been a moral one: Arthur Machen was to an incomparable degree the best — the most truly *good* man — that either of us has ever met, and one simply has to love the highest when one sees it'.

Some of the light from that goodness shines through the following pages.

ROGER DOBSON

LETTERS TO COLIN SUMMERFORD

1924 – 1947

12 Melina Place,
London, N.W.8
Feb. 12th 1924

My dear Sir,

I am much obliged by your letter. The 'Celtic Church and Grail' motive in 'The Secret Glory' is founded on six months' research in the British Museum.[1] Not, I hasten to add, that I 'read up' the subject in order to make a book, but having read to satisfy my curiosity, the topic occurred to me a year afterwards, when I was planning 'The Secret Glory'.

I find it difficult to give you any leading authorities; as the result was obtained from a very large number of books. I look into my old notebooks at haphazard, and see a title: 'Early Xtian Monuments of Scotland'[2] (Allen and Anderson authors) and find a passage underlined about the *Cathach* (I think a Book of the Gospels that had belonged to St Columba). The passage underlined is: '*it is not lawful to open it*'. This was important to me as illustrating one of the distinctions between the Roman and the Celtic Churches: the Romans exhibit their relics as much as possible to excite the devotion of the faithful: the Celts kept their relics in secrecy; it was dangerous for the unqualified to look on them. You see how this bears on the Grail legend; how it is one of the many small points which tend to establish the general conclusion: the Legend of the Grail is, in one of its aspects, the Legend of the Celtic Church.

Now here is a case of a book read through for the sake of one passage; and there are many dozen cases like it.

I wish you would call on me when you are next in town. I could then shew you these old notebooks of mine. We are always in on Saturdays at nine p.m.

Believe me,
Yours sincerely,

Arthur Machen

[1]   Machen studied the Grail legends in 1906. See pp. 36–43 and p. 221.

[2]   John Romily Allen, *The Early Christian Monuments of Scotland*, Introduction by Joseph Anderson (Society of Antiquaries of Scotland, 1903).

12 Melina Place,
London, N.W.8
March 13. '24

Dear Summerford,

Many thanks: I should like to see the Abbé's book[1] very much. I will return it to you with my notebooks and with Miss Jessie Weston's fallacious 'From Ritual to Romance',[2] when you write from your home.

I said 'fallacious'; but we are all fallacious, more or less, in this quest: chiefly because we never know whence information may come. A certain Venerable Head appears in one of the Grail visions. That Head is no doubt from the *Mabinogion* story of Bran Bendigeid. But how astonishing to find in a Red Indian myth, cited by Mark Twain in his 'Life on the Mississippi', a Head of very similar character! So it is impossible to exclude any source; and that means that the search is hopeless. The word of the enigma may be lurking in a bound volume of 'The Pink 'Un'!

                         Yours sincerely,

                         Arthur Machen

For the Mozarabic Rite: try Messrs Cope and Fenwick, Liturgical Publishers, London. I am afraid I have no more exact address.

---

[1]   Louis Gougaud, *Les Chrétientés Celtiques* (Paris: J. Gabalda, 1911).

[2]   Jessie L. Weston, *From Ritual to Romance* (Cambridge University Press, 1920).

---

12 Melina Place,
London, N.W.8
March 25th '24

Dear Summerford,

I hope 'this finds you' completely recovered. Will you let me know the dates of your stay within reach of London. I should like you to come and lunch with me at Stones in Panton Street. I will bring along the notebooks and 'From Ritual to Romance' and you might bring the *Chrétientés Celtiques*. Stones is far from being a good place, I am sorry to say; but it was founded in 1770, and there is a little old mahogany left.

Yours sincerely,

Arthur Machen

Harrow is Lupton![1] I forgot to tell you how queer it seemed to me that a passage from 'The Secret Glory' should be recited at a great public school. I am glad it was liked.

---

[1]   Lupton is the public school in *The Secret Glory* (Martin Secker, 1922) where Ambrose Meyrick endures an unhappy exile from Gwent. During a visit to Harrow in 1904 the Benson company members, Machen among them, were insulted and abused by pupils in the High Street. The incident was partially reponsible for Machen's blistering attack on the ethos of such schools in the novel. See *Arthur Machen: A Bibliography* (Henry Danielson, 1923), pp. 52–55.

---

12 Melina Place,
N.W.8
March 29th 1924

Dear Summerford,

Can you meet me outside Stone's in Panton Street, next Thursday, April 3rd at noon?

Herewith is a little book[1] which may interest you. The Welsh in it is, I am afraid, dubious. I got my friend, Caradoc Evans,[2] to read the proofs, but I believe he knows Welsh by ear, not by letter.

Yours sincerely,

Arthur Machen

---

[1]   *The Great Return* (The Faith Press, 1915).

[2]   Caradoc Evans (David Evans, 1878–1945), the Welsh novelist, short-story writer and

journalist whose sardonic depiction of Welsh life created much resentment among his fellow countrymen. Machen was one of several authors who contributed appreciations of Evans to Oliver Sandys' memoir of her husband, *Caradoc Evans* (Hurst & Blackett, 1946).

---

12 Melina Place,
London, N.W.8
April 23rd 1924

Dear Summerford,

Pray keep the notebooks and the Weston book as long as you like. I can't see that the lady makes out any real case for the existence of a Gnostic Sect in Britain in the XIth century. Though, oddly enough, there is a passage in the Introduction to the *Grand St Graal* that might be patient of such an interpretation.

I am glad you liked St Mark's Mass. That unhappy choir! They have suffered for the last iii years from a succession of bad organists. Now they have an organist who is an artist — too much of an artist for them.

With all good wishes
Yours sincerely,

Arthur Machen

---

12 Melina Place,
London, N.W.8
May 12. 1924

My dear Summerford,

In the first place; keep the book and the notebooks as long as you like. You will probably be having an exeat in the course of the term? If so you might bring up the books and I will lend you in exchange A. E. Waite's 'Hidden Church of the Holy Grail'.[1]

Now, of course, your request for advice is impossible. No man can advise another; fortunately or unfortunately. But, putting this objection on one side for the moment, you do not tell me of your immediate dispositions. That is:

how long are you staying at Winchester? Does your father desire that you should go to Oxford and take a degree? I need not tell you that you owe him absolute obedience up to the age of 21, and after that a very reverent consideration of his desires.

I doubt whether there is much to be said for the publishing proposition. I have seen a little of it (getting on for forty years ago) and I don't see that you could expect to get much out of it. A great deal depends, of course, on the question of means. Will you have enough to keep alive on? That is, I suppose, £200 a year. If so, you might go to a publisher and ask to be allowed to loaf about his office and do what you are told for nothing. You would soon find out whether the business appealed to you; and if your services appealed to the publisher, he would put you on the salary list. As for journalism: keep out of it. In my opinion, it is not the profession of a gentleman, and I had eleven years of it. You will see what I think of it, if you read my autobiographical book 'Things Near and Far'.[2]

Have you any feeling for the stage? If so, I can tell you where to get a training for a moderate fee. That has been one of my many crafts and I look back on it with the fondest affection.

But at last the fatal difficulty recurs. I cannot advise you because I do not know you, and you cannot tell me for you do not know yourself!

Yours sincerely,

Arthur Machen

Evelyn Underhill's[3] book is called 'A Column of Dust' — not very good.

---

[1]   *The Hidden Church of the Holy Graal* had been published in 1909. Machen provided Waite with material on the Celtic Church. See pp. 37–39.

[2]   Machen expressed his relief at being released from the *Evening News* by quoting the second verse of the 40th Psalm in the conclusion to *Things Near and Far* (Martin Secker, 1923), p. 176.

[3]   Evelyn Underhill (1875–1941), the poet, novelist and authority on mysticism, joined Waite's Independent and Rectified Rite of the Golden Dawn in 1904. She dedicated her supernatural novel *The Column of Dust* (Methuen, 1909) to Machen and Purefoy.

12 Melina Place,
London, N.W.8
May 20. 1924

My dear Summerford,

I was very glad to get your letter of May 16: and pray write to me whenever you feel inclined.

I note what you say about your stay at Winchester. Then you need not worry for the next two years, or perhaps three. You may have to settle things then, or possibly four years after that, on leaving the University. So get all the learning you can and do not trouble about what will happen in 3 or 7 years time. A man wrote to me last year of his approaching financial troubles: 'I do not know what will happen at the beginning of next year.' I wrote back sending him to 'the Book': 'let the beginning of next year take thought for the things of itself'. And nothing in particular did happen!

I am glad you liked 'Dog and Duck'. Did you note that the destruction of Geometry[1] was really a strong argument for the Faith?

Yours sincerely,

Arthur Machen

If necessary and when the time comes I will tell you how to live on £2 a week.

---

[1]   In the essay 'Stuff — and Science'. *Dog and Duck* had been published in America by Alfred A. Knopf on 8 February 1924 and in Britain by Jonathan Cape on 29 February 1924.

---

12 Melina Place,
London, N.W.8
July 11th 1924

Dear Summerford,

I am very glad to hear you are all right. You are wise to leave the future to take care of the future; let it take thought for the things of itself.

Many thanks for Miss Weston's book, and pray do not distress yourself for one moment about the trifling patch on the binding.[1] It doesn't matter in the least. I don't believe in her thesis for one moment: she has entirely failed to prove that a Gnostic sect persisted in Britain up to the XIth century. She is beset by two opposing absurdities: the folly of the 'fertility' people, and the of the occultists. She talks in her book of secrets having been communicated to her, and when people talk like that, sense is over.

Pray keep the notebooks as long as you wish.

Could you come round here on August 9th (Saturday) at 9 p.m.? We are always at home on Saturdays at that hour.

You speak of Glastonbury. It is a sad thing; but that holy place is possessed or obsessed by occultists of the worst type, who get messages from the ghosts of medieval monks in sham-antique English.[2]

You will find 'Things Near and Far' inferior to the earlier book.[3]

Yours sincerely,

Arthur Machen

---

[1] Colin Summerford recalls: 'After spilling ink or something on the binding I bought another copy. I then spilt something else over it! Fortunately Machen cared nothing for first editions or the condition of his books.'

[2] For the controversy over F. Bligh Bond and Geraldine Cummins, see pp. 54–5.

[3] Machen's first volume of impressionistic memoirs was *Far Off Things* (Martin Secker, 1922). He wrote to Vincent Starrett on 28 December 1922: 'You will be disappointed in "Things Near and Far". There is only one good sequel in the world: the second part of "Don Quixote".' See Michael Murphy (ed.), *Starrett vs Machen: A Record of Discovery and Correspondence* (St Louis, Missouri: Autolycus Press, 1977), p. 99.

---

12 Melina Place,
London, N.W.8
July 25. 1924

Dear Summerford,

You need not bother to write: we are always here on Saturday evenings at 9 p.m. But if some other evening be more convenient: then let me have a line two or three days beforehand.

I have just been engaged in the agreeable task of 'going for' Miss Weston. A series of Graal articles that I wrote in 1907[1] are to be reprinted, with other matter, some time early next year; and I have written an introduction to them. (Did you order a copy of 'Precious Balms'? I believe the whole edition was subscribed before publication. Only very few copies were sent out for review.)

There was once a habit of making an antithesis between St Paul and St John, as if between intellect and intuition. This is mostly false.

I forget whether I ever drew your attention to Coventry Patmore's *Religio Poetae* and 'Rod, Root and Flower'. I am sure you would be deeply interested in both.

Yours sincerely,

Arthur Machen

You are going to Brittany? Polish up your Welsh!

---

[1] The articles, first published in *The Academy* in August 1907, appeared as 'The Secret of the Sangraal' in *The Shining Pyramid* (Martin Secker, 1925). A limited edition of 250 signed and numbered copies was published in December 1924. Machen had a copy of the book sent to Jessie L. Weston.

Station House,
Penally,
Pembrokeshire[1]
Aug. 23 – I think –
1924

Dear Summerford,

I only hope you are having better weather than we are!

Of course the connection of the Dove with the Mass[2] — or *Offeren* as we said in Wales — is not peculiar to Celtdom. The medieval tabernacle in England was usually in the form of a Dove suspended by chains. It is highly curious that the Roman Missal ignores the work of the Holy Spirit in the Mass. It would be interesting to enquire — if enquiry were possible — whether the Dove and Host and Stone motive in the *Parzival* of von Eschenbach is not a Legend or Mythos constructed on a pictorial symbol; such as is the Nigg stone.

I am happy to hear of the good results produced on a Unitarian by 'The Secret Glory'. I think I had rather be an Atheist than a Unitarian.

My new book 'The London Adventure'[3] will be published on the 28th. It is very bad; and very sad for me. You in your day will find out the misery of failing or failed powers.

With all good wishes
Yours very sincerely,

Arthur Machen

[1]   The Machens regularly took their holidays here from 1909-28.

[2]   See p. 40.

[3]   *The London Adventure* was the autobiographical coda to *Far Off Things* and *Things Near and Far*. A limited edition of 200 signed and numbered copies had been published in March 1924.

---

12 Melina Place,
London, N.W.8
Nov. 22nd '24

Dear Summerford,

A bankrupt never feels his beggary so keenly as when he is called on for aid! The first measure I would commend to you is to write to:

The Revd J.N. Newland Smith[1]
The Vicarage
Kingskerswell
Devon.

You saw him, you remember, at the door of his church, and had a word or two with him. I know that he is capable of helping you, and I am sure that he will be willing to do so. He left St Mark's last July much to our regret.

Do not believe for a moment that one must be a Celt to see God! Every race has its own way of approach, its own manner of excellence. The Celts have their peculiar advantages — and also their deep defects. You will note, in the imaginative world, how little they have actually *done*, achieved. The Romance Literature of Europe was, doubtless, inspired by the Celt; but *written* by the Anglo-Norman.

I am delighted to hear about the Unitarian: may he prosper within and without.

There is one thing I would like to impress upon you. Among those who follow the interior life, there is a tendency, latent though often undefined and unexpressed, to belittle the moral law, the chiefly negative precepts of the Decalogue. And it is true that these are to the End as the rules of Grammar are to the achievement of Shakespeare. And it is true that those who have attained rarely or never think of them. It is moreover undoubtedly true that no man can get to heaven by *not* stealing, by *not* committing adultery. But, on the other hand, none of these is to be disobeyed with impunity, for one moment.

I think the case is this. The Decalogue is *intus et foris scriptus*. For the majority it preserves the decencies and moralities of the social order. For those of a more interior order; it is the condition, though not the cause, of their light. Covet your neighbour's ox; and that light will begin to grow dim.

You have all my prayers and good wishes

Yours sincerely,

Arthur Machen

You may mention my name of course to Newland Smith.

---

[1] For J. N. Newland-Smith, see p. 46. Colin Summerford, a High Anglican at this period, was considering entering the Church. He became a convert to Roman Catholicism in the 1930s.

---

12 Melina Place,
London, N.W.8
March 24th 1925

Dear Summerford,

Could you look in here on Monday, April 6th at 9 p.m.? Or, if not, mention some time and place more convenient. I shall have Notebook No. II at your disposal; though I think I embodied all the results of my research in the Graal Essay.[1] It is amusing in its way: but owing to the fact that very few of the Reviewers know anything whatever about the subject, they slide nervously past the Essay, murmuring 'Stimulating' or 'somewhat tedious' as the case may be. So I am deprived of the pleasure of being attacked.

I was very much obliged to you for giving me the information as to 'The Shining Pyramid'.[2] I came to the conclusion that no fraud was involved; only the grossest carelessness and mismanagement. A large 'only' for me, who have to live on what my books bring me.

Dr Frere's[3] book is very fine indeed. The Responses and verses have somewhat in them which is extraordinarily noble and compelling: thank you.

Urquhart's translation of Rabelais is *the* translation; and perhaps there can be none better. My impression on reading and comparing the original with the English version was that the book had been, somehow, thickened — rather than coarsened. It is as if one had translated Burgundy into whiskey — into a very fine whiskey, indeed.

The aim of the 'Secret Glory' was higher than the aim of the 'Hill of Dreams'; but alas! the former book broke in my hands. I got on a wrong track, cancelled about 20,000 words; and published a fragment.[4]

You say you will never do anything at writing. You don't know; the only receipt is: try hard for a dozen years or more, break your heart half-a-dozen times, go down into desolation and come up again, and then begin all anew. A nice life, isn't it?

Sebastian Evans's 'High History' is a fine piece of work. It is a pity that he let himself be ensnared into a very foolish theory of the matter.[5]

Yours very sincerely,

Arthur Machen

---

[1] 'The Secret of the Sangraal', in *The Shining Pyramid*.

[2] Machen had asked Colin Summerford on 11 February 1925: 'Would you mind telling me the (approximate) date on which you got "The Shining Pyramid", and whether it was a signed, Large Paper, edition, or an unsigned copy? I ask because I suspect my publisher of falsifying the date of publication, to suit his private ends.' The trade edition of the book was published in February and it seems that Machen was kept waiting for his royalties because of a dispute with Martin Secker over Vincent Starrett's collection of stories and essays, also titled *The Shining Pyramid* (Chicago: Covici-McGee, 1923).

[3] The Rt Revd Walter Howard Frere (1863–1938) was the Bishop of Truro from 1923–35 and the author and editor of liturgical works.

[4] Machen sent the excised portion of *The Secret Glory* to Vincent Starrett on 25 October 1921, having instructed him on 15 January 1918 'not to print, or to allow anyone else to print' the work (*Starrett vs Machen: A Record of Discovery and Correspondence*, p. 37).

The manuscript, which is now held by the Beinecke Rare Book Library at Yale University, consists of two long concluding chapters (V and VI) amounting to some 30,000 words and concerns Ambrose Meyrick's return to Gwent. Although clearly not revised to Machen's satisfaction — 'The composition of the book was broken by a visit to some friends; and the damage was fatal,' he told Starrett (*op. cit.*, p. 48) — its publication would not damage his literary reputation.

[5] In his *In Quest of the Holy Graal* Evans interpreted the Grail legends as an allegory of the political and religious conflict that occurred during the reign of King John, when the kingdom was laid under an interdict by Pope Innocent III. See pp. 38-39.

---

12 Melina Place,
London, N.W.8
April 15th 1925

Dear Summerford,

I have known my very dear friend A. E. Waite for 38 years; and I have not the faintest notion as to his real beliefs.[1] In hopeful moods I am inclined to think that he is a Deist; but in stern fact I should think that Pantheism is his veritable label. He was brought up strictly in the Roman Faith, and has always had the warmest enthusiasm for the Roman Church — 'as a great system of symbolism', as he once explained to me. I have often told him that his case is exactly like that of the late President Thiers, who once said: '*Je ne suis pas Chrétien: mais je suis toujours Catholique Romain.*' It is a strange case.

I will certainly write my name in 'Stiggins'[2] whenever you like to bring it along. And I hope that will be soon. Remember, if you find yourself by chance in London over Saturday, we are always in that night at 9.

Yours very sincerely,

Arthur Machen

---

[1] An analysis of Waite's beliefs is given in R. A. Gilbert, *A. E. Waite: Magician of Many Parts* (Crucible, 1987), pp. 163-65.

[2] *Dr Stiggins: His Views and Principles* (Francis Griffiths, 1906).

12 Melina Place,
London, N.W.8
Sept. 30th '25

Dear Summerford,

By all means keep the Grail book and the notebook as long as you please.

I hope you enjoyed your holiday. For once, I believe the West had better weather than the East. We had a great deal of noble sunshine and a very good and leisurely time. It was a little spoilt for me by the necessity of writing a weekly article for the *Graphic* and also writing Introductions: to a portfolio of symbolic drawings[1] which I did not understand, to Brillat-Savarin's *Physiologie du Goût*,[2] to 'The Canning Wonder'[3] (my own book) and to Lady Benson's[4] 'Overture and Beginners, Please' — stage annals and reminiscences. I brought into this the last chapter of 'The Secret Glory' about 'The Hathaway Company'; the Benson Company being intended when I wrote it.

I have some notion of trying to find a French book on the Compagnonnage, the ancient Freemasonry of French workmen, very curious in its way. If the material seemed likely I would translate it — and vex old Waite horribly; he having a theory of Freemasonry which makes the existence of the Compagnonnage highly inconvenient.

Pray let me know when you are to be in town: I want you to lunch with me.

With our best wishes
Yours sincerely,

Arthur Machen

My last work is the composition of an inscription for a new sacring bell at St Mark's: *Mater Dei Maria ora pro nobis in via.*

---

[1] Frederick Carter, *The Dragon of the Alchemists* (Elkin Mathews, 1926).

[2] J. A. Brillat-Savarin, *The Physiology of Taste* (Peter Davies, 1925).

[3] Published by Chatto & Windus on 28 October 1925.

[4] Lady Constance Fetherstonhaugh Benson (Gertrude Constance Cockburn Samwell, 1863–1946), the actress and writer. She joined Frank Benson's theatrical company in

1884 and married Benson in 1886. Her book was published as *Mainly Players: Bensonian Memories* (Thornton Butterworth, 1926).

---

12 Melina Place,
London, N.W.8
Oct. 21st, 1925

Dear Summerford,

Many thanks for your letter of Oct. 2nd.

What a very odd circumstance; this offering of earth, carrots and twigs! I can make nothing of it; but I should have made a good deal of it about thirty years ago! Indeed, I invented something of the kind in one of my short stories.[1]

Alas! It is sad to grow old. A couple of years ago, a man was telling me a very striking notion for a story which he wanted me to use. I said: 'Talk to me about that in 1890'!

I hope the Canning book will be out directly, but, likely enough, the publishers will put it off to February next. Publishers often do the displeasing thing.

Translate the Grail Books! They are a Library: they would fill a large room: it would be the task of a lifetime. *You* might think of it.

I shall be most happy to sign 'The Secret Glory' whenever you will.

We have begun to use the new Sacring Bell at St Mark's; it has a reverend sound.

With all our good wishes
Yours sincerely,

Arthur Machen

Mind you let me know when you have a day in town: you must lunch with me.

---

[1] Presumably 'The Ceremony', one of the tales in *Ornaments in Jade* (Alfred A. Knopf, 1924) and reprinted in *The Cosy Room* (Rich & Cowan, 1936) and *Holy Terrors* (Penguin, 1946).

---

12 Melina Place
Jan. 14. 1926

Dear Summerford,

Thinking it over, I feel that it would not be very good manners to send a savage assault on the schoolmaster's craft[1] — to a schoolmaster. I have a reverence for the College motto.[2] Your venerated founder had certainly 'a message for this age'.

I once went to the Rite of Irving at their 'Cathedral' in Gordon Square. You know the subtitle of the sect; what they call themselves? It is 'The Catholic and Apostolic Church'! Their 'Mass' is quite dignified. All present (of the sect) communicate, being marshalled from their seats in due order by two deacons. In the midst of the service a silence; then a voice suddenly uplifted, wailing on vowels, or so it seemed to me, in a somewhat terrifying manner. As you may be aware, I know something of the matter of sorcery; and it is curious that the Tongues (as it is called) is very like an Incantation. It is supposed to be a heavenly language, as a courteous deacon informed me.

I trust you have succeeded with the Scholarship.

Yours sincerely,

Arthur Machen

[1] *The Secret Glory*. Machen was evidently persuaded to change his mind. See p. 104.

[2] William of Wykeham's 'Manners makyth man'.

12 Melina Place,
N.W.8
Jan. 30th 1926

Dear Summerford,

The heartiest congratulations of us both on your success.[1] You are one of the very few people who are elected to be round pegs in round holes. You are deeply interested in Theology, Liturgiology, and the history of the early British

Church — and you are bidden to study all these subjects! It is wonderful.

One note of the connection between the Grail Romances and the Celtic Church has occurred to me lately. In the Romances and the C. Church, it is only the elect who may see the Holy Things — Lancelot, you remember, is blasted, not healed, by the *theoria* of the Grail. Amongst the Latins this is not so: the more of a sinner you are, the more need of seeing and revering the mysteries.

As to the Irvingites: the 'Angel' (Bishop) celebrates in a Gothic Chasuble. But what is the story of the transformation of a Presbyterian Congregation that went crazy into what we must call a Catholic sect? I do not know.

Yours sincerely,

Arthur Machen

The Merchant Taylors' School[2] Badge is the Lamb and Flag.

[1] Colin Summerford had won a scholarship to read theology at Exeter College, Oxford.

[2] Hilary Machen was a pupil at the school.

---

12 Melina Place,
N.W.8
March 3rd 1926

Dear Summerford,

'First there comes David,
Then there comes Chad,
Then comes Wenwoloc
As though he were mad.'

I was born on his day in the year 1863. He has variant names: Gwynllyw and (oddly) Woolos.

I am ordering a copy of 'The Secret Glory' to be sent to you. Will you pass it on to Mr Robinson?[1] I shall be obliged.

I never met Dr Warren.[2] I think I told you that I wrote to him for information — and in a short time found myself giving it. There is the necessary defect of specialism; you have no time to go outside your subject, and indeed, being a specialist, you do not know where to go. I, being a smatterer, could bear the Celtic Church in mind while I was investigating the Grail Romances.

I expect the stacks of 'The Great Return'[3] have gone down a bit, but I don't know. Somebody told me the other day that the book now fetched 5/-.

I will remember the good Canon of whom you speak.

Yours sincerely,

Arthur Machen

[1]   Cyril Edward Robinson, a master at Winchester.

[2]   The Revd Frederick Edward Warren (1842-1930), the liturgiologist and writer on religious matters; author of *Liturgy and Ritual of the Celtic Church* (1881).

[3]   Unlike its predecessor, *The Bowmen and Other Legends of the War*, *The Great Return* had not been a success. See *Arthur Machen: A Bibliography* (Henry Danielson, 1923), pp. 44 – 46.

---

12 Melina Place,
N.W.8
March 5. '26

Dear Summerford,

Forty years ago I read in *The Tablet* a sonorous and satisfying phrase which has always remained in my memory. Some position was being condemned, and of it the writer said that it was:

'injuriosa, perniciosa, male sonans, et plurium errorum productrix'.

These words apply admirably to the *Ch. Times* position as to the iconostasis, or Rood screen. It is absolutely false. The screen is an image of the Veil through which we pass (see Epistle to the Hebrews) into the Holy Place. It also signifies that the Holy Sacrifice is a Holy *Mystery*; a thing discerned in part, *per speculum in aenigmate*. It was in use in the East where there was no sudden irruption of half-taught barbarians. It was pierced in the West and became the Rood screen, as the sense of the *Mysteries* — not to be viewed too clearly — grew dim: this was the period when the 'squints' were made, to enable people in the aisles to see the altar. The end of the process is manifest in the Modern Roman Church, where the altar is to stand high and dry, the most visible object in the church.

The Romans of Southwark pulled down the Screen that Pugin had made in their Cathedral some years ago.★

As for the rest of the article; it is a mass of falsities and hypocrises: full of *suppressio veri et suggestio falsi*.

'The shabby leavings of the Middle Ages'.

I like that. Are the Gothic Cathedrals shabby? And if, on the surface they became so, who made them so?

I never see the *Church Times*. It became the organ of Satan many years ago.

Yours sincerely,

Arthur Machen

★ But the Romans utter the same symbolism when the priest lowers his voice in the Canon: inaudible signifies the same as invisible.

---

12 Melina Place,
N.W.8
March 12. 1926

Dear Summerford,

Did you get 'The Secret Glory' all right? Denny the bookseller says he has sent it.

If Mr Robinson talks to you about the book, point out to him that whereas most writers dwell on the vices of public schools, it is their virtues, all that they are most proud of, which stink in my nostrils. Individual vices are, comparatively, of little consequence. My friend Waite said once, very truly, that the crimes of the Borgias are of no account when compared with the Nonconformist Conscience.

Is there a chance of seeing you about Eastertide?

Yours sincerely,

Arthur Machen

12 Melina Place
N.W.8
July 19. 1926

Dear Summerford,

Tell me when you can have lunch with me. We are in town up to and including August 14th; then for Penvro. Why don't you arrange to take a short holiday of your own at Tenby or Penally? I want to show you the place where the heroes heard the singing of the Three Fairy Birds of Rhiannon at the Entertainment of the Venerable Head, and, unhappily, opened the door which looked on Cornwall.[1]

I had a letter from Dom Robinson. He said that 'The Secret Glory' was a travesty of the system of the Great Public Schools. I replied that we did not seem in perfect agreement on the matter.

Yours sincerely,

Arthur Machen

[1] In the story of 'Branwen Daughter of Llŷr' in *The Mabinogion*.

12 Melina Place,
N.W.8
Nov. 15. '26

Dear Summerford,

I hope you are having a very good time. Remember it is your duty to enjoy yourself enormously at Oxford.

One of your Winchester masters, Leeson,[1] has been appointed Head of the Merchant Taylors'. What character do you give him?

Have you looked up David Kimpton, whom you met here just before going up? I wish you would, if you could manage it. I think he is a very good fellow. I believe he proposes to take Orders. Worcester is his college.

If, after your Degree, you still think of going into a Publisher's House; I believe I know of one that you would like. This is Peter Davies,[2] who, if I recollect, was about the night you were here. A long, thin, somewhat sombre looking man. He is, in fact, the original of Barrie's 'Peter Pan'. But he has grown up, and issues, so far, only books of real interest.

How do you get on with Waite's book on the Grail?

With the best wishes of us both

Yours very sincerely,

Arthur Machen

[1] Spencer Leeson (1892-1956), the headmaster of Merchant Taylors' School 1927-35, the headmaster of Winchester 1935-46, and the Bishop of Peterborough 1949-56.

[2] Peter Llewelyn Davies (1897-1960) had founded his publishing company earlier that year. For his views on Machen, see p. 198.

---

12 Melina Place,
N.W.8
Nov. 24. '26

Dear Summerford,

Many thanks for your letter. I am glad you give Leeson such a good character.

I suppose it is the corruption of our nature which makes us in practice equate 'duty' with the disagreeable. But it is no doubt a high duty to enjoy the delightful. See the awful fate of the people who didn't enjoy life — the accidious — in Dante. This grievous sin is laid, justly or unjustly, against the University to which you belong. It is externally manifest in that affected weariness and languor which is called 'the Oxford manner'. I have known sufferers who cannot say: 'That is very beautiful', but will drawl out, as if half-asleep, 'it seems raaaather interesting'. The Publicans and Sinners, you will remember, did their very best to enjoy life. Their methods were doubtless mistaken in some particulars; but they were preferred before the Scribes and Pharisees — the Dons of their day!

I don't know where you can find the Grail Texts. Write to A. E. Waite, 156 High Street, Ramsgate, and say that I told you to do so.

Tell the new Cope and Fenwick[1] to let us have — if not the whole liturgy — a sample chunk of the Mozarabic Rite, displaying the Epiclesis, in Latin and English.

If you will let me know a day when you will be in town in the vacation, I will let you know where you shall lunch with me. I am glad you take to Kimpton. It will, perhaps, be your business to lead him to the Catholic Faith.

Yours very sincerely,

Arthur Machen

[1] Colin Summerford was now involved in running the publishing firm which had been acquired by his friend Lance Fairtlough.

---

12 Melina Place,
N.W.8
Dec. 13 1926

Dear Summerford,

I am much pleased that Waite gave you the information that you wanted.[1] I have written him a line; reminding him that next month it will be forty years since we met. Alas, Postumus![2]

Pray bring Mr Lane[3] — poor man! — with you next Saturday: and bring Mr Fairtlough too, if he will come. But what day can you appoint to meet me at Stone's, at 1 p.m. for a beefy lunch? Saturdays, in the afternoon, is a *dies non* for me: any other weekday save Friday, when Stone's is no place for a Catholic.

I note the Cope and Fenwick policy: a judicious one, I am sure. 'Ornaments in Jade'[4] is more or less Knopf's property. And as for 'the new book': I fear there is little prospect of any such thing.

Yours very sincerely,

Arthur Machen

[1] Waite had replied on 5 December. See p. 47.

[2] Horace, *Odes*, Book II, xiv.

[3] Allen Lane Williams (1902–70), the founder of Penguin Books, had been appointed to the board of The Bodley Head at the end of 1924 by his cousin John Lane. He was a friend of Colin Summerford.

[4] *Ornaments in Jade*, a collection of prose poems written in 1897, was published by
     Alfred A. Knopf in September 1924. Colin Summerford had suggested that Cope &
     Fenwick publish the book.

---

12 Melina Place,
N.W.8.
March 3rd 1927

Dear Summerford,

It is lucky for the Firm that it is not employing me as a translator of the
Mozarabic Liturgy. I finished my serious study of the Latin tongue just 47 years
ago![1]

Thank you very much for writing to Lane. I will await his letter with due
serenity. Of course you and Fairtlough will not expect to make 'real money' out
of Liturgies. From the nature of the case, the public for such matter is and will
be a very small one. I suppose the average liturgical book, published at 10/6 —
16/- is lucky if it sells 1000 copies; and this is probably an optimistic estimate.
Such books are bought by the inner circle of experts: if you could tap the *Church
Times* public with 2/6 translations, you *might* get a circle of 3000 readers: again
an optimistic forecast. I think it would be idle to expect anything better.

Yours very sincerely,

Arthur Machen

[1] Machen was a pupil at Hereford Cathedral School from 1874-80.

---

12 Melina Place,
N.W.8
Holy Wednesday,
1927

Dear Summerford,

'London Calendar'? That is the subtitle of 'Dog and Duck', a volume of
essays. I think they are very decent essays. As for 'The Dragon of the

Alchemists'; I wrote the Introduction to it, but I really have not the remotest notion of what it is about! I met the author[1] once or twice and found him a singularly pleasant man, but I didn't like to ask him what he meant by his book.

St Mark's uses black apparel in Holy Week; I don't know how the Sarum order is.

We saw John Davenport[2] the other day. He was just going to meet his father:[3] a subject for an historical painter.

May your Easter be blessed.

Yours sincerely,

Arthur Machen

You know how St Philip Neri, meeting the students of the English College at Rome (*temp.* Eliz. R.) used to hail them — *Salvete flores Martyrum*? Well, the young man[4] next to Fairtlough — Saturday night — has just resigned his desk in the family building business for the career of letters. May he intercede for us in the time of his glory.

---

[1] Frederick Carter (1885-1967), the painter, engraver and writer. Machen admired his work.

[2] John Lancelot Davenport (1908-66), the journalist, author and screenwriter. At this period he was an undergraduate at Corpus Christi College, Cambridge.

[3] Robin Davenport, the songwriter and long-time friend of the Machens, was cousin to the late Christopher Wilson.

[4] Frederic Field Stoner (1903-87), the novelist and journalist who wrote as Oliver Stonor and Morchard Bishop, joined the Machen circle in 1926. His tribute to his mentor, *The Table Talk of Arthur Machen*, which he compiled in the 1950s, still remains unpublished.

28 Loudoun Road,
N.W.8
25.II.'28

Dear Summerford,

Many thanks for your letter. I did not know that I had attracted the favourable notice of that ruffian[1] and his friends. He was abominable, no doubt; and he was also an ass and a quack. The combination is not a very usual one. One cannot be very serious in one's condemnation of a man who says he is Therion, the Apocalyptic Beast.

I hope all goes well and happily with you; and I hope that you and Mr Fairtlough will not fail to appear on a Saturday night, when you are next in town.

Hilary has begun studying Hebrew, and seems to like it. He began the other night to tell me about Tetragrammaton!

As to Loudoun Road:[2] it is only the smallest portion of the terrors, afflictions, and dismays with which it has pleased Tetragrammaton (blessed be his Name!) to lay upon these my later years.

Yours very sincerely,

Arthur Machen

[1] Edward Alexander 'Aleister' Crowley (1875-1947), the notorious occultist, poet and author, and the self-proclaimed Messiah of Thelemic magic. Although Crowley and Machen had been members of the Hermetic Order of the Golden Dawn at the turn of the century, they do not seem to have met. Crowley's animus towards W. B. Yeats in the schism which destroyed the Golden Dawn is dealt with in a veiled manner in *Things Near and Far* (pp. 148-49). Colin Summerford encountered the Great Beast at the Café Monico in Shaftesbury Avenue. 'He was the most boring famous man I ever met,' he recalls.

[2] The family had to leave their much loved home in Melina Place in December 1927 when it was sold by their landlady. They hated the house in nearby Loudoun Road. See p. 233.

28 Loudoun Road,
N.W.8
St Denis, '28

Dear Summerford,

Many thanks for your letter with its most entertaining account of your doings at Molesey.[1] I would think that our V.H. Frater, Sacramentum Regis, otherwise, A. E. Waite, would declare that the Rite of Molesey was voided, the sanctuary stripped and bare, the lamps extinguished, and the Relics taken away into a deep concealment.

Indeed there is a certain sacred story, as to which there were profane (uninitiated) references in verses by Sybil Waite, quoted to you when you were here last.

'When London's mighty city
With orgies seemed to scorch.'

But it is related, with due veils and concealments, that on the morning of the Coronation of our Sovereign Lord, King Edward of happy memory, seventh of that name since the Conquest, Mrs Menteith came out of Gray's Inn at about eight of the morning, and was seen to get into a four wheeler. And, indeed (και δη και) it is declared by Waite *that she never got out of it*; that a mere simulacrum and appearance arrived at Molesey; that the word was lost; and that a mere substituted word took its place.[2]

But these are sacred matters.

Your Mass of the Rocks reminds me somewhat of the Mass of Lavenham, Suffolk. But the Priest of Lavenham lights XVIII candles for Low Mass!

With all good wishes from Mrs and myself.

Yours very sincerely,

Arthur Machen

Pray excuse pencil.

---

[1]   Colin Summerford had visited Granville and Dora Stuart-Menteath, for whom see p. 32, at their home 'Toftrees' at East Molesey, Surrey.

[2]   The celebration, at Machen's rooms at 4 Verulam Buildings, Gray's Inn, in August 1902, evidently marked the end of the liaison between Waite and Dora. For the

relationship between the two, see R. A. Gilbert, *A. E. Waite: Magician of Many Parts*, Chapter 7, 'Dora and the Coming of Love'.

---

28 Loudoun Road,
N.W.8
Dec. 27. '28

My dear Summerford,

All our thanks for your good wishes; and the same to you for the coming year. I suppose you will go down finally in a year's time, and begin what is called life. I have seen John [Davenport] twice, and was very glad to see him well, and pleased with Cambridge and his college. If the oddly named 'intelligentzia' has no worse effect on him than that of causing him to utter rhyming jingles; then it is very well indeed. For the hatred of rhyme is, often, a very marked and malignant symptom of the disease in question, causing that monstrosity called *vers libre*.

We hope to see you and Mr Fairtlough on the first Saturday night that you can manage. Old Waite was in town about three weeks ago. I thought him in excellent health and spirits. I again urged him to write that book which is to let us know what he really believes. I am inclined to think that he may find the task a difficult one.

Yours very sincerely,

Arthur Machen

I agree with you about Christmas cards. I don't like them nearly so much as I did about 1868-74.

---

28 Loudoun Road,
London, N.W.8
Jan. 12. '29

My dear Summerford,

Could you put in a word for me with that young Lane of whom we were talking the other day? *Not* to influence him favourably on behalf of a literary masterpiece; but to ask him if the Firm can give me any 'reading'. I have some experience in that art.[1] I should be much obliged if you could manage this.

I hope your party went off to rights. (My spouse once rebuked me for using this phrase; but I showed it to her in 'Gulliver's Travels'.)

Yours sincerely,

Arthur Machen

[1] Machen was a reader for Ernest Benn's publishing company.

---

28 Loudoun Road,
London, N.W.8
Jan.18. '29

My dear Summerford,

Your course is obvious. Tell the young woman to buy 'The Shining Pyramid' (Secker) and read the Note on the Graal there contained. I do not know that any valid new light has been thrown on the question in later years. I am sure that the late Miss Jessie Weston was quite misguided. As for telling all about the Graal in a letter: that is nonsense. I speak with authority, since I once, in accordance with orders, put the Graal in a box,[1] to use a technical phrase, which I hope you do not understand.

Yours sincerely,

Arthur Machen

[1] A newspaper or magazine article, usually brief, enclosed by a rule or border.

---

28 Loudoun Road,
N.W.8
Jan. 21. '29

My dear Summerford,

You are most kind in all you say, and I hope I shall be able to fall in with your benevolent schemes. I will let you know when I hear what plans the Club

Secretary has made for me.[1] I do not quite know, by the way, why I am lecturing at Oxford. I know, very well indeed, that I do not want to lecture at Oxford, or at any other place. I suppose the truth is that with a man of the constitution called 'easy-going', it is more unpleasant to refuse a request rather than to grant it — provided the discomfort attached is not very great. I flung down an invitation to lecture in the Bishoprick of Durham for a week, with a small fee, without hesitation; the misery involved being very great.

If that girl delays to get 'The Shining Pyramid' the consequences are on her own head.

I remain
Yours very sincerely,

Arthur Machen

---

[1] Machen had been invited to lecture at Oxford University's English Club in February. Because of illness he was unable to fulfil the engagement.

---

28 Loudoun Road,
London, N.W.8
June 22nd 1929

Dear Summerford,

Uncertain as to your present address, I am writing to Exeter, where there is, no doubt, a manciple or Protonotary, or something of the kind who will forward letters.

On Monday next, June 24, we move to

> Lynwood,[1]
> Amersham,
> Bucks.

I thought at first that the house was called 'Latimer' or 'Ridley' or something friendly. However, its actual title recalls that agreeable historical romance, 'The Lances of Lynwood' by the late Charlotte M. Yonge.

When we have settled, we propose to institute monthly Saturdays, 4-7 p.m. at which we shall hope to see you and Mr Fairtlough. Amersham, or more properly, Agmondesham, is an hour from Baker St or Marylebone.

Kindly peruse the enclosed character.[2] Would it be any good to show it to young Lane? If you think it would, you would oblige me very much by doing so, if the opportunity should arise: if not, throw it away.

Yours very sincerely,

Arthur Machen

1   A flat, on the first floor of Lynwood, a red-brick terraced house in the High Street of Old Amersham, had been found for the Machens by Purefoy's niece, Sylvia Townsend Warner.

2   Ernest Benn had provided a reference. Machen wrote to Colin Summerford on 25 June 1929: 'Pray approach Lane exactly as you think fit; or, maybe, not at all. I am ashamed to trouble you with my troubles. But a wife and children make a man a villain in this way.' The attempt to secure Machen some reading came to nothing. Machen wrote on 1 August 1929: 'I had forgotten about the Bodley Head Directors doing their own reading. Pray destroy Benn's Blessing forthwith and say nothing to your Lane.'

Lynwood,
Amersham, Bucks.
Aug. 14. '29

Dear Summerford,
    Thank you so much for your very kindly thought. But I am not going to the Benson Dinner; the last Benson Dinner; for what is to come hereafter, with women at the board, will be nothing.[1]
    Hilary's schooling will end next Christmas. I believe his present notion is to go and build organs, but nothing is settled. It is a pity that Leeson, a most amiable man, is a Liberal — in the broad sense of the word. How is it, said the Doctor, that we hear the loudest yelps for liberty from the drivers of slaves?[2] So it was, and so it is, however; and so Liberal Leeson makes my boy learn history out of a book warmly commending Henry VIII, one of the filthiest tyrants that the world has seen.
    When you do come to Amersham you will be welcome.
                    Yours very sincerely,

                    Arthur Machen

---

1   The Benson company dinners were traditionally Bohemian affairs lasting into the early hours. Machen had made his final appearance with the Bensonians, walking on as 'Sir Thomas Morgan' — a character of his own invention — in a matinée of *The Merry Wives of Windsor*, at the Wimbledon Theatre in 1928.

2   Samuel Johnson, *Taxation no Tyranny* (1775). See Boswell's *Life of Johnson*, 23
    September 1777.

Lynwood,
Amersham, Bucks.
Feb. 21. 1930

Dear Summerford,

It is extremely good of you to forgive my silence and total neglect of your kind Christmas wishes. My negligence is partly due to an obstinate *accidia*, and partly to the fact that just before Christmas I fell down stairs and gave myself a very nasty shock, and a few days later had a severe and lasting fit of gout. Like the clergyman in *Hamlet* I lay howling. Now, I am glad to say, we are all as well as we are likely to be.

Will you and Fairtlough come along Saturday sennight about nine, to drink Punch? It is St David's day — *Dydd Dewi Sant* — and should be a good day. And would Fairtlough do us the great favour of conveying a passenger — Mrs Lynch whom I think you have met? If you can come, we will write to Mrs Lynch and fix it up.

I am afraid I can think of nothing for Peter Davies. I am glad he is doing well.

I suppose Waite is still talking of that 'Secret Church' of the H.G. — which has no existence, and in which he doesn't believe himself. I sent him some time ago 'From Ritual to Romance'. And that is about another Secret Church which has no existence. But Miss Weston's Church is quite different; being a Gnostic Sect, which survived in Wales up to the XIth century!

Do I look as if I knew a Mercer?

Hilary has taken the Apron,[1] and so far likes his job very well, and, I gather, promises well at it. He lodges during the week with the Clerk of St Mark's,[2] our cousin.

Thanks very much for your kind offer of Bed and Brandy. You do not express the latter easement; but I have gathered that it is annexed.

Let me know as soon as may be, whether you can both come on March 1st.

Yours,

Arthur Machen

---

1   Hilary had become an apprentice organ builder in London.

2   The Revd Cecil Lamb, the successor to J. N. Newland-Smith at St Mark's Church, was Purefoy's cousin.

Lynwood,
Amersham, Bucks.
March 4th 1930

Dear Summerford,

To begin at the beginning: we were very sorry indeed that you and Fairtlough could not come on Saturday; more especially as your letter seemed to say that there was not much prospect of your being able to come on any discernible Saturday. I hope you will both reconsider this?

Thank you so much for your good wishes. It seems a long time since March 3rd, 1863. I cannot think the date was a well chosen one. March 3rd 1820 would, I think, have been more suitable, with a run up to, say, 1890. In that event, I should not have had the pain of living into an age which I regard with ever increasing horror, hatred and contempt. For example: I hear rumours that the squire here, Tyrwhitt Drake, is thinking of selling his estate. You will find somewhere in Coventry Patmore the most wise sentence: that the ploughboy, though he does not know it, is the happier because of the existence of the duke.

'The Rod, the Root and the Flower' is, indeed, a most profound book: more difficult than the *Religio Poetae*, also a treasure of wisdom. You know that some of the articles in *Religio* were contributed to the *St James Gazette*? *There* is a measure of the change that has come upon us. It strikes me that the difference between the end of the Roman world and our own will be this: that our barbarians are from within, not without.

The method of Wason's[1] promotion — I hope it will be so — pleases me very well. It has a certain ancient, homely touch about it which is very comfortable.

I have just been reading for the first time, 'Antic Hay'.[2] 'Pooh': that is my criticism. The fellow is quite aware that he is being very shocking; he means to be very shocking. Compare him with Casanova: the Italian knows that his method of living is completely right, the only method for a man of sense, education and sensibility.

May Fairtlough's cold be a decent old-fashioned cold, such as one used to get; not the six weeks venom of these days.

Yours,

Arthur Machen

The saint of March 3rd is variously spelt
  Wenwoloc
  Gwynllyw
  Woolos

---

[1]   The Revd Leighton Sandys Wason (1867-1950), the Anglo-Catholic cleric and poet whose principles brought him into conflict with his ecclesiastical superiors. His comic novel *Palafox* was published by Colin Summerford at Cope & Fenwick in 1927. Wason's friend Compton Mackenzie wrote the Introduction.

[2]   Aldous Huxley's novel had appeared in 1923.

                                                   Lynwood,
                                                   Amersham, Bucks.
                                                   July 26. '30

My dear Summerford,
    For some time past, I have been thinking of searching The Book with respect to you. I am sure there is some text, 'Forsake not the counsel of the aged' — or words to that effect, as the stage manager used to say to beginners who had to take their cues from Benson.
    You know you are always welcome here; and the question of time is for you. If you have a car, come along at 8.30 and drink punch. If not, take the 3.25 from Marylebone, and have tea, with a drink in the xvjth century King's Arms to follow. Aug. 2 will suit us perfectly. Will Fairtlough come also? And John Davenport?
    What a book is *Belle and the Dragon*![1] But *I* would not revisit the scene. The souls have gone thence: they that seem to be there are but *Klippoth*, shells. But on this see *Kabala Denudata* of Knorr von Rosenroth.
                                        Yours,

                                   Arthur Machen

---

[1]   A. E. Waite, *Belle and the Dragon: An Elfin Comedy* (James Elliott, 1894) is a fairy *roman-à-clef* concerning Waite's relationship with the Stuart-Menteaths. Waite

depicts himself as The Mystic, Dora as Belle, Granville Stuart-Menteath as The Gadfly and Ada Waite as Lucasta.

Lynwood,
Amersham, Bucks.
July 31st '30

My dear Summerford,

The 3.25 from Marylebone is a handy train; and if your friend can come, pray bring him along. I am sorry we do not grow *urtica pilulifera*[1] here. But we have curious herbs: tansy, hyssop, marjoram, savory and rue. One or all of these might do good. But there is not any right Anticyran Hellebore.

Remind me to show you a Thesis[2] for the Degree of Master of Arts, submitted to the Faculty of Vanderbilt University, Nashville, Tenn. U.S.A. If it is received with boisterous mirth, I shall be very much hurt!

I told you long ago that the true doctrine is that Mrs Menteith *never got home* on the morrow of the sacring of King Edward VII of happy memory.[3]

Yours,

Arthur Machen

[1]   The Roman nettle; it is mentioned in *The Hill of Dreams* (1907), p. 25.

[2]   Ralph Grainger Morrissey, 'Arthur Machen: A Study'. See pp. 236–238.

[3]   See p. 113.

Lynwood,
Amersham, Bucks.
March 3rd 1931

My dear Summerford,

Thank you very much. I think Wenwoloc *means* all right, but . . .

Well, for one thing, he hardly seems to have made up his mind about the spelling of his name. There is your version, and the one I have just used; and I think that in the Gentility of the Saints of the Isle of Britain it is Gwynllyw; and as the Patron Saint of Newport, Mon., he is Woolos. So, perhaps, on the whole . . .

Moreover . . .

(You know the Great Legend of that last word? In the days when things were, perhaps, better managed at *The Times* office — and in other places — than they are now; the rule was that when a gentleman was to write a leading article, a bottle of port was taken to his room. Dr Wace,[1] afterwards Dean of Canterbury, was on one occasion asked to write two leaders, and two bottles of port were taken to his room. The hours passed on, no bell was rung for the copy messengers. Finally, Dr Wace was found fast asleep, his head on the table. On the pile of 'blue slips' beside him was the one word 'Moreover'. The two bottles of port were empty.)

Did you see that, on analysis, the soil of Cornwall proved to reek with arsenic? There is more poison in a handful of Cornish soil than in the dead, poisoned body buried in it. I always thought so. I always put the letters 'G.H.' after Cornwall, in addressing anybody there. They signify, 'God help'.

Well, you have got a queer job in Talbot Square;[2] but there is an element of waggery — to quote Waite on the constitution of the universe — in it. It would suit me better than the other job at the Stock Exchange.

Have you heard anything of John Davenport? I am afraid he is distressing those excellent people of his.[3] He won't even take the trouble to write to his mother: a sad fellow.

Do come down for tea and a drink any Saturday — March 14 excepted. Name your day and take a Day Return ticket, Marylebone, 3.25.

What was the notion of making the Café Royal like the waiting room of a gaol?

Yours,

Arthur Machen

[1]   The Very Revd Henry Wace (1836-1924) was the author and editor of religious works and the Dean of Canterbury from 1903.

[2]   Colin Summerford, then working as a statistician for a stockjobbing company, had been appointed moral overseer of his employer's son and was living at Talbot Square, W2.

[3]   Davenport had begun his wayward career of heavy drinking.

Lynwood,
Amersham, Bucks.
Thursday
[9 July 1931]

Dear Summerford,

Thank you, indeed. A gorgeous book,[1] one of the finest I have seen. That is, *foris*; as to *intus*, I will write you later; since, as it happens, I have a big bundle of Benn books this week, and nearly all of them have to be read. That is, they are not good, but their badness does not appear in the first chapter.

I am delighted to have such a good report of A. E. W. and Sybil. The old man is evidently in the height of health, in body and mind. I should love to hear him expounding his latest doctrine of the Hidden Church: as false as hell, I am sure, but what does that matter? In my latest letter to him, I suggested that to many of the Graal problems there is no answer; no vital answer that is: I cited Hamlet: people are still enquiring what is deeply hidden in that matter of the ghost: Hamlet talks to his father's ghost, and then speaks of that bourne from which no traveller returns. The answer is, simply, that Shakespeare was a careless fellow, who wrote in a hurry.

When you write to Brightman[2] again, do ask him if he considers this a valid formula:

Car chou est li sanc di ma nouviele loy, li miens meismes.[3]

I should be most interested to hear his judgement on this, and on the *mysterium fidei*. I did not know that there was an answer to the latter question. Has Brightman ever considered the possibility of fervent improvisation as a liturgical source?

How are we to account for the fact that the *hwyl*, the singing eloquence of the Welsh Methodists, is, pretty nearly, the Preface Tone?

On July 27 we visit niece Sylvia Warner[4] for 10 days. Do fix a day before that: a wire in the morning ample notice.

Yours,

Arthur Machen

---

[1] Presumably *Mandolinata*, a collection of short stories by Faith Compton Mackenzie, published by Colin Summerford at Cope & Fenwick in 1931.

[2] The Revd Frank Edward Brightman (1856–1932), a Fellow of Magdalen College,

Oxford, and the author of *Liturgies Eastern and Western* (1896).

[3] Part of the mass which appears in the 13th century *Grand Saint Graal*.

[4] Sylvia Townsend Warner (1893-1978), the novelist and poet; the daughter of George Townsend Warner, head of the modern side of Harrow School, and Nora Hudleston, Purefoy's sister. Her first novel, *Lolly Willowes*, a witchcraft fantasy, had been published in 1926, and *Opus 7* (1931), a novel in verse, was dedicated to Machen.

Lynwood,
Amersham, Bucks.
July 24, '31

Dear Summerford,

He works in a mysterious way: in a sense I am sorry not to see you tomorrow; but on the whole it is well, for tomorrow my chief admirer, Fytton Armstrong,[1] aged 19, comes, and he would not amuse you. It was only by threats that I dissuaded him from reprinting *Eleusinia*: pitiable doggerel that I wrote when I was 17, that would have disgraced 7.

The formulae of the *Grand Saint Graal* (? *c.* 1200) runs as follows:

'Come and eat, and this is my body which shall be delivered to martyrdom and torment for you and for many other people.'

'Take and drink, for this is the blood of my new law, my very same, which shall be shed for you in remission of sins.'

I suppose 'my very same', *li miens meismes*, means, 'my very own (blood)'.

Of course, I did not suppose that Brightman would know or care anything about the Grail Legend, but it struck me that he might be interested in the extraordinary formula: of questionable validity, though, I suppose, *li miens meismes* might be held to supply the defect of *li sanc di ma nouviele loy*. In the formula of the break; I know of no parallel to the phrase 'delivered to martyrdom and torment', not even in the wild Liturgies of Arabia and Ethiopia.

Of course, to the Grail student this account of 'the first Mass that was ever said' by the — wholly imaginary — Josephus, son of Joseph of Aramathea, opens difficult questions:[2]

1. How did the Romance Writer, almost certainly a cleric, dare to distort the sacred history in this manner?

2. Why didn't he use the Roman formulae — or go to the Gospels?

3. Where did he get his formulae?

4. Why didn't the ecclesiastical authorities come down on him?

We shall return on Aug. 6. How about that weekend for you? I am glad you are to be released from the tents of Kedar.[3]

Yours,

Arthur Machen

How I envy A.E.W. that struggle to write 300,000 words![4] May he prosper.

[1] For Fytton Armstrong, 'John Gawsworth', see pp. 169-70ff.

[2] Machen's tentative theory, presented in 'The Secret of the Sangraal', was that the Eucharist in the *Grand Saint Graal* may have been a fragment of the lost liturgy of the Celtic Church. He writes: 'Wales conformed to the Roman Church between 750-809; and therefore we may conclude that the prescription of the Celtic Liturgy began towards the end of the eighth and the beginning of the ninth centuries. It is quite likely that the native ritual was not extinguished without a struggle; it is quite likely that it continued to be celebrated by patriot recluses, by "saints" who had oratories among the rocks and among the woods for a long period after the Roman Missal had become the only legal use; it is quite likely that the primitive Liturgy endured long enough for the rumour of it to have reached the ears of the Romance writers.' *The Shining Pyramid* (1925), p. 120.

[3] Colin Summerford was leaving the stockjobbing company.

[4] Waite was working on *The Holy Grail* (1933), his revised and expanded version of *The Hidden Church of the Holy Graal* (1909).

Lynwood,
Amersham, Bucks.
Sept. 3rd 1931

Dear Summerford,

I have left your letter unanswered for a month; since you intimated that throughout August you would be here and there. Now, let me try to fix you up for Saturday Sept. 19th. It is Fair Day here, and the sight of the booths all along the old street, flaming and gay, is good for the eyes. I hope you will come. I have fixed Armstrong up for Sept. 12th.

I should like very much to have the views of the Egg-headed Divine[1] on that Formula. I think I had better translate the whole passage; since, apart from the wording of the Formula, the question arises: is a mass which consists solely of the words of Institution, a mass at all? And that, according to the text, was the Mass of 'Josephe'. 'It was very soon done, for he only said these words which Jesus Christ said to His disciples at the Supper.'

To me, there is an evil Protestant stench about this — 'It's so simple', as Drage used to say — and the puzzle is, where does it come from? — the date being *c.* 1200 and the general trend of the Grail Romances being highly to exalt the Sacrament of the Altar.

I heard from Waite the other day: he has compelled Walter Hutchinson[2] to consent to the Grail book running to 350,000 words! There are powers for you.

As you have despised the Venusian Bard and (I am sure) no end of General Councils and Provincial Synods, and have consulted Babylonian Numbers: well, I hope it may all come true and soon.[3] But I wish you could make it Duckworth. Putnam's head man once treated me to lunch at Gatti's.

> Yours very sincerely,
>
> Arthur Machen

[1] Brightman.

[2] For Walter Hutchinson, see p. 60.

[3] Colin Summerford was seeking a job in publishing. He began working for Methuen at the beginning of 1932.

> Lynwood,
> Amersham, Bucks.
> Oct. 12. '31

Dear Summerford,

We will despatch the Bergamots this day. They are snail-bitten, I regret to say, but the fact does not impair their vitality.

By removing 'The Circle'[1] from the range of the little typist, you diminish the miracle, but you increase your chance of success. Do not think of 'The Witch Review' as a title. It sounds funny, and people would hate to ask for it. Years ago, Harry Furniss tried to found a comic paper. He called it 'Lika Joko' after his signature in *Punch*; but, though a good paper, it did not do. People don't like going into a shop with an apologetic grin on their faces. That objection applies also to 'The Ghost'.

Waite's title for a magazine he ran 40 years ago was good:

The Unknown World

or

The Unseen World

or

The Wizard World   (rather cheap)

or

Magic   (apt to suggest Maskelyne and Devant)

or

The Veil   (melodramatic)

My favourite is *The Unseen World*.

In my opinion, the two dangers chiefly to be guarded against are credulity and insincerity. A.E.W. put no end of stuff into 'The Unknown World' that he knew to be balderdash: 'The Occult Review' — is it going still? — put in lots of stuff that it *ought* to have known to be balderdash: my friend Gow,[2] when editor of 'Light', wallowed in balderdash.

Two guineas is exactly the sum I thought of. As to length:? 1200 words.

You know, of course, how important the make-up, setting and cover are? Here my unsolicited advice is to avoid all funny stunts, such as using l.c. where custom prescribes caps: as

the unseen world

And, pray, nothing of Euclid's geometry on the cover! I mean, in the depiction of the human form; for it occurs to me that a Red Pentacle on a Green Ground would be in every way appropriate, effective, and cheap.

Here is a suggestion for a No. 1 article. 'Old Moore's' almanac for the current year, greatly to my surprise, contrived to predict, exactly not generally, the present political to-do. Let someone get all the astrological almanacs for 1931 and go through the predictions, comparing prophecy with fact.

Yours,

Arthur Machen

Many thanks for B.B.C. exertions.

[1] Colin Summerford was planning a periodical devoted to the mysteries.

[2] For David Gow, see p. 48.

Lynwood,
Amersham, Bucks.
Dec. 12. '31

Dear Summerford,

Then I will find out what Saturday after Xmas young Mr Armstrong is likely to turn up — he is impending — and we can fix up a day for you.

Are you settled at Dryden Chambers?[1] I took over the site nearly 40 years ago and built an extremely agreeable French Café.[2] On fine, warm days, one drank red wine of Touraine there, sitting at little tables in the courtyard. See, *The Three Impostors*. A friend of mine once kept a gay lady freely in his chambers there, and afterwards, by ill advice, married her. He was much amazed when he was instantly turned out. The strange thing is that he was the son of Tommy Case, Waynflete Professor of Moral Philosophy in the University of Oxford: since his conduct was neither moral nor philosophic. The poor fellow is said to have ended, sadly enough, as a schoolmaster; so we see what Waynfleterie leads to.

I am not astonished at the delay in producing *The Riddle*; I am afraid that my getting two quid[3] out of you was rather on the Waynflete side of morals. Still; miracles do happen.

Per speculum in aenigmate: our translators rendered the phrase, 'in a glass darkly'. But there is a shade in the Latin which they did not get. I do not know what the original Greek phrase is. I hope you will get into Methuens: a good firm, I should think. We saw about Peter Davies. The Great Oes will soon be upon us.

Yours,

Arthur Machen

---

[1] Colin Summerford was staying with Faith and Compton Mackenzie at Dryden Chambers, 119 Oxford Street, W1.

[2] In 'The Encounter of the Pavement' in *The Three Impostors* (John Lane, 1895)

Machen's hero Mr Dyson is told the 'singular tale' of the 'Novel of the Dark Valley' by one of Dr Lipsius's associates at the imaginary Café de la Touraine.

3 Machen had written an article on Spiritualism for Colin Summerford's proposed magazine.

Amersham, Bucks.
Feb. 12. '32

Dear Summerford,

I have a proposition of a publishing kind: it is to make a selection of the best things in the works of Charles Dickens. Of course the true Dickensian has these works complete on his shelves; but they would make a bulky addition to his baggage on a journey to Baile-Atha-Cliath or Samarkand. The notion is, to give him the quintessence of his author in a handy book, the size of which would be a matter for the publisher's judgement. One can conjure a great deal into a small compass, using India paper. If you think there is anything in it: would you put it to the House?[1] Or would it be better for me to write, direct? There is nobody ill here at present; and I hope Dryden Chambers can speak as fairly.

Yours,

Arthur Machen

My selections would, generally, be made with the view of getting rid of the 'Little Nell' element in Dickens.

---

1 The proposal was rejected by Methuen's chairman and managing director E. V. Lucas. Machen accepted the decision philosophically. 'A learned tongue, I think I remember, adjures us to trust the expert,' he wrote to Colin Summerford on 22 February 1932. The selection was published as *A Handy Dickens* by Constable in December 1941.

Amersham, Bucks.
July 8. '32

Dear Summerford,

I am very sorry. Not hearing from you, I thought that the typing job was, for one reason or another, unacceptable to your man. Time pressed, and a week ago, I sent all the stuff I had done to an agency. I wish I had written to you again.

Poor Uncle Ernest![1] What he will say to 'The Green Round' I do not know. Gollancz[2] told me that Sir Ernest was a man absolutely without religion; but I trust that this is not the case. He will want consolation.

I am afraid that the task of rendering the *Conte del Graal* is quite definitely beyond my powers. But why do you approach me? Is there not one[3] who probably knows the *Conte* backwards; who would grumble, indeed, at the offer — on the ground that the poem has only 32,000 lines instead of 64,000 or, better still, 164,000? Surely you cannot hesitate.

Yours,

Arthur Machen

---

[1]   Sir Ernest John Pickstone Benn (1875–1954) was the founder of Ernest Benn Ltd and the author of many books and pamphlets championing the rights of the individual against the bureaucratic State.

[2]   For Victor Gollancz, see p. 51.

[3]   Machen is suggesting Waite for the task. Colin Summerford cannot recall whether he approached Waite with the proposal, but the scholar was busy with his revision of *The Hidden Church of the Holy Graal.*

Amersham, Bucks.
July 20, '32

Dear Summerford,

Many thanks for your felicitations. Who am I to bandy compliments with my sovereign?[1] I am pleased to see that the other winner of the £100 prize is

Aylmer Maude;[2] the Tolstoy man. He once wrote to me, very civilly, asking me to write an introduction to one of the volumes in his new edition of Tolstoy. I replied, civilly also, I trust, but mentioning my profound conviction that no Russian should be taught to read or write.

Do not let me mislead you as to the Grail book and A.E.W. One man cannot guarantee another man's work. I can only say that he strikes me as the obvious man for the job. He has an enthusiasm for the subject; though that enthusiasm may not always be according to reason. Still; for all I know, your ends may be served better by hunting in the Schools for a Scholar well taught in Middle French, who will undertake to render the poem exactly into Grammatical English.

Miss Mary Butts and Rodker [3]

Long ago, I lunched with Rodker. There was a lady, lean, dark, haggard. She had cooked plovers for lunch. They were a dull blue within. I had a whole one, and I ate it, and declared that it was altogether excellent upon my word of honour. That was what the French Marquis said in *Peregrine Pickle* about the soup flavoured with assafetida, a substitute for the nitron of the ancients. Unlike him, I was not carried away in a chair directly afterwards. I wonder whether this amiable woman, if indifferent cook, was the Mrs Butts of today.[4]

Do not dream that I shall ever write an authoritative article on Geomancy — or anything else. I am a smatterer; not an authority. (See pp. 21, 22 'Things Near and Far'.) But I am sorry for your contributors.[5] For your Encyclopaedia will have to make all the others look silly. 'Geomancy, a form of Divination known from very ancient times' — but that won't do for you. *You* want to know: exactly how ancient? Egypt, Babylonia, Jews, China? Savage races? earliest and simplest form to be found where and when? Western form derived from Eastern? Distinctions between the two? Tampered with by Renaissance, or modern, occultists? I am content to know that the magician's brother in Aladdin used Geomancy. He practised the art with sand, kept in a box.

Yours,

Arthur Machen

[1]   Machen, who had been awarded a Civil List pension of £100 a year, is quoting Dr Johnson. See Boswell's *Life of Johnson*, February 1767.

[2]   Aylmer Maude (1858-1938) was the translator and biographer of Tolstoy.

[3]   Mary Francis Butts (1892-1937), the novelist and short-story writer, was the second wife of the publisher John Rodker (1894-1955). Rodker reprinted Machen's *Casanova* in 1922 under the imprint of The Casanova Society.

[4]   After hearing from Colin Summerford, who knew Mary Butts, Machen commented in a letter of 15 August 1932: 'It is quite clear that Mary Butts is not the Mrs Rodker that cooked the Blue Plover.'

[5]   Colin Summerford was considering publishing an encyclopaedia on the occult.

Amersham, Bucks.

Oct. 28 '32

Dear Summerford,

I hope you have got over that gastric influenza by this time? I believe it is a hideous malady.

When are we to look for you down here? A post card a day or two in advance; and we will await you.

Do you remember my notion of a Dickens selection: not a substitute for complete works, but a viaticum to take away in your pocket? Well, without any communication from me, Sylvia Warner has done just the book that was in my mind, and done it admirably. It is called 'The Week End Dickens'.[1]

If you *do* go on with that Grail notion, and don't find the obvious man; give Oliver Stonor a chance, if it may be. He would find it child's play after *Le Moyen de Parvenir*.[2]

When is Aleister Crowley going to bring his action against Nina Hamnett?[3] When muck meets mud . . .

Yours,

Arthur Machen

Conte de Graal: poem by Chrétien de Troyes and others, who continued it. *Percival le Gallois*: prose, translated by Sebastian Evans under the title, 'The High History of the Holy Graal'.

[1]   *The Week End Dickens*, with an Introduction by Sylvia Townsend Warner, was published by Alexander Maclehose.

[2]   François Béroalde de Verville, *The Way to Succeed*, translated by Oliver Stonor (The Hesperides Press, 1930). Machen was invited by the publishers to continue his

bawdy translation of the seventeenth-century pastiche of Rabelais, publication of which had been disrupted in 1889 when the printers refused to continue work because of its indecencies (see pp. 180-81). He declined but suggested Oliver Stonor for the task and provided an Introduction.

3 Crowley claimed that the artist Nina Hamnett (1890–1956) had libelled him in her book *Laughing Torso* (Constable, 1932) by associating him with the practice of Black Magic at his villa near Cefalu in Sicily. When the case was heard at the High Court in April 1934 the defence presented details of Crowley's unsavoury life and he lost his lawsuit.

Amersham, Bucks.
Nov. 29. '32

My dear Summerford,

We were delighted to see you. The notice business is merely to ensure that you shall find somebody at home at the end of a tiresome journey: though it is rarely indeed that we are out of an evening.

I had been reflecting — and I never explained that Grail business. Here enclosed is the distinction between the two Romances. I do not think that the *Conte* has ever been translated; but I am not sure. Both books are concerned with Percival, but they differ widely, both in matter and in spirit. The prose Romance (The 'High History') has the singular episode of an ecclesiastical regulation ascribed to King Arthur, which, in fact, was made by St Columba. The regulation, providing that every church must have a chalice,[1] is in itself highly significant; and its provenance and ascription are significant also as shewing how a Grail romancer went to work: he took his goods wherever he found them; in this case in an Irish Book of the XI or XIIth century; the *Leabhar Breac* — Freckled Book.

Mrs and Miss are looking forward to Friday night: 6.30 as arranged.

I have been consulting the Old Man's book[2] for those data as to the *Conte* and the *Percival*: it is a confusion, but what a golden and glorious confusion: a noble book, indeed.

When you wish to give us a good evening: repeat your visit.

Yours,

Arthur Machen

[1]   See 'The Secret of the Sangraal', *The Shining Pyramid* (1925), pp. 92-93.

[2]   *The Hidden Church of the Holy Graal.*

Amersham, Bucks.
April 8. '33

Dear Summerford,

Very many thanks: I shall be there. I know the Ivy: I once dined there with Caradoc Evans and a strange meinie. I shall not recall myself to Constance Collier;[1] but, long ago, when she was a Merry Wife of Windsor, I was Mr Justice Shallow.

I don't think I have seen the Old One since '27; and I believe that it was in your flat that we met. It will be a very great pleasure to me to see him again.

You should have a great time at Dublin. The word must be: *Usquebaugh yn aur*: whiskey in a crock of gold. I once spent three or four days in Belfast with drunken Protestants who believed in — and dreaded — the *daoine sidhe*. They nearly killed me. I will get Norah Hoult's[2] Dublin address: you might — or might not — look her up.

Benn are dispensing with my services in three months' time. There is something solemn in being sacked at seventy.

You will let me know the hour and place of meeting on April 20?

Yours,

Arthur Machen

Should we, then, go to Barbary also? Is there balm in Barbary that will minister to a purse diseased?

---

[1]   Constance Collier (Laura Constance Hardie, 1878-1955), the distinguished actress who appeared with Sir Herbert Beerbohm Tree's company before building a screen career in Hollywood playing eccentric *grandes dames*.

[2]   Norah Hoult (1898-1984), the Anglo-Irish journalist and novelist, was the first wife of Oliver Stonor.

Amersham, Bucks.
April 21. '33

Dear Summerford,

I hoped to hear from Stonor this morning, and so to send you Norah Hoult's address. But I have not; and no doubt he is away on holiday. As soon as I get that address, I will forward it.

Let me thank you most heartily for one of the pleasantest days I have had for a very long time. I don't know when I have enjoyed myself so much. Good company, good meat, and good drink: a rare combination. I confess I had at the time and afterwards certain qualms on your behalf. I greatly fear that you heard too much about St David's Altar, and other matters congruous therewith. If so; set it down to your account of charity!

I thought the Old One in famous condition of body and mind. I confess I was a little put out when he said he was quite well: the first time I had heard that *ab initio symboli*; otherwise, all the years I have known him.

Enjoy yourself well in Dublin: I crave pardon: in Baile-Atha-Cliath. I wonder how it is that in the Welsh branch of the Celtic tongues, every letter is pronounced: in the Scoto-Irish, very few. In Welsh that name would be called 'Byley Atha Clee-ath'.

Pray give Mr Stephens[1] my respectful admiration.

Yours sincerely,

Arthur Machen

---

[1] James Stephens (1880-1950), the Dublin-born poet, novelist and broadcaster, who like Machen drew on myth and folklore for his works. Colin Summerford got to know him while planning an anthology of Irish writing for Methuen. His relish for fantasy may have led him to fabricate a birthdate of 2 February 1882 — James Joyce's birthday.

Amersham, Bucks.
April 27. '33

Dear Summerford,

Very many thanks for your kind offices with the *Observer*. I shall look out for the Grail review with interest. So far, I have seen nothing at all adequate about the Old One's book.[1] Whatever one may think of his theories: it is the only book in existence which gives a full account of all attempted solutions of the puzzle.

I have heard Stonor talk of A.E.[2] with much reverence. I know nothing or next to nothing about him; but I think the spectacle of A.E. leading George Moore[3] into caverns and clefts of the rock, if haply he might find the gods of pagan Ireland, belongs distinctly to the Comic Muse. It seems to me in the vein of Aristophanes. I once saw George Moore when they were 'putting him through it' — 'it' being the world of hidden things. Yeats arrived one evening, with George Moore in tow, at the Society of the Three Kings. They gave, as it were, a stool to George to sit on; and he was to be a good boy and listen heedfully.

You are having an admirable time in Dublin, it is clear. I once stayed a brief while in Belfast of the Black North. I perceive that there are links between the two capitals, however great their severances.

In the main, this matter of the Celtic Spirit seems to me to be comparable to the matter of making bread. You put a little, a very little barm (the froth of fermenting beer) into the great mass of dough; and it *rose*, it was leavened. But, you couldn't have done much with the barm by itself. But do not speak of this till you are away from Baile-Atha-Cliath.

All our best,

Arthur Machen

---

[1] *The Holy Grail* was published by Rider on 1 February 1933. Colin Summerford was a reviewer for *The Observer* at this time.

[2] A.E. was the pseudonym of George William Russell (1867-1935), the poet, painter, economist and mystic, who was one of the leading figures of the Irish literary renaissance.

3   George Augustus Moore (1852–1933), the Anglo-Irish novelist, poet and dramatist. Machen and Moore did not care for one another's work. See p. 228.

Amersham, Bucks.
May 31. '33

Dear Summerford,
   You must now be quite all right again after Dublin. Do you feel once more a Saxon; or, should I say, perhaps, a Brython, not a Gael?
   I heard from Stonor the other day. He seemed a little anxious about Norah. It would relieve him, I think, if I could pass on a report from you that she was well and flourishing. I am cadging and mumping around and about; but I have not yet found my fortune.

> Yours sincerely,
>
> Arthur Machen

Amersham, Bucks.
June 20 '33

Dear Summerford,
   It is strange; but not long ago I heard from a Lisbon friend,[1] who has been suffering horribly from sinuses, even to the extent of the surgeon's knife; and now you write from Jethou of antrums. I hope they are quite right by this. I remember Jethou as a great green hill, in line with Herm, rising out of the sea, and I hope it has not altered since I saw it — in the year 1877. Then, St Peter Port was a pleasant old town: that, probably, is not quite so pleasant now.
   I was afraid you would not be able to do much with the *Observer*. I did a weekly article for them in 1926, '27, called 'Queer Things'; and suddenly I was thrown out. I never heard what my sin had been.
   With this letter, or, perhaps, shortly after it, you will be getting a book called 'The Green Round'. Let us annotate this book in the proper scholastic manner; let us cf. it. And in the first place;
   Cf. The Apothecary[2] (*Romeo and Juliet*).
   Cf. also, the story of the Chelsea Pensioners. Evans, the editor of the

Evening News, loved to pull the leg of J. M. Dick, the Sporting Editor, so one ugly Saturday in winter, he began:

'Well, Dick, got any big football story today?'

'Villa versus Pensioners, of course,' said Dick.

'Pensioners! Do you mean to tell me you dig out those poor old . . . gentlemen and make them play football on an afternoon like this. It's a bloody shame!'

Dick just escapes apoplexy.

I am glad to hear that Norah Hoult is flourishing so famously.

Is it your first reading of *Don Quixote?* If so you are to be highly envied. Note amongst the wealth of proverbs: The laws follow the Prince's will. This refers to the trial by Ordeal of Fire between the Roman and Mozarabic Rites. The Roman Missal went up in blazes: the Spanish Ritual remained unscorched; and the King said: 'We will use the Roman Missal.'

With all our best

Yours,

Arthur Machen

[1] Undoubtedly Luiz Marques, the editor of the *Anglo-Portuguese News,* who became a friend of Machen while working in London during the 1920s. He had returned to Portugal in 1932.

[2] The Apothecary is described by Romeo as

> . . .so bare and full of wretchedness . . .
>
> . . .famine is in thy cheeks,
>
> Need and oppression starveth in thine eyes,
>
> Contempt and beggary hangs upon thy back . . .
>
> (Act V, Scene 1)

Amersham

July 12. '33

Dear Summerford,

This, in the hope that you are back again and utterly restored to health and strength. Gogarty;[1] and he to be a poet, too: I should not have anticipated felicity from his knife. But, I confess, I am extremely anti-Irish.

We hope to see you and Mrs Mackenzie[2] down here before long: do make the journey. And I want to hear your first impressions of 'Don Quixote', which I read first just about 60 years ago.[3] It has been one of my great companions through life.

I hope Guernsey has kept its old constitution. I described it to the American Wister[4] — author of 'The Virginian' — and he expressed the most fervent wish that his country could have so happy and just a form of government.

Well; let us hear your news and see your face.

Yours,

Arthur Machen

---

[1] Oliver Joseph St John Gogarty (1878–1957), the Dublin-born poet, playwright and surgeon, and the original of Buck Mulligan in James Joyce's *Ulysses*, had operated on Colin Summerford for a sinus problem.

[2] Faith Compton Mackenzie (d. 1960), the authoress and wife of Compton Mackenzie, was a close friend of Colin Summerford.

[3] Machen discovered *Don Quixote* on a visit to Llanfrechfa Rectory in Gwent with his mother. See *Far Off Things* (pp. 43–44).

[4] Owen Wister (1860–1938), the American novelist. The conversation concerning Guernsey is referred to in 'A Thorough Change', *Dog and Duck* (p. 74).

Amersham, Bucks.
25 July '33

Dear Summerford,

Your letter was a great relief. We were afraid that you were making a slow recovery; this especially, after a too brief visit from Sibyll Ray,[1] who gave us the notion that you had been very ill indeed. Hence our joy at hearing that, at length, all is well.

I *won't* say 'it's very good of you to praise "The Green Round"', because I am sure that you would not speak well of it unless you thought well of it. But I may say that I often hesitate as I wrap up my 'presentation copies'. Here I am — I meditate — sending a copy of my book to this poor man, and practically compelling him not only to read it, but to write a brief favourable review of it! But I am resolved to believe that you and Mrs Mackenzie are right, and that I am wrong. As for press notices; I have never been much in the way of getting a pretty press. Haven't I shewn you my little compilation, entitled — pleasantly, I think — 'Precious Balms'?

I should like very much to get a commission to write another 40,000 word story;[2] but my agent has not succeeded in getting anything of the kind; though Cape very handsomely promised to read such a story, if I liked to send it along. But this offer, though immensely gratifying, won't do. It was the fact that I had received £50 on account that carried me through over 'The Green Round'. I knew I *had* to finish it, to send in something by a certain date.

Now here is a difficult business, this Stonor-Hoult affair . . .[3] Do not, please, imagine that we claim any jurisdiction over other people's morals: I hope we heed the Apostle's: 'study to be quiet and mind your own business' . . .

Try and come down before long. We are well — save that Mrs finds the heat very trying.

Yours,

Arthur Machen

[1]   Sibyll Ray, an elderly friend of Colin Summerford, had joined the Machen circle.

[2]   Machen had written to Ernest Benn on 29 April asking: 'Would you consider another short novel from me on the same terms as "The Green Round" — save that I should like 6 months instead of 4 for completing the Ms?' The proposal was evidently rejected.

[3]   Two brief passages dealing with the marriage breakdown of Oliver Stonor and Norah Hoult have been omitted as Machen later revised his opinion of the matter. 'We grieve very much that two good friends have fallen out,' he wrote to Colin Summerford on 31 July 1933.

Amersham, Bucks.
Sept. 22nd '33

Dear Summerford,

In the first place; I am charged by Mrs with love, and many thanks for your letter.

As to Besterman;[1] I recommended him for the Besant life, because he is both a Theosophist and a critical man. This seems a contradiction; but B. has somehow managed to reconcile the one attitude with the other. If you see him, get him to show you how Spiritualists produce their raps: very impressive.

As to the other Life[2] which is contemplated: the unhappy Armstrong. Gawsworth turned up here the next morning. It seems — according to him — that the publishers, Rich and Cowan, proposed the book to him, commissioned him to write it, and paid him money in advance. I told him, therefore, that I would not forbid, denounce, or commit any other malignant act against it; on condition that I became censor, and struck out anything that I held to be actively objectionable: Rich and Cowan to take the resultant copy or leave it, as they pleased. So, refrain, if you will, from speaking to Secker[3] (G.H.) on the matter. I have instructed Armstrong (G.H.) to be very little biographical and as fiercely critical as he pleases. It is a bad business:

Excuse the lack of accents.

It *was* a jolly evening — thanks to you, Norah Hoult, and the green-fingered Absinthe, child of the sea.

Yours,

Arthur Machen

Somebody should feel the bumps of Rich and Cowan.

---

[1]   Theodore Deodatus Nathaniel Besterman (1904–76), the author of numerous works on psychical research and bibliography and the biographer of Voltaire, was Investigation Officer of the Society for Psychical Research from 1927–35. He wrote and edited several books about Annie Besant.

[2]   John Gawsworth was planning to write a biography of Machen. See pp. 182–90.

[3]   For Martin Secker, see p. 230.

Amersham, Bucks.
Sept. 26. '33

Dear Summerford,

I am sincerely sorry to have bothered you about nothing. If (I am afraid) it were not too late, I would countermand the *Plain Dealer*.

This is what has happened. Two years ago, or so, I transcribed *Eleusinia* for

Armstrong (£10). At his request, I wrote a brief Intro,[1] showing how it was done. It is that, no doubt, which he has sent to the paper. Of course, it is his property.

(*Sub sigillo*) And, by the way, never have any dealings of any kind with M. P. Shiel;[2] if you can help it. He took in Gollancz. You know what that means. That, I daresay, is no secret; but *my* speaking of M.P.S. and the matter is.

Our best
Yours,

Arthur Machen

They are still talking of how Dowsett,[3] the amiable Gasman, knocked down 30 coconuts at the Fair. In a generous spirit, he declares that his muscles were invigorated and his vision rectified by Dog and Duck Punch.

---

[1] The article appeared as 'My First Book "Eleusinia"' in *The Plain Dealer*, Vol. I, September 1933. See p. 180.

[2] For M. P. Shiel, see pp. 50-1. Shiel possessed idiosyncratic ideas about the law of copyright, believing that when a book was out of print the rights automatically reverted to the author. This created problems for Victor Gollancz when he began publishing Shiel's novels in 1929. See Sheila Hodges, *Gollancz: The Story of a Publishing House 1928-1978* (Victor Gollancz, 1978), pp. 77-78.

[3] The editor of *Gas World*.

Amersham, Bucks.
Nov. 25 '33

Dear Summerford,

Can you lend me £10? We are absolutely down and out. My 'Reading', as I think I told you, came to an end in June. Shortly after, Sir Ernest Benn engaged me to write for his new weekly 'The Independent',[1] at 'the old salary' = £5 a week. When November came, and payment for October, I got a cheque for £14.10.0. I remonstrated, and Sir Ernest assured me that my impressions of our interview were mistaken; and that he was paying by space — with a limitation, by the way, on the amount of space I am to occupy. So there you are. If you can lend me the money, I promise you, you shall be paid; but I should be dishonest if I named a date.

Here is the sort of thing I am doing for 'The Independent'. Don't return.

Yours very sincerely,

Arthur Machen

---

[1] Machen contributed a weekly column, 'Radio Reflections', and general articles on literature, folklore, the Grail, music and other subjects to *The Independent* from 7 October 1933 until the last number on 2 March 1935.

Amersham, Bucks.
June 21. '34

My dear Summerford,

It has given us great pleasure to hear from you. It will give us greater, if you and Mrs Mackenzie will be so kind as to come and see us. If you can manage it, let us know a couple of days ahead, so that we may have our party to ourselves.

I am very sorry to hear that you have been suffering from depression: that most horrible of maladies, rightly called *Balneum Diaboli*[1] by ancient authors. I suppose the jaundice bore its part in the offence? If a man's liver is amiss, though all else be well, it makes him ready to hang himself.

As to our finances (G.H.) we just manage to hang on by a narrow margin, which trembles and wavers terribly at times, in sympathy with Uncle Ernest's humours and careers. Perhaps I might enjoy it if I were a younger man. I remember some grim sports of my youth in which there was a certain relish. But at 71!

As to editors, you know: thank you very much. But will they bear it? I daresay my writing is old-fashioned; but if that review I did for the *Observer* be passable: I should very much like any reviewing that is going, anywhere.

Hilary ceased to be the Catholic Organ Builder's Guild, and turned himself into a Small Holder. He was here a week ago and seemed well and happy: I hope he will be able to live by the job. It is a hard one; but a good deal better, he tells me, since the Government stuck a duty on foreign stuff.

By the way; if the opportunity offers, would you show the enclosed to

Desmond MacCarthy,[2] and ask him if he agrees? I don't want it back.
Now name an early date for a joint visit.

Yours,

Arthur Machen

---

[1] The complaint afflicts Gervase Perrot at the beginning of *The Chronicle of Clemendy* (Carbonnek, 1888), pp. 13–14.

[2] Desmond MacCarthy (1877–1952), the literary and dramatic critic, essayist and author. With Colin Summerford he organized the appeal for Machen's eightieth birthday in 1943.

Amersham, Bucks.
March 19. '35

My dear Summerford,

I don't approve of your plans at all — since if they be carried out we shall hardly ever see you. But I think you will like Caldy very much: a beautiful island by a beautiful coast: a country very well called by the old bards, 'the land of illusion and enchantment'. Note the old parish church at Caldy: compare it with Gumfreston church[1] on the mainland, and decide whether they are pre-Norman or no. I think that they may well be of the 8th century.

It is a good thing that the island is purged of that dubious breed of Anglo-Roman monks. They were no credit to Angles or Romans. When I first encountered them there was one of them called Father Iltud. They had copied his name in its earliest spelling out of the books, to be correct, and pronounced it as if it were English. The saint is called, and usually spelt, 'Iltyd'. Cf. *'uffern dan'*, a military expression, used in drilling Welsh regiments. It is pronounced 'iffairne dahn'. Literally, it means 'hell fire': technically, it may be equivalent to 'shun!' for all I know.

Alas, poor Benn! He says that he lost £10,000 on the first twelve months of 'The Independent', and I daresay he did. Anyhow, he shut it down three weeks ago, and I am left howling. Oddly enough, it was 'given me' a few days before the end that I had better look out, so the 'Sunday Times' is wondering whether it would like a column something in the manner of the 'Radio Reflections' that I contributed to 'The Independent'; while Ellis Roberts[2] is (I hope) doing his best with another bundle of samples.

By the way; you will have a competitor in the solitary way, and in the contempt of riches. Stonor was here a few weeks ago. His complaint was that he was working so hard at quantity surveying that he had no leisure for books or literature; and secondly that he was earning so much money that he was in danger of becoming a dipsomaniac. That was his *gravamen*, his *reformandum* was to take a cottage by Dunkery Beacon, Exmoor, at a rental of 4/- a week and there support himself by writing.

Let us hear from you again soon.

With our very best wishes

Yours,

Arthur Machen

We hear from Muriel George[3] that John has had a book accepted and is 'better'.

---

[1] Gumfreston Church, near Tenby, appears in *The Great Return* as Llantrisant Church.

[2] Richard Ellis Roberts (1879-1953), the journalist and author, was the literary editor of the *New Statesman* from 1930-32.

[3] Muriel George, the former stage performer, was the wife of Robin Davenport and John Davenport's mother.

Amersham, Bucks.

May 7. '35

My dear Summerford,

Many thanks for the card. I thought you would like Caldy: a place of old enchantment: island and mainland are a second home to me. You know the prehistoric export of the county? — a kind of bluish rock, essential to the Rite of Stonehenge, Avebury and such temples: whatever that rite may have been.

Give our very best to Norah Hoult. I hope she got Purefoy's letter.

To use the idiom of a friendly nation: the Jubilee[1] was a wow. The roar of cheering coming over the wireless was tremendous. Amersham kept it up tremendously. Janet waited on six old men at the banquet for the aged and made it her pious care to fill and re-fill every glass with beer all through the proceedings. At night a torch light procession, a most famous sight, going through the street on the way to the Bonfire and Fireworks in the Park.

I have been soothed — the word is Boswell's — by a very pleasant article,[2] 'Arthur Machen, *Théoricien de L'Esthétisme'* by Madame M. L. Cazamian, *Professeur à la Sorbonne,* in the *Revue Anglo-Americaine* of Paris.

Let me hear from you again

Yours,

Arthur Machen

[1]   The Silver Jubilee celebrations of King George V.

[2]   The article, in the *Revue Anglo-Americaine,* Vol. XII, April 1935, was a chapter from Madeleine L. Cazamian, *L'Anti-Intellectualisme et L'Esthétisme: 1880–1900,* Vol. II of *Le Roman et Les Idées en Angleterre* (Paris: Les Belles Lettres, 1935).

Amersham, Bucks.
May 23. '35

My dear Summerford,

There is something moving (in my opinion) in the spectacle of a bad old man struggling with adversity.

I know that you and Mrs Mackenzie will do whatever you can, but I know also that formes are not elastic. If there is no room; well, there isn't.

I am afraid research *is* out of the question. Do you think Gollancz would give me something on account of a 'shocker'? If I were paid money in advance I should be forced to write the book — as in the case of 'The Green Round'. You and other people have said kind things to me about it, but my own opinion of it, in the process of writing, was so bad, that nothing but the sheer compulsion of £50 received on a/c could have made me finish it.

I have a subject floating in my mind — a gang of children murderers (that is, of children who murder, not are murdered) with horrid suggestions and implications.[1]

You know how welcome will be the visit of Mrs Mackenzie and yourself; but beware the 3rd of June. We have one of our rare engagements on that day.

Yours,

Arthur Machen

1   This story may have developed into 'The Bright Boy', published in *The Children of the Pool* (Hutchinson, 1936), in which the evil 'Henry Marsh', who appears to be a boy of seven, is actually an adult with arrested growth.

Amersham, Bucks.
Oct. 4. '35

My dear Summerford,

Whenever more than two or three people come here, I awake next morning with the profound conviction that I have grossly neglected every one of them. I beg forgiveness.

How is the 'Life'?[1] Does it move, does it march, does it trot? If so, I hope that understanding of which you spoke has been reduced to fair black and white, and that it is a good understanding.

Janet is enjoying herself vastly, walking on in the *Merchant*.[2] She finds the conversation of Property Men, Wardrobe Mistresses, and such like most entertaining. This is a good sign of a vocation.

I once went into a pub with a young and solemn journalist. A quiet man at the bar: 'Don't you remember me, sir? I made the crossbows for the Scottish Archers.' The young journalist's notions of history became a heap of confusion.

Note for the 'Life'. There is no better introduction to me than any connection with the stage, down to the Stage Doorkeeper. I shall never cease to regret that I once spent an evening with E. Nesbit,[3] her husband, Bland, and a sandy young man from Balliol, when I might have spent it with Charley Pounds.[4] It is a satisfaction to recall that I told the Balliol man that he ought to go to Salamanca or Valladolid: a counsel which he received in a very sullen manner.

Mrs enquires when Mrs Mackenzie is coming to see her again. She says she finds it necessary, like dram drinking; and I know that she means this well, though it may sound oddly. I second the invitation cordially, and include yourself.

Our Greenwood is going to Sofia, on film business.[5]

Arthur Machen

Is there such a thing as a Dictionary of Folklore 'motives'? If not, there ought to be. How handy it would be to turn up *Exile, Return, and Vengeance* and find that it is current among the Bhils, the Aborigines of Papua, and the Hottentots. The fact is, that I have been reading Map's *De Nugis Curialium* lately, and came across a note on two 'motives': the *Lapse of Time in Fairyland* and the *Wild Hunt* or *Miesnie Furieuse* — and the notion of a Folklore Dictionary struck me.

1   Problems with John Gawsworth's biography of Machen led to a suggestion that Colin Summerford should revise the text for Rich and Cowan.

2   Janet Machen was appearing at the Lyric Theatre, Hammersmith, with the Arthur Phillips company. She went on to appear in the Stratford season in 1936.

3   Edith Nesbit (1858–1924), the creator of enduring children's books, and her husband Hubert Bland (1856–1914), the author and essayist, had enlisted Machen as a contributor to their periodical, *The Neolith*, which ran to four numbers in 1907–08.

4   Charles Courtice Pounds (1862–1927), the actor and singer who appeared in the original Gilbert and Sullivan productions at the Savoy Theatre.

5   For Edwin Greenwood, see p. 64. He worked for the Gaumont-British film company.

Lynwood,
Amersham, Bucks.
March 3rd, 1936

My dear Summerford,

1863 is a while ago, isn't it? Thank you so much.

Can't you bring those Riches and Cowans to the point of yea or nay?[1] I detest indecision. I believe they are obligated by a bond to bring out my collection called 'The Cosy Room'.[2] There are things in it, dating from 1890, that make me sick to look at. Nevertheless, since Armstrong went through the pains of digging them all out, typing them when dug, finding an agent, getting them published, and getting me some money: — I felt forced in mere decency to dedicate the book to him.

Spurred by this fine example of Armstrong's, I have entered into a contract with Hutchinson to produce, by the end of July, a collection of short stories[3] amounting to 50,000 words. I have already done 10,000 of them. I am sure that, in the words of Dryden (more or less) you will not, from the dregs of Art, think to receive what the first sprightly running could not give.

We do hope that in April we may see you and Mrs Mackenzie again.

With all our best wishes

Yours,

Arthur Machen

---

1   This may relate to the question of whether Rich & Cowan wished to publish John Gawsworth's biography of Machen.

2   *The Cosy Room*, a collection of stories written by Machen throughout his career, was published later in the month.

3   *The Children of the Pool* was published by Hutchinson in September 1936.

Lynwood,
Amersham, Bucks.
May 4. '36

My dear Summerford,

What an excellent notion. I am writing to Norah Hoult about it.

It is some time since you have come from London to this place; so let me recommend the 3.25 from Marylebone: the train that is always there. Norah came by it with great success a couple of weeks ago. Once, she trusted to Baker Street, a station where doubt and treachery lurk hidden, and in consequence she got to Amersham rather late, as the result of travelling via Watford, the Circular Route, which I do not recommend.

I am mentioning this train to N.H. — still it is not compulsory; and if you both choose another way, only let us know what time you are to be expected.

Saturday next is *not* May 11. It is May 9.

I have just finished another volume of short stories[1] — long shorts: 50,000 words.

The Doctor, being asked his views as to the preaching of women, said: 'Why, Sir, it is like a dog standing on his hind legs. He does not do it well; but the wonder is that he should do it at all.'[2]

Yours,

Arthur Machen

Methuen again? Good.

1   Machen had written the stories in *The Children of the Pool* in little more than two
     months.

2   See Boswell's *Life of Johnson*, 31 July 1763.

High Street,
Amersham, Bucks.
St Martin's Morrow
'36

My dear Summerford,
   When will you learn that from the literary-business point of view I am quite
hopeless?[1]
   A little over 40 years ago, it was proposed to me to write a history of French
Gardening from the earliest times to that present day. The fee was to be £20, but
that is not to the point. I declined — greatly to the wrath of the Old One, who
said he would have taken the offer and knocked off the book in a brace of shakes:
and I have no doubt that he would have done it, sufficiently well.
   You know that Martinez Pasquale said to Louis Claude de St Martin:[2] 'We
must be content with what we have.' It is also necessary to be content with what
we are. I often used to wish that I could write a novel.
   Did you note the L.C.J.'s address on Horace? He suggested 'artistic neatness'
for '*curiosa felicitas*'. I suggested 'exquisite felicity' to Peterborough, the
'columnist' of the *Daily Telegraph*. He wrote me a civil note, approving of the
emendation, but doubting whether exquisite quite got *curiosa*. However, he
added, 'Horace at his best is always untranslatable.'
   Was it Petronius Arbiter who used the phrase in question? Lord, Lord. It
sounds as if it might be connected with John Jershom Jezreel, the New and
Latter House of Israel, and that Tower at Chatham, built for the Hundred and
Forty Four Thousand.
   I do, now and then, receive jejune typewritten letters from the Old One, *per*
Somebody. He writes of his getting on with a little work on Secret Rituals,
amounting, up to the present, to some 600 pp. in quarto. The people at
Hutchinson's wonder how it is that they often find Walter sobbing quietly

when they bring in his afternoon tea. He is as helpless as a little child in the hands of the Mighty Old One.[3]

As to the Life; would you like to do it?[4] If so, by all means, so far as I am concerned, go ahead. My own opinion is that no life can properly be written — published, let us say, while the subject lives. Then, in this particular case, I am very sure that it would be a disastrous commercial failure.

We are both deeply grieved to hear that the car is going. Make an effort, before it is too late, and give us a couple of days' notice of the visit. There are lots of nuts, waiting to be salted, peppered and toasted.

Janet is engaged: to one Martin Pollock, of that respectable family which has given us many esteemed judges in the last hundred years. Aged 21, a B.A. of the University of Cambridge, proceeds next year to a London Hospital for the practical part of his medical instruction, spent a month of the long vacation at Moscow, sent Janet a picture postcard shewing Lenin's Tomb. The world is a wide place and I daresay that it holds still more horrible objects.

> And the days darken round me, and the years,
> Among new men, strange faces, other minds.[5]

All our loves to you and to Mrs Mackenzie,

Arthur Machen

---

[1] Presumably Colin Summerford had suggested a literary project which Machen felt unable to fulfil.

[2] Machen was familiar with Waite's work on the mystic. Waite's biography, *The Life of Louis Claude de Saint-Martin, the Unknown Philosopher*, was published by Philip Wellby in 1901. Waite also wrote a short study, *Saint-Martin, the French Mystic and the Story of Modern Martinism* (Rider's 'Mystics and Occultists' series, 1922).

[3] See p. 59.

[4] This question suggests that the earlier plan for Colin Summerford to revise Machen's biography had been only tentative. Nothing came of the proposal.

[5] Alfred Tennyson, 'The Passing of Arthur', *The Holy Grail and Other Poems* (1869).

Lynwood,
Amersham, Bucks.
Monday. July '37

Dear Summerford,

Please receive my most grateful thanks;[1] I am fortunate to have such a friend. Again and again: thank you.

What astonished in my latest little encounter with Fleet Street — the Street of Adventure, as it has been beautifully called — was not the fact; I have known publishers, editors, all the tribe too long for that to cause me any surprise; but rather the discovery so constantly renewed that it is worth while for well to do, even very wealthy men, to cheat a very poor man out of pitiful little sums, monies that these people can hardly see. But if one brings the instance under general principles, one ceases to be amazed: neither the Saint nor the man of letters ever neglects the little things.

It will be a very great pleasure if you and Mrs Mackenzie and your company will come and see us. Let me have a line a day or two ahead. We are very rarely away, but we are sometimes away: for instance, we are keeping Thanksgiving with an American gentleman[2] next Saturday.

I am delighted to hear of your Oxford appointment; you could not do better.

Yours,

Arthur Machen

I note what you say about cheque date.

---

[1] Colin Summerford had evidently procured an outstanding payment for an article written by Machen.

[2] This was doubtless Montgomery Evans, a friend of the Machens since 1923, who regularly celebrated American festivals.

Would next Monday   High Street,
suit you both to   Old Amersham,
come down here?   Bucks.
                                   July '37

My dear Summerford,

I am sure that you had a very splendid holiday in Provence. I had — 41 years ago.

'The Hill of Dreams' has had its best compliment. You say Provence reminded you of the book: I could wish for nothing better. And, as it oddly happens, there is a connection between the *terra fabulosa* and the tale. When I was writing the first chapter, in February, 1896, in Verulam Buildings, Gray's Inn, in describing a hot summer, it came upon me to utter the sentence: 'and white walls of old farm houses blaze in the sunlight as if they stood in Arles or Avignon or famed Tarascon by Rhone'.[1]

Whereupon I said to myself: (more or less) 'that sounds good to me; I'll go there' — and did so the following August.

We have just returned from a very delightful visit to Clomendy Wood, between Caerleon and Usk; guests of Mr and Mrs Laybourne.[2] They took us all over the country in a big car for the highways and a little car for the narrow lanes; by all sorts of places, open and secret, that I had not seen since I tramped them in the 'seventies and 'eighties. We talked Llangibby Hunt, of what Efan the Huntsman said to Old Lawrence the Master on a proposition to feed the hounds in a new way, of Lord Raglan's nose bleeding over the Hunt Supper, of how a member of the congregation of Llanddewi Fach (my father's old church) wondered whether he would be strong enough to hold down the Rector A. Williams if he suddenly developed Homicidal Mania in the pulpit — which seemed more than likely. I was happy to give Mrs Williams, Llangibby, a bit of hot news: that Tom Parr, the man who spoilt Caerleon, was an illegitimate descendant of the family of Ambrose, Waun-y-pwll, extinct *c.* 1860. I am sorry to say that Purefoy, listening attentively to all the stories of the good old days, came to the conclusion that the Nobility and Gentry of Gwent were a race of madmen.

When are you and Mrs Mackenzie — to whom our loves — renewing your acquaintance with the kitchen of the King's Arms? Please name an early date — excepting July, 10, 13 and 16. I have been thinking how strangely holidays and changes differ: Provence, Paris with the Greenwoods,[3] Clomendy Wood — all admirable, but *immane quantum discrepant.*

And by the way: Laybourne said to me: 'I can't imagine how you managed to give such an admirable description of Penhow Castle in "The Chronicle of Clemendy".' 'Well,' said I, 'I saw it for the first time yesterday, when you drove past the Castle.'

I could see he didn't believe me; not a word. I mention this, not for the sake of the personal compliment, but because the circumstance illustrates the true theory of Literature as distinct from Journalism. *Prius in mente quam in corpore*; and *corpus* doesn't matter much anyhow in Literature. Yet Mr Blank still goes to Dashe in search of Local Colour for his forthcoming book.

Yours,

Arthur Machen

[1]   *The Hill of Dreams* (p. 11).

[2]   Talbot Laybourne and his wife were admirers of Machen's works.

[3]   Machen and Purefoy visited Paris with Edwin and Mollie Greenwood in April 1937.

High St.,
Old Amersham,
Bucks.
Sept. 7. '37

My dear Summerford,

I hope you are most thoroughly enjoying Paris, after your dip into Teutonism. Two things occur to me concerning Paris.

Do you know the stained glass of the Sacré Coeur, Montmartre? It struck me as very remarkable — and very beautiful.

And

What a pity the Government added sugar to the official Pernod. I always like mine unsweetened.

We celebrate the Fair on Sept. 20. Be here about, or rather at, 7 p.m. I do hope Mrs Mackenzie will be available: Purefoy is writing to her.

Yours,

Arthur Machen

High St.,
Old Amersham,
Bucks.
Dec. 23 '37

My dear Summerford,

Not long after the war, I was accustomed every Saturday to take a glass of dubious and metallic absinthe in a Mooney pub in a turning off Fleet Street. The barman came from County Tipperary; and on one occasion, after serving me with my absinthe, he gave the next customer his dose of Irish from the same measure.

'What's this you're giving me? It's got a quare taste.'

The barman leant over the bar and said in a confidential, impressive, stage whisper:

'*There's good in it*. It's absinthe. It's very dear.'

The customer was satisfied, as one having the best of the bargain.

And so I am sure there is good in 'The Crystal Cabinet'[1] for which I thank you very much. But what made the woman think that the verb may be omitted in an English sentence? Thus:

> I walked under the trees. Green trees. Leafy trees. Old trees. Trees that Dr Johnson might have admired, if he had happened to care twopence about trees of any kind or sort.

This painful gibberish was introduced by one Bart Kennedy[2] 30–40 years ago and was highly approved by Lord Northcliffe.[3]

We must fix that January meeting. Till then may you make the merriest Xmas.

Yours,

Arthur Machen

Mrs says that she has not read the book, that her taste was formed in extreme youth by 'Comin' Through the Rye'[4] and 'Cometh up as a Flower',[5] and so she may love 'The Crystal Cabinet'.

The following recipes were enclosed with the letter of 23 December 1937.

PUNCH

Dog and Duck No. 1.

Take Gin and Sauternes, the latter the sweeter the better, and mix according to the taste and capacity of yourself and your friends. N.B. the white Burgundies won't do.

Dog and Duck No. 2.

As above: but with the addition of any small Burgundy or Bordeaux. The quantities have never been measured; they are ascertained in mixing and follow the taste of the mixer. Or, as one has said: 'Dog and Duck Punch is an essentially fluid conception.'

Rum Punch (hot)
  1 Bottle Rum★
  1 Quart Green Tea — after 3 or 4 minutes decoction
  Juice of 4 Lemons
  ''   '' 3 Oranges
  Peel of Lemon and Orange
  Sugar to taste

Grate 6 lumps of sugar on the lemons
Keep hot and covered.

★ Rum is weaker now than in 1905. Perhaps another ½ bottle?

[1]   Mary Butts, *The Crystal Cabinet: My Childhood at Salterns* (Methuen, 1937).

[2]   Bart Kennedy (1861-1930) was an author and journalist who experienced an adventurous life in America before turning to writing.

[3]   Alfred Charles William Harmsworth, Viscount Northcliffe (1865-1922), the newspaper proprietor whose techniques of mass circulation journalism revolutionized Fleet Street. Machen was not complimentary about him in his memoirs.

[4]   Helen Mathers, *Comin' Thro' the Rye* (1875).

[5]   Rhoda Broughton, *Cometh up as a Flower* (1867).

High St., Amersham,
Bucks.
May 17, '38

My dear Summerford,

It is benevolent of you to tell me that you liked the Waite review.[1] I hope the Old 'Un liked it! I am sitting in the shade and keeping quiet. But we cannot let you away to the misty islands[2] without a word. When are you going? If not immediately; then, will you and Mrs Faith come down between 5-6 Saturday, May 28? If immediately: will next Saturday May 21 serve? I insist on Saturday because that is the best chance of getting something eatable. I think the Henry VII Arms have found out that the rebuilt Crown is not a formidable competitor — and so *canis reversus* . . .

Yours,

Arthur Machen

[1]   Machen's notice of *Shadows of Life and Thought* was published in the *New Statesman and Nation* on 7 May 1938. See pp. 62-3.

[2]   Colin Summerford was going to live at Compton Mackenzie's home, Suidheachan, on Barra in the Outer Hebrides.

High St.,
Old Amersham,
Bucks.
Oct. 14. '41

My dear Summerford,

I write to urge on you the performance of a Corporal Work of Mercy.

The case is thus. You know, I think, that A. E. Waite has been very ill for the last year or more. For some reason, I know not what, Mrs Waite is now resident in North Wales;[1] so there is no one at hand to type letters; while Sybil suffers badly from a Neuritis in the arms, which makes writing very painful for her. I

have kept up a sort of one-sided correspondence with Waite, with a very
occasional note from Sybil. In the last of these she says:

'What has happened to Colin? He came to see us before he went into the
monastery, but we have not had a line since he left it.'

The address is:

Gordon House

Bridge

Nr Canterbury, Kent.

And there is another Corporal Work of Mercy which is also to be urged on
you: that is, to show yourself here. We have been vaguely hoping for the last
few weeks that you and Norah would manifest at the King's Arms some
Sunday; or turn up here, morning or evening, at about the time when 'they'
open.

I hope all goes well with you. In case you do not see the horrible paper, I
enclose a leaf of it. Who would have thought that modern Eire could furnish a
new version — 'The man who disliked MacNeice' — of the ancient, 'The man
who struck O'Hara?'[2]

Arthur Machen

---

[1]   Waite and his wife lived apart because Sybil Waite intensely disliked her stepmother.

[2]   James Bridie's article, 'Dublin in Wartime', in the *New Statesman and Nation* of
      4 October 1941 told of an epic fight that erupted in a public-house after Louis
      MacNeice's poetry had been criticized.

Amersham, Bucks.

July 9. '44

My dear Summerford,

We had a very cheerful and smiling time with you and Baker,[1] and I am glad
indeed to understand that the experience was common. Talk not of the 'feast'; it
was not in any proper sense a meal; it might pass, monastically, as a collation.
But it may be said, I think, that the Griffin's decent *ordinaire* mitigates, to some
extent, the austerities of the board.

It was a great pleasure to write to you at the Friary; I like jawing, both by
script and mouth; and in the region of script, I herewith enclose a very delightful

tribute to my faculties in that department. The document — non-returnable — consists of extracts kindly made for me by a friend, from an article in *The Manchester Guardian*, by one Hogan.[2] I found a great relish in being carried back to the old Verulam Buildings' age, and to the business that employed me there. I wrote to Hogan, thanking him, and telling him about the Barnsbury House with the Green Stain:[3] how I used to urge it to Waite as a desirable residence for him; merely causing the First Mrs Waite to regard me with a greater and deeper loathing than before.

I have put your remarks before Purefoy; and she just says she is quite well. What is one to do?

There is really something extremely exhilarating in being told that there is 'lots more money where that came from'.[4] I can't imagine how you do it, but I believe, with my grateful, amazed recollection of your achievement of March 3. '43. But I think there is no immediate need to meditate manoeuvres. At present, I have in bank just £1690, and I think I ought to worry along on this for some while yet.

Many thanks for the Tree of 'Gentility' (as the Welsh lists of the Saints call such a document) of the late Mrs John Davenport.[5] I was once quite familiar with the aspect of her grandfather and grandmother. They were opposite to me in Great Russell Street, period '93–'95 — and I often saw Ian at the window, script in his hand, learning a part, and illustrating it with the other hand in gesture: a grim, lean man. More smiling, more gracious, the moving apparition of Mrs Ian, daughter of Joe, beloved of the Airs and Graces. She would, like rosy fingered dawn, leap from her dim couch and appear at her window, in what looked like scanty pink fleshings, smile at Great Russell Street and the world, and proceed to do her hair. She was like the isle of Zacynthus in Homer: 'Very conspicuous'.

Yours,

Arthur Machen

---

[1]   Frank Baker (1908–82), the novelist, musician and actor. He wrote and presented a radio documentary, *Remembering Arthur Machen*, in 1963 and devoted a chapter to his friend in his reminiscences, *I Follow But Myself* (Peter Davies, 1968).

[2]   The article in the *Manchester Guardian* of 22 May 1944 was reprinted in J. P. Hogan, *Hair Under a Hat* (Chaterson, 1949). Hogan said he had visited 4 Verulam Buildings, Gray's Inn, 'to salute the doorstep which knew Mr Arthur Machen's tread fifty years ago'.

[3]   The house with the green stain appears under various guises in Machen's works: as

the decaying mansion in the Prologue and the 'Adventure of the Deserted Residence' in *The Three Impostors*; as the abode of the Barnsbury Hermit in *Hieroglyphics* (Grant Richards, 1902); and as the ruined dwelling in Chapter VII of *The Hill of Dreams*.

4   The national appeal for Machen's eightieth birthday raised more than £2,000, enabling him and Purefoy to live their remaining years free of financial worries. A cheque for the first instalment of the sum was presented to Machen at the celebration lunch in his honour at the Hungaria Restaurant in Regent Street, SW1. See p. 200.

5   A reference to Clement Forbes-Robertson, the stage designer and John Davenport's first wife. Her grandfather was the actor Ian Robertson, the younger brother of Sir Johnston Forbes-Robertson. Her grandmother was Gertrude Knight, daughter of the drama critic Joseph Knight.

Amersham, Bucks.
Dec. 4. '44

My dear Summerford,

Here is the odd gipsy story. What emerges, for me, is the tribal view that the tribe is quite competent to settle its own little troubles by its own law and custom and dislikes the intervention of the Gentile Magistrate. We used to have them about us in Llanddewi: my father used to compare phrases from Borrow with the local idiom in his progress through the lanes. He once baptized a gipsy baby by the odd name of Gentilee.

I get up now after breakfast and lounge about. I believe the Dr thinks I go on as well as may be. She hints that I am rather old.

Sorry to hear the last news of Norah: that she has got a cold. Her colds are apt to be bad colds. And she will be vexed by the death of Heinemann Evans,[1] who liked her work. She found him, I believe, a very pleasant fellow. I did not; partly, because he told me that a chapter of mine was a recollection of a former life;[2] partly, because he wrote me a pretty curt letter when I applied for some 'reading' for his firm.

When you write to the Bakers[3] pray put in our very cordial regards.

Arthur Machen

1   Charles Seddon Evans (1883-1944) was the chairman and managing director of William Heinemann and the author of *Nash and Some Others* (1913).

[2]   In Chapter IV of *The Hill of Dreams* Lucian Taylor retreats into a dream world, conjuring up the lost Roman splendours of Caermaen, Machen's light disguise for Caerleon.

[3]   Frank Baker and his wife Kathleen.

Amersham, Bucks.
March 5. '45

My dear Summerford,

Very many thanks for your good letter and your good wishes. I have been feeling a good deal brighter for the last 2 or 3 weeks; not so limp as I was when you last saw me.[1] Conveyed by the family I was again at the King's Arms yesterday and felt no worse for the trip.

Pray dismiss from your mind, utterly and entirely all anxieties about that money. Just don't think of it at all. These are the small bothers that are solved by time.

I am never quite sure what year it was when we met, but I think it must have been in '24 or '25. I believe you were under 16 at the time. You can still relish 'The Secret Glory'? I am surprised and pleased too, I do assure you. There are so few books, I find, that 'keep' well. I read a book, enjoy it very much: look at it again in 5 or 10 years time and find that it has all turned to dust.

Pray remember me very cordially to Fr Wason. Has he tried 'Things Near and Far'? I incline to think the former book the better of the two, but I have heard the reverse opinion expressed.

I hope that someone will be 'raised up' — see A.E. Waite — to take the place of the Swedenborgian; and that before long.

Our love and best wishes
Yours,

Arthur Machen

---

[1]   Machen was now very infirm, having almost died from pneumonia during the winter of 1943-44.

Amersham, Bucks.
July 9. '45

My dear Summerford,

Now then! Will you do your best to collect at the Griffin, on Tuesday, July 17, at 12.30: —

Yourself, Norah, James Stephens, Barbara?[1] And will you let me hear as soon as ever you can? Things are in such a state here that it is necessary to give notice. The King's Arms is mostly shut, so the other places are apt to be crowded out. At the Griffin, the little *ordinaire* is finished. The cooking remains; but if you will look on the visit as the Visitation of the Sick, you will be all right. Of course I should very much like to meet Stephens. I praised 'The Crock of Gold'[2] as well as I could in the *Evening News* about 30 years ago.

I do assure you that little matter of money does not cause me the slightest inconvenience. In the past I have dimly noted little yellow slips among cheques from the Bank, signifying payments from you. But you will attend to all that, since I am not capable of attending to anything much.

When you are in Barra, keep a sharp look out for Fairies, Peechts, and that sort of people. There was a correspondence in the *Sunday Times* a few weeks ago on odd numeral words and 'Fairy Counting' which recalled old interests of mine very vividly. It would have been very useful for a story[3] I was writing in '95.

Now let me hear directly that you are all coming on Tuesday, July 17.

Yours,

Arthur Machen

---

[1] Barbara Josephine Pickup (1910-69) was Oliver Stonor's youngest sister. Machen had convalesced at her home at Gerrards Cross, Buckinghamshire, after his illness in 1944.

[2] *The Crock of Gold*, Stephens' best known fantasy, was published in 1912.

[3] This was the 'Novel of the Black Seal', an episode in *The Three Impostors* which concerns the 'Little People'. See pp. 203-4.

Amersham, Bucks.
Sept. 25. '45

My dear Summerford,

It is very pleasant to hear that you relished the little party at the Griffin: but let the praise be given to Stephens; a very rare fellow and fine company. It must be 34 years since I did my best for 'The Crock of Gold' in the *Evening News*. About the same time there was another good companion discovered; a very different one, Caradoc Evans, very turbulent, highly entertaining. He united a strong dislike of Calvinist Preachers with extreme delight in and reverence for their 'singing religious eloquence' which you know as the *Tonus Prefationis*. On one occasion he had gone to a Welsh chapel in the London suburbs to hear a famous preacher, and told me: 'Indeed, it was lucky I thought of it beforehand and had a couple of pints, or he would have got me.'

How did the gale go with you on Barra? I read of it, and murmured the lines of Burns in his Address to the De[v]il: 'I'm wae to think upo' yon den (Hell!) E'en for thy sake.' But there is one thing: your P[aying] G[uest][1] got his value and more: he who goes to the Hebrides does not look for the weather of the Hesperides.

Of Sheep's Head, the following moral story is told. All my days I had a peculiar distaste for all the odds and ends of animals: all the materials which went to Don Quixote's Saturday dinner, which the author calls 'pains and breakings'. I had never so much as looked on any of them, save only kidneys — till I came to inhabit theatrical rooms in Rupert St., Soho. On a certain day there, midday dinner was Sheep's Heart. I found it sorry eating, tough and tasteless. Hoping, I think, to mend this, I went out at a venture to cadge a supper from Sandy Stewart, a journalist, in Gray's Inn. The supper was Sheep's Head. I call this, rubbing it in.

Much in the style of the recent gale at Galway: it just took off the roof of the Anglican Cathedral: very marked, it seems to me.

You would like to Journalize a bit? I suppose the recipe is to write to a friend in Fleet Street. Have you asked Norah about it? Reverting to the kitchen: I once knew an actor who felt bound to abstain from Blood and from things Strangled. He never told me what his attitude was as to Things Offered to Idols.

Purefoy sends her love, and sends two recent discoveries: Turbot in white sauce, with corncobs. Bream: white sauce and young artichokes; both excellent.

We light a candle to St Mary of Amersham for your safe return.
Yours,

Arthur Machen

---

¹ Colin Summerford's guest at Suidheachan was Philip Leaver, the playwright and
actor.

Amersham, Bucks.
7 Oct. '46

My dear Summerford,

If I were in communion with the See of Rome, I should ask you to procure
for me everything of a plenary kind that the Holy Father has in stock, since
infirm old age is in need of any number of indulgences, absolution, pardon and
remission, that is to be had. I can see very little, I forget everything, and I never
know where it is. 'It' = anything. Which reminds me somewhat of the last will
and testament of Rabelais. I have nothing, I owe a great deal, and the rest I leave
to the poor. Or, more concisely, I should have written to you long ago. I assure
you that you have not been out of mind; but you have certainly been out of sight
for a sadly long day.[1] For our sake and your own I wish you could offer a
clearer, nearer prospect of return. If you could have reported that the smuggling
industry was in a flourishing condition, and that Schiedam and Rightnantz were
nestling under every rock: there might be something to be said for Barra; but as
it is — *fuge crudelis terras, fuge litus avarum* as soon as you can.

News. Janet and her husband[2] are still in the purlieus of Bristol. He has some
sort of a job there. But they can find no place to live in, and so are quartered on
mother-in-law, not an ideal position for either party. Hilary has set up as
Electrician at Northampton, and I hope he will do well. But I should have been
better pleased if he could have got back to his old firm, who always treated him
and his family very well indeed. But: not a house to be found in all Penvro
within possible vicinity of his job. And, I gather, from an American
correspondent of the B.B.C. that housing is in an ever more horrible condition
in U.S.A., where, let it be noted, they have not a Labour government. A day or
two ago, we lunched at the King's Arms with Oliver Stonor and Sister Barbara.
Stonor has had a novel[3] accepted by Gollancz, on good terms, he says. I expect
you have heard that Barbara is parted from Pickup. We both thought that

Norah had made a great success out of difficult material in her latest book.[4] Indeed, I wrote to her that the result was grubby but grand. And I do hope that she will do well out of it financially.

Ours is the guinea-fowl's cry: 'Come back.'

Yours,

Arthur Machen

Purefoy's Postscript.
'Tell him I am madly pickling white cabbage instead of red: just as good!'
P.S. (mine) Were you aware that Broad Beans, picked much too soon, make a delicious dish?

[1]   Colin Summerford was still living on Barra.

[2]   Janet had married in Rome, where she was working for the British Red Cross, at the end of 1945.

[3]   *The Song and the Silence* (1947).

[4]   *House Under Mars* (Heinemann, 1946).

High St.,
Old A.,
Bucks.
Ap. 1 '47

My dear Dpt,[1]
Alas! It is all off. My dear wife died suddenly on Palm Sunday. Yesterday.[2] Don't bother to write. Tell Tommy.[3] I think he will be sorry.

Yours,

Arthur Machen

[1]   This pencilled note to John Davenport was forwarded to Colin Summerford. It is now held in the Machen collection at Newport Central Library in Gwent.

[2]   This suggests that the letter was, in fact, written on 31 March, since Palm Sunday fell on 30 March.

3   Thomas Wade Earp (1892–1958), the art critic and writer.

Amersham
Wednesday
[9 April 1947]

My dear Summerford,
   Many many thanks. You were always dear to her, in the early years and in
the late. I hope we shall meet before very long. But you will see only half of me.
                    Your grateful

                    Arthur Machen

Amersham, Bucks.
A sunny day in Sept.
[Postmark 25
September 1947]

My dear Summerford,
   Thank you yet again for your cheerful cheering letter. I was more particularly
pleased, because I have been meditating for some time that the spectacle of the
old one on his last legs could not be very exhilarating. You reassure me, and I
hope you are right.
   Janet and her husband departed to Bristol a few days ago, and Mrs Hilary
does her very best, and gives me every possible care, early and late. Hilary, in
view of the Basic Petrol Charge, gave up his job at High Amersham and has got
a new one, which pleases him better, because purely electrical, at the Euston
Road. He goes off at 7 and comes back at 7. He likes the people at the new place,
as well as the work, particularly a workman who is an Austrian Jew, who is
amusing.
   He and I, I gather, both owe you our thanks for promoting the kind offices of
Mrs Glock, who introduced him to the electric chief of Covent Garden. There
was a good job for him there and he would have liked it very much, but he
would have had to be about the theatre, or, at least, within call, from 10 to after
the fall of the curtain. This, he felt, would shatter 'the home'. He was sorry, and
I was sorry.
   I think Norah Hoult, Cook aiding her, managed to slip away to Italy, and I

hope she is having a great time there. I shall be very glad to see her back, for I am badly in need of cheering, and she always cheers. Did you hear on the wireless the case of Henriquez, who met a Commando, was taken back to camp a bag of broken bones, was given up by the Army Surgeons, and then cured in three weeks by sitting on the banks of a river and doing a little mild fishing — this on the orders of a person described merely as 'the great surgeon'? Henriquez said he left his hearers to judge how it was done: he didn't know. But the bones, which had been obstinately apart, under all the Army surgeon's efforts, including a sort of iron cage, joined up securely after the three weeks spent by the river. Curious?

Janet says the inside of her (prefabricated) house is rather like a ship's cabin: everything folds back on the wall. It amuses her. The Fair is just over: to me a rather sad reminder of the old days.

Yours,

Arthur Machen

Amersham
Monday
[6 October 1947]

My dear Summerford,

Storm and rain in Barra, and here we wonder gratefully whether the summer will ever end. The finest since 1921. I almost think the finest I have ever known. Though '68 or '69 was amazing when the mountain caught fire.[1]

Come when you will; we have no appointments. I hope we may be able to get a drink at the K[ing's] A[rms]. Coleridge said Swift was the *anima Rabelaisii habitans in sicco*. We all dwell in a dry place.

Yours,

Arthur Machen

[1]   See *Far Off Things* (p. 28).

This was Machen's penultimate letter to Colin Summerford. In a final note, written on 16 October 1947, he warned his old friend, who intended visiting him: 'Don't look for anything bright, but rather a smoking flicker.' Machen died in the early morning of 15 December 1947 at St Joseph's Nursing Home, Beaconsfield, with his daughter Janet and Colin Summerford at his bedside.

John Gawsworth

JOHN GAWSWORTH
Introduction

Friendships can develop at many different levels, depending on the degree of intimacy involved. When Randolph Bourne wrote, 'Our friends are chosen for us by some hidden law of sympathy and not by our conscious wills', he might well have been describing the relationship between the poet and critic John Gawsworth and Arthur Machen.

Gawsworth was born Terence Ian Fytton Armstrong in London in 1912. He claimed to be of both Celtic and Jacobean descent; also a kinsman, on his father's side, of Ben Jonson and the 1890s classicist Lionel Johnson. Gawsworth was educated at Merchant Taylors' School, as indeed was the tragic Edwardian poet Richard Middleton, whose works he admired so much.

In 1931, when still only 19 years of age, his first collection of poetry, *Confession*, was published, and more remarkably within a further two years another four works were in print. The originator and leader of the Neo-Georgian Movement in the 1930s, Gawsworth was awarded the Royal Society of Literature's Benson Medal in 1939, and subsequently made a Freeman of the City of London. In addition, he founded the *English Digest*, which he edited 1939-41, moving on to the editorship of the *Literary Digest* in 1946. He was also an anthologist, critic and avid book collector, the latter — in the form of buying and selling antiquarian volumes — provided financial sustenance in his later years.

He served during the Second World War in Italy and the Middle East, and even there he managed to find time for literary pursuits. Almost inevitably after the war a slow decline in his fortunes set in, undoubtedly exacerbated by his dismissal — on the grounds of economy — from the post of editor of the *Poetry Review*.

His final years were a nightmarish reminder of the fate of many neglected writers, marked by disillusionment, ill-health and the eventual solace of alcohol. He was often homeless, wandering the streets of London at night, with a Hyde Park bench serving him as a bed till morn. A plea for a fund to be set up to help him was made in the 'Diary' column of *The Times*, but continual heavy drinking had taken its toll and by the autumn of 1970, when still only in his fifty-ninth year, he was dead.

His obsession with the works of Arthur Machen — and no other word can be used to describe Gawsworth's interest — began in the late 1920s. Whether the subject matter or the quality of Machen's writings evoked this adulation is not immediately apparent. Perhaps Machen's ornate and incantatory style of prose appealed to the lyrical nature of Gawsworth. It is of interest to note that Oliver Stonor, in a 1963 radio broadcast entitled *Remembering Arthur Machen*, says at one point 'although he [Machen] never wrote a line of memorable verse in his life, he was *essentially a poet*'. Later in the same programme, Stonor refers to the booklet, *A Note on Poetry*, where Machen himself writes, 'There is a world elsewhere; its speech is called poetry.'

Whatever the reason, Gawsworth certainly took up the now elderly writer's cause with extraordinary enthusiasm; and indeed, as the letters show, he often came generously to his aid when times were lean. It is, of course, understandable that there must have been occasions when Machen, living at Amersham, wearied of the seemingly eternal presence of Gawsworth. The letters, however, reveal nothing of this; on the contrary, Machen is unfailingly polite and receptive to the many topics that arose during their nineteen years of correspondence. On this theme, the author Henry Savage, in a letter written a decade after Machen's death, described his old friend as 'being excessively, as I thought, polite with me'. Whilst Oliver Stonor named his mentor's outstanding qualities as 'urbanity, geniality and benevolence'.

The letters themselves constitute a unique and remarkable insight into the literary and philosophical landscape inhabited by Arthur Machen in his later years.

GODFREY BRANGHAM

LETTERS TO JOHN GAWSWORTH
1929 – 1947

28 Loudoun Road,
NW8
Jan. 22nd '29

Dear Mr Armstrong,

I will sign the book with great pleasure, and write something about Caerleon-on-Usk on the first page. Caerleon = *castra legionum*. It was the headquarters of the second Augustan Legion for about 300 years. In Welsh, the word is pronounced 'Kirelayon'. The people who live there call it 'Care-lee-on', and I have heard a porter on the platform name it 'Ca'leen'.

If you are interested in my Clarendon Road days; you will find a full account of them in Chapter V of my book *Far Off Things* — whence I suppose, S. P. B. Mais[1] got his materials. I have never seen his article. My number was 23 and I lived behind the little window on the top floor, next to the bow window. The period was 1883-84-85.

With all good wishes,
I remain
Yours sincerely,

Arthur Machen

---

[1]   S. P. B. Mais, *Some Modern Authors* (1923) contains a short essay on Machen, ending with the prophetic, 'His first editions are fetching high prices. People are beginning to collect his work.'

Lynwood,
Amersham, Bucks.
March 31 1930

Dear Mr Armstrong,

Many thanks for your letter. I will begin with two counsels, one particular, the other general.

1. If I were you, I would not do any business with the ingenious Mr Searle,[1] of Wardour Street.
2. I should think that the collecting of 'Machen Items', save at prices under

10/-, is a pursuit of doubtful — or not at all doubtful — wisdom. There may be a recovery, of course; but I should think probably not. This week I am 'reading' for the House of Benn, a MS dealing with collecting modern authors. My name is not even mentioned . . .

I have no duplicate copies of my books. I know nothing of the Book Market, so I don't know whether £6 is high for *Anatomy*.[2]

I have the most pleasant memories of my interview with Stephen Graham. He was everything that was kind and courteous. I congratulate you on the 2 strings to your bow. I have found the House of Benn most pleasant to serve. And, by the way, I do not believe for one moment, that Quiller Couch said anything about 'slime'.[3] He probably said that he had spent a whole day in being interviewed, and that he was bored to tears; and I don't wonder. But Swete, I am sorry to say, a man of many qualities and accomplishments, liked hurting people's feelings — or trying to hurt them.

Thank you very much for *Strange Roads*.[4] It was found t'other day among Hilary's props. He had never given it to me . . .

Yours sincerely,

Arthur Machen

---

[1] R. Townley Searle, proprietor of the First Edition Bookshop. Machen wrote *The Grande Trouvaille* as an Introduction to his catalogue No. 3 (March 1923) and *The Collector's Craft* for catalogue No. 6 (1923).

[2] *The Anatomy of Tobacco* (George Redway, 1884), Machen's second published work which was reprinted in 1926.

[3] Sir Arthur Quiller-Couch (1863–1944) was producing *The Mayor of Troy* in the West End in 1916 and Machen was sent to interview him. Shortly afterwards Lyall Swete, an actor in the play, told Machen that after being interviewed by journalists Quiller-Couch felt covered in slime. See *Arthur Machen: A Bibliography* (Henry Danielson, 1923), p. 31.

[4] *Strange Roads and With the Gods in Spring* (1923).

Lynwood,
Amersham, Bucks.
St George 1930

Dear Mr Armstrong,

I am afraid I have got to be disappointing. Thinking over your *Residences* proposal,[1] I have come to the conclusion that I must not be concerned in it, either in signing or preface-writing. If I were thus concerned, people would say: 'Whom does he think himself: Shakespeare, Milton, or only Charles Dickens?' I should look a terrible ass.

If you go on with the scheme, minus signatures and preface, you would be prudent if you took samples around the trade, and found out how many orders you could secure.

I don't know the Hereford street numbers. The Castle St. house — red brick — was on the left hand side of the street, as you pass out of the Cathedral Close, towards the upper end — nearer to the Close gate, that is. The St Ethelbert st. house — St E. st. continues Castle st. at an angle — is the last of a stucco row, a corner house: it being understood that you are still going away from the Close. But of course both houses may have been pulled down long ago.[2] I should think you could get a trip to Newport on as good terms as the Hereford ticket and Newport commands Caerleon, Llanthewy Rectory, and what I somewhat egoistically call 'my country'.

I am sorry for the matter of the *Residences*: but it would not do.

Yours sincerely,

Arthur Machen

---

[1] Published as *Fifty Years in London. The Residences of Arthur Machen: 1880-1930* (1930); also *Residences of Arthur Machen. Second Series: 1863-1930* (1930).

[2] They are in fact still standing to this day.

Lynwood,
Amersham, Bucks.
June 28. '30

Dear Mr Armstrong,

Any Saturday or Sunday (July 5 excepted) that suits your uncle will suit us; and pray give him our best thanks.

One of the best of the photos is my cloaked figure in the wet street; I think that both the street and I are most picturesque.

You mistake the force of the phrase I used about Parsons.[1] I am sure he is the last person to borrow money. The phrase: 'I don't think I'll borrow half a crown to get drunk with Chose', means: 'I don't care much for Chose's company'. I found Parsons a gloomy man. Of course I will sign your typescript of *Eleusinia*.[2] An American named Evans[3] has asked me to reserve the *Fleet Street* MS. I have told him that £20 is a preposterous price, but that I do not care to sell it for less. No; I am not selling the Note Book.

Yours sincerely,

Arthur Machen

By the way: I don't think I impressed on you strongly enough the utter — and malignant — falsity of that gossip you heard about Savage[4] sponging on Middleton.[5] I speak with authority and know the tale to be an infernal lie. A.M.

---

[1] Charles Parsons, a Yale alumnus, book collector and acquaintance of Machen.

[2] *Eleusinia* was Machen's first published work (1881). The only officially recorded copy is held by Yale University Library.

[3] Montgomery Evans, the American bookseller and ardent Machenite. According to Evans he possessed the unpublished manuscript, then titled *Fleet Street Recollections*, in December 1949.

[4] For Henry Savage, see p. 233.

[5] Richard Barham Middleton (1882-1911), the poet and short-story writer who committed suicide in Brussels. Savage wrote a biography of him entitled *Richard Middleton: The Man and His Work* (1922).

Lynwood,
Amersham, Bucks.
July 10. 1930

Dear Mr Armstrong,

Thank you very much for the prints: they are excellent. And so were the Maids of Honour, for which all thanks.

Fleet Street is not really a nice street; I don't wonder you find it distasteful. But you have the resisting power of youth. You are 18, and there are some diseases which comparatively trifling to the young, are serious matters when they make their attack on the middle-aged and elderly. I was 48 when I caught Fleet Street, and 55 when I caught chickenpox. They were both severe attacks; but *you* can laugh at 'the Street'.

Can you come here on Aug. 10? I shall be very glad to sign anything going.

Thank your uncle for myself and Mrs. He gave us both a delightful afternoon. And remember us to your cousin;[1] who is being held up to Janet as an example.

Yours sincerely,

Arthur Machen

[1]   Elizabeth Armstrong.

Lynwood,
Amersham, Bucks.
July 16. 1930

Dear Mr Armstrong,

The photographs are superb; thank you very much. We shall expect you on Aug. 10 at 4.30.

A wonderful feat to get a letter from Waite.[1] I didn't know there was any method of getting *Horlicks*[2] — beyond advertising for it. There are some admirable and curious articles by Waite in it; and the marvel is that he persuaded old Horlick to run such a magazine; which would do the milk more harm than good.

As to Fleet Street: again I would say that it is good to get the drudgery over young. I tried to learn Welsh at fifty — I should like to know Welsh — but I found I couldn't stand grinding the elements.

I hope your uncle and Elizabeth and all the family will have a great time at Dawlish. It is a delicious country.

Yours sincerely,

Arthur Machen

---

[1] There is a hint of irony here as Waite did not write to Gawsworth until the following month.

[2] *Horlick's Magazine*, edited by A. E. Waite. In 1904 he printed Machen's 'The White People' and serialized *A Fragment of Life* and *The Garden of Avallaunius* (later published as *The Hill of Dreams*).

Lynwood,
Amersham, Bucks.
Oct. 28 '30

Dear Armstrong,

. . . Now as to your tour in Monmouthshire. The best train for Newport leaves Paddington about ten to nine a.m., arriving at 11.30 or thereabouts. Three miles away (train or bus) is Caerleon. Four miles from Caerleon is Llanthewy Vach Rectory: no bus. But unless I know how long you propose to stay, and whether you intend to hire a car; it is difficult to guide you about the country. However, we will suppose that you put up at the Hanbury Arms, Caerleon, and have no car.

You first of all go to the Vicarage, and inspect the Register for March 1863: name Arthur Llewelyn Jones.[1] I do not know anything about registers: the particulars may include the name of the house where I was born: if so you will be able to find it — unless pulled down. This done; set out to walk to Llanthewy; passing through Ponthir (Pont-heor) and keeping to the right. You will climb up and up, and the top of the hill is Common Cefn Llwyn. There is no common: somewhere to the left is *imagined* to be the Roman Fort in *The Hill of Dreams*. Down the hill to the level where I used to await the postman with my *Heptameron* copy: up again: Llanthewy Church to the right, grave of my father and mother in churchyard — approach by lane. Back to main road, up hill: Llanthewy Rectory on right. You return to Caerleon. The head of the Faun[2] was in the hall of what is now the doctor's house. Hardby is the Roman amphitheatre but this is now excavated; in my time it was all green.

Next day: go over Caerleon bridge, and passing through Caerleon-ultra-Pontem, take the old Usk road. Kemeys (*A Fragment of Life*) on right. Newbridge (5 miles from Caerleon). Turn up to right, and pass Bertholly (1st Chapter *Great God Pan*: summer residence of Professor Gregg),[3] and if you will get into Wentwood, and if you go to the top, I think you will see the Grey Hills where the Professor was taken by the fairies. But these you should look out for in the train, after you have come out of Severn Tunnel on the right . . .

N.B. Returning from Llanthewy (1st day), ask at Common Cefn Llwyn for the lane to Llanfrechfa (*f* sounds *v*), the ruin was on the left; and if you like to go on, you will come out of the 'turnpike' road, and can get to Caerleon that way.

3rd day. Take train from Caerleon to Llantarnam, and there ask the way to Twyn Barlwm: 3 or 4 miles, but a steep climb at the end. Mynydd Maen (pronounced Munnith Mayne) is of the same range, to the north. When you get back to Caerleon, ask for Pont Sadwrn (Pons Saturni) and you will see the Soar Brook fall into the Usk.

4th day. Take train from Caerleon to Abergavenny (see *Chronicle of Clemendy*) and returning, get out, if you will, at Pontypool Road Station.[4] You can wait for the next train, or walk back to Caerleon . . .

Yours sincerely,

Arthur Machen

[1]   Machen's given name.

[2]   See *The Great God Pan*, 'Mr Clarke's Memoirs'.

[3]   See *The Three Impostors*, the 'Novel of the Black Seal'.

[4]   'And another event of like importance was my seeing De Quincey's *Confessions of an English Opium Eater* at Pontypool Road Station' (*Far Off Things*, p. 41).

Lynwood,
Amersham, Bucks.
Jan. 8 '31

Dear Armstrong,

You will be glad to hear that I have written the Introductory Note to *Eleusinia*, and am preserving the draught in accordance with your desire.

As to Pembrokeshire: the journey takes from about 9 a.m. to about 3.30 p.m. A return ticket costs about £3. The scene, of wonderful beauty, is the background of *The Great Return, The Terror*,[1] one of the 'Strange Roads' and the short story, called, I think, 'Out of the Earth'.[2] It deserves more than two days. I finished *Things Near and Far* on the sand dunes at Penally. All the places are close to each other, and a pub at Tenby or Penally would be a convenient head quarters.

I will keep the pen for you. Earache gone but deafness tiresome.

Yours sincerely,

Arthur Machen

[1]   *The Terror* was serialized in the *Evening News* in October 1916 and published by Duckworth in 1917.

[2]   'Out of the Earth' was first published in *T.P.'s Weekly* in 1915 and subsequently reprinted in *The Shining Pyramid* (1923 and 1925).

Lynwood,
Amersham, Bucks.
Jan. 23. '31

Dear Armstrong,

Answering two letters. Do send your list of residences and firms when ready: I will look them over.

The Hesperides Press is mistaken. The Preface to their *Way to Succeed*[1] is a revised version of the Boni and Liveright Preface.

The Red Priest of Castletown (or Castleton; I am not certain which. Consult Glamorgan Gazetteer).

fferiad coch: he had red hair. He was the Revd Hezekiah Jones. One of his brothers was the Revd Daniel Jones, who died *c*. 1820 Curate of St Fagan's, near Cardiff. His son was the Revd Daniel Jones, sometime Vicar of Caerleon-on-Usk — my grandfather. I believe this race of Joneses came (*c*. 1750) from Carmarthenshire. There were branches (cousins of mine) in Anglesea and London, 50 years ago. About that time I met 15 Jones cousins one Sunday afternoon — disliked them all, and never saw them more. A distant cousin is Mrs Priestley (Mrs Priestley the novelist, as we should say in Wales) who is descended from Daniel of St Fagan's.

Richard Middleton. I was never a Reader for Unwin. The only proof I could have read for them was the proof of my Introduction.[2] The truth of the Middleton Savage friendship is very simple. The two men were great friends, and if there were any question of money between them, it would be Savage's, since Middleton had no money, and, at that time, Savage had. A further reason is, that Savage is one of the most generous men I have ever met. Not for one moment would I say that Middleton 'sponged' on Savage: between friends, real friends, there can be no question of any such thing. I never got on with Middleton; an ungenial, gloomy fellow, with a grievance against life.

I never fix myself down to appointments in prospect. Come, by the usual train, Saturday, Feb. 7. I am not well: deaf, with an evil chill hanging about me.

I would like to see a Jordan-Smith[3] photograph.

Yours,

Arthur Machen

---

[1] The Hesperides Press approached Machen for a new translation of *Le Moyen de Parvenir*, but he felt that his age was against him and the commission went to Oliver Stonor. Boni & Liveright in New York reprinted Machen's earlier translation of Béroalde de Verville's book as *Fantastic Tales* in 1923.

[2] Despite his antipathy to Middleton exhibited in this letter, Machen composed a charming Introduction to the writer's posthumous *The Ghost-Ship and Other Stories* (1912).

[3] Paul Jordan-Smith, the American academic and author who wrote about Machen at length in his outstanding trilogy, *On Strange Altars* (1923), *For the Love of Books* (1934) and *The Road I Came By* (1960).

Amersham, Bucks.
Aug: 8: '32

Dear Armstrong,

Pray quote me on 'Gold Like Glass',[1] if it will do you any service.

I should like to see the 'Anthology'[2] proofs if convenient. We are not going away until the end of the month.

My price for the MS of *The Green Round* is £25.[3] I have quoted it to Spurr,[4] in answer to his question. I was pleased to find that he and I had arrived at the same estimate.

Yours sincerely,

Arthur Machen

[1]   'Gold Like Glass' was a short story by the artist and mystical writer Frederick Carter which Machen admired.

[2]   Gawsworth's *Strange Assembly* (1932), containing Machen's stories 'The Gift of Tongues' and 'The Rose Garden'.

[3]   This manuscript was offered for sale by a London bookseller for £4,200 in 1987. *The Green Round* was Machen's last full-length work of fiction, in which he reworked some old themes.

[4]   For Harry Spurr, see p. 211.

Lynwood,
Amersham, Bucks.
Feb. 8. '33

Dear Armstrong,

In the first place; it is my bounden duty to warn you against undertaking the work you propose to undertake. There are minor reasons against it; but chief of all, is the major premise (see *Whately*, not *Whateley):*[1]

Major Books about Machen are interesting to very few people.
Minor This is a book about Machen.
Conclusion: Therefore, this book is interesting to very few people.

There you are: irresistible in *Barbara* and I hope you see the next syllogism in *Celarent*: books interesting to very few people don't sell etc. etc.

I remember three years ago or so having a very glowing letter from America; I think the writer was Van Patten,[2] but I am not sure. But, anyhow, it was glowing, and ended up with something about holding a Machen Dinner: I wrote back that I was delighted; and scarcely liked mentioning the fact that my total American Royalties for the past year amounted to a little under £5.

So there you are; and if you resolve to go on I can only say, 'And God give you a good deliverance' — as the Clerk of the Court used to remark to the Prisoner of the Bar, when they had quite made up their minds that he must hang.

I said there were minor objections. One is that it is a ticklish thing to write a man's life during his lifetime. For example; I might not care to have any letters to Lane[3] printed; and what a nuisance that would be for you . . .

Yours sincerely,

Arthur Machen

[1] One of Machen's favourite books was Richard Whately's *Elements of Logic*. In *Far Off Things* (pp. 135-37) Whately and scholastic logic are discussed in some detail.

[2] Nathan van Patten (1884-1956), the director of the Universities Libraries at Stanford University, founded the Arthur Machen Society in America in 1948. In an obituary of Machen, *There Are Some Who Mourn* (Canton, Ohio: 1948), van Patten wrote: 'Machen has gone and the mysteries remain.'

[3] For some of Machen's letters to the publisher John Lane, see pp. 216-19.

Lynwood,
Amersham, Bucks.
June 13. '33

Dear Armstrong,

It is extremely good of you to take all this trouble:[1] a thankless job — and I shall be a good deal astonished if it is a successful one, I have long parted with illusions; not that I ever harboured many.

Pray look around on Saturday next. Your plan of sending a list of questions is a good one: consideration makes for accuracy. Nothing like black and white.

My copies of 'The Green Round' have come. At the request of the firm, I wrote the 'blurb' for the jacket. To this they have prefixed an imbecile paragraph of their own, telling the world what a splendid fellow I am. It is the sort of thing that moves the sensible reviewer to just a contemptuous comment.

Pray give our best regards to Mrs. And, by the way, I hope the uncertain prospects of *Everyman* of which she spoke to me some time ago, are now both certain and good.

Yours sincerely,

Arthur Machen

[1]   This is presumably a reference to Gawsworth's work on the Machen biography.

Lynwood,
Amersham, Bucks.
Aug. 11. '33

Dear Armstrong,

I think you have done nobly: thank you very much. It must have been a vile task.

As to *Clemendy*,[1] £20 to 14/-; what does the Psalmist say; put not your trust in *prices*. This book business is just a small chapter in a big volume of depreciation, following naturally on a monstrous appreciation. Before long there will be a readjustment, but not to the high watermark of the early twenties.

We shall see you, then, next Saturday, and I trust Mrs with you. I have not yet received your questions.

I have been wanting to say: present my compliments to Miss Dorothy Sayers, and beg her from me to make a study, biographical and critical, of Wilkie Collins. From a few things she has written about him, I am sure she would make a very choice book. I believe he was a queer customer: all the better for her purpose.

Yours sincerely,

Arthur Machen

¹ *The Chronicle of Clemendy* (1888).

Amersham, Bucks.
Aug. 14. '33

Dear Armstrong,

I am writing this day to *The New Statesman* re *The Pantomime Man.*[1] I am doubtful of success since Ellis Roberts,[2] the former Literary Editor, who sent me an occasional book for review, has left the paper some time ago.

Have you got a copy of 'The Cosy Room'?[3] I should be much obliged. I am putting up a notion for a series in this vein to some agents, and they want to see *The Cosy Room* before they start.

Your number up with R[ich] & Cowan, if *Pantomime Man* doesn't do well? Don't bother about that: your number there will be up all right a very few weeks after the issue of your book about me.[4] However, I did my best to dissuade you in *Barbara* and, I think, in *Celarent*.

We hope to see you both next Satdy.

Yours sincerely,

Arthur Machen

---

[1] *The Pantomime Man* was a collection of stories by Richard Middleton, edited by Gawsworth.

[2] For R. Ellis Roberts, see pp. 144–5.

[3] 'The Cosy Room' was first published in Cynthia Asquith (ed.), *Shudders*, (Hutchinson, 1928).

[4] It was — after delivery of the manuscript.

High St.,
Amersham, Bucks.
23 Aug. '33

Dear Armstrong,

The Sunday Times sent its proofs in duplicate,[1] so I send you the enclosed, knowing your fondness for these curiosities. The sentence in the margin is not in the article.

'The Machens' Little French Maid'

Let me beg you not to make Shiel[2] the authority for any statement about me or my life. The man is an inveterate liar.

Our best regards to you and Mrs.

Yours sincerely,

Arthur Machen

[1]   Machen reviewed *The Pantomime Man* in *The Sunday Times* on 3 September 1933.

[2]   For M. P. Shiel, see pp. 50–1. In a letter to Gawsworth Shiel claimed that while he was living at Gray's Inn Place in the 1890s the Machens' maid had come to his apartment and offered to sleep with him. Gawsworth was collecting information for his biography, despite Machen warning him against the project.

Lynwood,
Amersham, Bucks.
Sept. 4. '33

Dear Armstrong,

In the first place, I hope that you and your wife are having a very pleasant time in Devon, and secondly that she may very soon find a better job. Not that I have ever thought much of the process of earning an honest livelihood. I remember writing in 1900 to my *confrère*, P. J. Toulet, (translator of *Pan*):[1] 'I shall soon be reduced to the sad and disgusting necessity of earning my own living.' He approved in the strongest terms of my choice of adjectives: I approve them still.

Thank you very much for your kind review and for the *Terror* cutting. I think it must have been in 1922 that I wrote the Benson article. F.R.B.[2] was going to South Africa. I don't remember anything about giving the staff to Foster; but it may be so, and anyhow it's of no consequence. I gave it to Benson, anyhow.

Yours sincerely,

Arthur Machen

[1]   *Le Grand Dieu Pan* (1901).

[2]   Sir Frank Robert Benson (1858–1939), the founder of the Benson company, with whom Machen toured as a 'bit' actor in the first decade of the century. See Constance Benson, *Mainly Players: Bensonian Memories* (1926), for which Machen provided the Introduction.

Amersham, Bucks.
Thursday
[7 September 1933]

Dear Armstrong,

Herewith the questions answered to the best of my abilities. But many of the matters you ask about are trifling, and I don't think I ever remembered them! As Edward Walford's 'devil', I wrote the Ballantyne obituary for him in the law paper[1] and met A. E. Waite for the first time while I was doing it, under the big Dome.

The photograph in the *Play Pictorial* is not of me. I suppose the groups of the subsidiary villains were unsatisfactory: none appeared.

Best regards to you both.

Yours sincerely,

Arthur Machen

[1]   *The Law Times*, 15 January 1887, Obituary: Serjeant Ballantine.

Lynwood,
Amersham, Bucks.
Sept. 19. '33

Dear Armstrong,

I accept your £5 proposition. I will not attempt to rewrite, but will correct any errors of fact, to the best of my ability . . .

Now look here. I must bring you a sense of your great blessing. You talk of your 'swan song'. And you 21! I must confess that I remember feeling in the year 1892 that I was finished. That was imbecile enough; though I was 8 or 9 years older. Swan song, indeed. Why you have hardly begun to say 'cheep, cheep', and you have your life before you. I am 70. I think it extremely unlikely that I shall ever write another line worth reading; but it is not impossible.

More advice. When you told me you were going to write this Life, I shewed you in *Barbara* and *Celarent* that it would do no good; that it wouldn't do. After glancing through the chapters you sent me, I am still sure that it won't do. On general principles, it is always undesirable to write the lives of the living. It is done sometimes, I believe, in the case of politicians; but such 'Lives' are mere election puffs. And when, as in my case, the subject of the life is practically unknown, commercial disaster is certain to attend literary impropriety.

Keep your five pounds: put your notes away — and wait a little.

You say, I see, that you are not attempting any critical estimate of my work. Now this is the kind of book that can be written in the subject's lifetime with propriety; though, in my case, it would be commercially worthless.

With best wishes to you both, and good counsel (believe me) to you.

Yours sincerely,

Arthur Machen

Amersham, Bucks.
Sept. 22. '33

Dear Armstrong,

Herewith your copy, duly clawed by me, according to the King's Arms Treaty of the 20th inst. And now; criticize the *Books* as freely as ever you please, and leave Man as much alone as may be — and so spare me the use of the Censor's pencil.

I am going to look up for you a bundle of letters to a dead friend,[1] returned to me. I believe they are somewhat interesting.

With our best wishes to your wife and hopes for a speedy job.

Yours sincerely,

Arthur Machen

[1]   For the letters to Paul England, see pp. 219-28.

Lynwood,
Amersham, Bucks.
Sept. 27. '33

Dear Armstrong,

Can you send along that £5 for my revising services?

Here are the letters I spoke of: they are less interesting than I thought, but you may get a bit here and a bit there. I have enclosed a note on dates and residences to give some guide — vague enough — as to the date of the letters. They were written to Paul England (*c.* 1865-1932) concert singer, translator of songs and librettos (several for Beecham), author of a volume of poems, teacher of singing, man of books.

  Best regards to your wife and yourself.

Yours sincerely,

Arthur Machen

High Street,
Old Amersham,
Bucks.
May 19. '37

Dear Armstrong,

Many thanks: I will send along the address to the French firm. Shall I suggest, '*Abandon-nos ces lieux*' for 'let us go hence'?[1] I will think it over.

The first edition of *Le Grand Dieu Pan* appeared in 1901; I hadn't heard of any other; it was in a green paper wrapper.

The Greenwoods were our hosts on the Paris visit. We started on April 23rd and returned on Tuesday April 27th.

I will return you the Yorick *menu* when I renew my stock of large envelopes. I was not at the dinner in question, though I have been Christopher Wilson's guest at the club. What has become of the series of portraits of members, painted by Sime?[2]

Colin Still,[3] as a practical man, has told Rich & Cowan exactly what I told you four or five years ago, on conclusions obtained *in modo et figura*. The coincidence of the theoretic and practical reason is striking.

With our best to you both.

Yours,

Arthur Machen

[1] The phrase appears in *The Great God Pan* (p. 12). The fourth edition of the French translation was published in 1938.

[2] Sidney H. Sime, the illustrator of Lord Dunsany's works and of Machen's *The House of Souls* and *The Hill of Dreams*.

[3] Colin Still was a new reader for Rich & Cowan who advised against Gawsworth's biography of Machen.

Clomendy Wood,
Nr Caerleon,
Mon.
Saturday
[1 July 1937]

Dear Armstrong,

We are staying with friends: let that explain all that is amiss.

As a matter of fact, we are having a most gorgeous time with the Laybournes of the above address, on the western slopes of Llanhenoc, looking on the trees about Llanthewy Rectory, and the full sweep of the mountain beyond. We are driven all over the country; in the Rolls car for the roads, and in the Morris for the lanes.

No doubt the Jones of the catalogue is my cousin. His father was a physician of Finsbury Sq. I had thought his Xtian name was Jacob; but evidently not so. I remember trying to read *Inez* or 'Iquez'[1] — a pamphlet in brown paper wrapper. I never heard of *Hood's Magazine*.

A pity about *Eleusinia* — as you want it.

Would you and your spouse come on Saturday *after next* at the usual hour; I have a trifle for you, a paged proof of 'The Shining Pyramid', to go into a publication of Faber's 'Welsh Stories'.

Our best remembrances to Rainey.[2]

Yours,

Arthur Machen

Would Rainey like to come with you, Saturday sen'night?

Forgot to put in catalogue; will keep it for you.

A.M.

[1] In *Far Off Things* (p. 87) Machen comments on a Welsh relative who composed a five-act heroic blank verse drama entitled *Inez de Castro*.

[2] Tristram Rainey, the poet, illustrator and friend of Gawsworth.

High St.,
Old Amersham,
Bucks.
Dec. 5. '38

Dear Armstrong,

If you can get a *Great Return*, will you send it along with invoice?

On the whole, if poor old Saintsbury can keep going, some portion of my Irving article will survive into his collection.[1] But no MSS; he sent me typescript.

I am booked to write a story for the *Welsh Review*, edited by Glyn Jones — a grave man, who spoke at the Newport Lunch.[2] The first number appears in February next. I haven't heard yet as to the date of the last number.

With our best to you both,
Yours sincerely,

Arthur Machen

Greenwood — you remember him at the pub? — is going filming shortly with Laughton[3] and wife.

[1] H. A. Saintsbury and Cecil Palmer (eds.), *We Saw Him Act* (1939). Machen contributed 'Irving as Don Quixote'.

[2] A civic lunch to celebrate Machen's seventy-fourth birthday had been held at the Westgate Hotel, Newport, in March 1937.

[3] Edwin Greenwood and Charles Laughton played smugglers in Alfred Hitchcock's *Jamaica Inn* (1939).

High St.,
Old Amersham,
Bucks.
Dec. 7. '38

Dear Armstrong,

I am extremely obliged. I wish I could give you the required date for the Astrologer; but I have no notion of the time; therefore, I fear, we shall never know who was the Lord of the Ascendant, or who was afflicted in the Twelfth House!

No hurry about Waite's book.

The other day I wanted three books: Mrs Earle's *Pot Pourri from a Surrey Garden*, Clement Shorter's[1] *Brontë Circle*, and Willa Cather's *One of Ours*. Each in its way is a real book; the Brontë book more especially. I have just heard that all are o. p., and am trying Foyles. But they are books which should not be out of print.

You never met Clement Shorter? He would say: 'Cub id, Bister Bachad, cub id'— and then talk of 'we Scandinavians'. He was very dark for a Scandinavian.

The best to you both.

Yours,

Arthur Machen

P.S. There comes into my mind the notion of a bit of honest work I think I could do, if anyone would pay me for it: *The Week End Dickens*[2] — a series of selections with an introduction. The notion is, not to provide for the man who has little of Dickens, and will only read him in scraps; but rather, for the man who knows and likes him so well that he is unwilling to be wholly destitute of Dickens in trains and by strange bedsides. Sylvia Townsend Warner did something like this five years ago; but she, or more likely her publishers, made the mistake of turning it into a sort of puzzle, by leaving some of the characters' names blank in the text, and filled in at the end of the book: a silly plan.

A.M.

[1]   Clement King Shorter (1857-1926), the journalist, critic and book collector.

[2]   See pp. 129, 132.

High St.,
Old Amersham,
Bucks.
Nov. 9. '39

Dear Armstrong,

What strikes me is that the *Digest*,[1] so far from dying of the Wars should fatten on them. It is a collection of chunks and very well selected chunks; and what can be more suitable for the trenches? And no mistake could be greater to suppose that the army as it is, here and abroad, is on the 'Comic Cuts' level.

The only thing against it is the title, which is Johnsonian, learned and obsolete — that is for the average mass of man. Still, I suppose the title must stand. It is extremely good of you to fish the publishing waters for the Dickens book. I have got the whole scheme of selections ready, and will sent it on to you in a day or two, with the information desired.

I didn't know there had been two shots at the notion. Sylvia Townsend Warner wrote a noble Intro to her *Week End Dickens*: but the mere format of the book, within and without damned it from the beginning. It looked, in binding and on page, exactly like an Educational Textbook. Moreover, it was done on the Snip Principle, instead of on the Chunk Principle.

Well; do let us have that date, as soon as you can manage it.

With our love to you both,
Yours,

Arthur Machen

---

[1]   *The English Digest* was founded by Gawsworth in 1939.

High St.,
Old Amersham,
Bucks.
Feb. 12. '40

Dear Armstrong,

Upon my word: you would have done better if my prophecy had been fulfilled in the letter. A few kicks, a goblet of liquid fire, and a few moral tableaux; not pleasant, perhaps, but better than your actual portion of — Itis, and Pneumonia and Gruel.

I hope you begin to mend seriously. Can't you get 'seconded' for editorial service in grand Cairo, under the sun?

We have had waterbursts, but only on the ground-floor — and that was untenanted at the time.

I note what you say about the Dickens book.[1] If Routledge should want to take it on, it will be necessary to look closely into the agreement. They had a director who called himself Stallibras — *un qui estale les bras* — his real name being Sonnenschein; and the firm may keep up the tradition. Somewhere in 1887, I copied out a Sonnenschein agreement at Redway's request. 'Even *we* may learn something from that', he said humbly, and yet with a touch of dishonest pride about him.

As to *Casanova*.[2] The article consists of the 12 vols of the Casanova's Society edition (as disrupted by the printer), the MS of the translated note, and the MS of my 'Translator's Preface' which runs to 8,500 words, with the first proof of this preface. For this, I should like £20.

Very many thanks; but we have *The New England Nun*;[3] a present, I think, from Goldsmith.[4]

Kidnapped Poets of Great James St.[5] I told you, I think, that I had once visited The Pines — in the post-Swinburnian age. I found Watts-Dunton[6] a feeble, amiable old man. You remember Wilfred Blunt's[7] phrase as to Swinburne's condition, when found: 'He was dying of drunkard's diarrhoea'.

You don't say what your spouse got for keeping Xmas in a Fire Escape. I hope they let her off lightly.

Well, as I say, with others, in the Chorus of the *Agamemnon* . . . rendered in our version

Yet, let the house's tale
How dark so e'er
Show yet an issue fair.

I am sorry to state that it didn't do anything of the kind; but let's hope that you and Mrs Armstrong and all of us may have better luck.

Yours,

Arthur Machen

[1] *A Handy Dickens* was published by Constable in 1941.

[2] Machen's translation of *The Memoirs of Casanova* was first published in 1894 in 12 volumes. He is referring here to the London reprint edition of 1922.

[3] Mary E. Wilkins Freeman, *A New England Nun and Other Stories* (1891). Machen greatly admired the works of the American authoress. See the Appendix to *Hieroglyphics*.

[4] Alfred G. Goldsmith was an American antiquarian bookseller.

[5] Swinburne and Gawsworth; both were red-bearded. This was a proposed article on the two poets by an American journalist.

[6] W. T. Watts-Dunton (1832-1914), the writer and critic who became Swinburne's guardian.

[7] Wilfred Scawen Blunt (1840-1922), the orientalist, poet and champion of nationalistic causes.

High St.,
Old Amersham,
Bucks.
Feb. 17. '40

Dear Armstrong,

Pistols pointed at your head? How would you like machine-gun nests?

I can only say: *Uffern Dan* — which means 'Hell Fire', and is understood to be a word of command in the Welch Regiment. Pronounce: 'Iffairn Dahn'.

I'll see what can be done with *Casanova*; but I am afraid the times are not very hopeful. I am beginning with Rota:[1] could you oblige with 2 or 3 other 'likelies'?

You do that *Digest* extraordinarily well. Big type and little: all very good. Rothenstein[2] commits one curious error: he speaks of Burne Jones as a Socialist. He was, in fact, a Gladstone Liberal, and, as it appears in his Life by Lady B-J, he was most distressed when Morris turned Socialist — anarchist, rather.

There won't be any Maginot Line or any other line — except the writing and editing line — for you.

With our love to you both
Yours,

Arthur Machen

[1]   Bertram Rota (1903–66), the London antiquarian bookseller specializing in modern first editions.

[2]   Sir William Rothenstein (1872–1945), the painter and writer. Gawsworth used some extracts from his memoirs.

High St.,
Old Amersham,
Bucks.
Feb. 25. '40

Dear Summerford [Armstrong],

I hope you are much better by this time; since I am going to bother you. But remember: 'The merciful man is mindful to his bothered, as well as to his beast.'

In the first place: will you address and post the enclosed — if there is a Peter Davies[1] firm still going? If not — put it in the fire or the W.P.B. No don't. There is a cutting enclosed which I should like back.

Secondly: as to the Dickens book. If Routledge doesn't want it, do you think that the other man you mentioned, who does want it, would make an advance now; I to furnish a Preface forthwith?

Tertio: I am in correspondence with Rota as to *Casanova*, and expect to settle one way or another before long.

Again, I hope you are better and that your spouse is well.

Our love to you both,
Yours sincerely,

Arthur Machen

[1]   For Peter Davies, see pp. 107-8. In a letter dated April 1954 Davies wrote: 'I knew him [Machen] quite well and loved him, and think the saddest letter I ever had in my life was the last I had from him, after his wife died . . .'; and later: 'Lucian Taylor [*The Hill of Dreams*] is a very one-sided self-portrait. There's quite a lot of Machen in the amusing Dyson of *The Three Impostors*, "The Inmost Light", etc.'

High St.,
Old Amersham,
Bucks.
March 20. '40

Dear Armstrong,

We are very much relieved to hear that you are all right again. It is true that you are, evidently, very hard at work; a condition that I have always cordially disliked. Still, it is better than pneumonia — I suppose. Do give Shiel my cordial congratulations;[1] I am delighted to hear the news. I suppose that his expedition[2] to Palestine will be delayed by the war. I remember the J.H.V.S. Syndicate, which was looking for the Ark of the Covenant, was held up by the Italo-Turkish War. They knew exactly where to go, being guided by the researches of Javelius, who discovered the cipher of Ezekiel.

I look forward to the promised booklet of verse. (*Mind of Man*)[3]

I should think it would be some time before I hear from Peter Davies! I had no notion he was gone to the Wars — or, most certainly, I would have refrained from troubling him.

Rota is not inclined to be optimistic. Still, as I reminded him, *Casanova* is a constant.

Send you back the Irishman with the thumb of the ready typist.

Yours,

Arthur Machen

---

[1]   Gawsworth was instrumental in getting Shiel's Civil List pension raised.

[2]   To seek the tomb of Jesus.

[3]   *The Mind of Man* (1940).

High St.,
Old Amersham,
Bucks.
Oct. 30. '41

Dear Armstrong,

Somewhere about 60 years ago, or, perhaps, a little more, at this season of the year, I remember hearing my father (who knew such scraps of Welsh as I possess) trying to persuade an old lady (who knew more Welsh than English) that the popular Welsh festival of Oct. 31st, known as *Noscyn à gaia*, should really be pronounced *Nos galan gaeaf*, which means 'the Eve of the Calends of Winter', otherwise, the Night before Winter. The old Welshwoman laughed consumedly, and held his doctrine in profound derision; but I saw a few nights ago a 'Welsh Talk' under the latter heading. It was a noisy discussion, as it appeared, on the celebration, and there were one or two references, derisory, from the eloquent tones of the speakers, to what they did at the feast as kept in 'Scotlahnd'. Nevertheless, and in spite of all, I hope you may keep Hallowe'en cheerfully.

We are both more sorry than I can say to hear your Marlow[1] news. I was grieved at the story you had to tell when you were here; and I am more greatly grieved now. In such a case third parties can do nothing better than be sorry. But it is a good thing that your interests are in capable hands.

But I think the great topic of consolation and hope is: that the game is a long one, and you have only just sat down at the table. I was born in 1863, you in 1912; so I can talk like that. Mark you; I don't say that it is a splendid game; but it has its great moments.

And now for nonsense. Constable is doing wonderful things with *The Handy Dickens*. Sadleir wrote triumphantly some time ago, that in spite of all difficulties, he has secured Ardizzone to do a Title – Frontispiece. I got the proof of this lately. Ardizzone has excelled himself. He has changed the title to *A Handy Dickens*. The design consists of 7 or 8 vignettes, illustrating scenes from the works of Dickens. The designs are not original; they are what I should call rough recollections of Phiz, covered with a pale pink wash. But the point about them is; that not one of them illustrated any passage or scene that occurs in the selection!

I must quote a line from a favourite classic of mine:

'Can Limburger smell worse?'

Yours sincerely,

Arthur Machen

[1]   This is presumably a reference to Gawsworth's *Marlow Hill* (1941). Machen is sympathizing over the break-up of Gawsworth's marriage.

High St.,
Old Amersham,
Bucks.
April 8. '43

Dear Armstrong,

. . . a piece of news. In February, Colin Summerford raised the cry that my eightieth birthday was coming, and sent round the hat. The result was a fund (to which your mother most kindly contributed in your name); a very comfortable cheque, and a Lunch.

Picture: 80 candles on the board, 40 people about it: myself sitting between Lady Benson[1] and Sir Max Beerbohm: Miss Lally[2] chatting to Augustus John: W. W. Jacobs and Stella Gibbons to Mrs Machen. The typescript of my brief oration will be at your disposition.

Hilary has been in Italian hands since last June. One gathers that his state is tedious, but tolerable.

Now, when you write, do make the address most clear, beyond the possibility of error.

Yours sincerely,

Arthur Machen

---

[1]   For Lady Constance Benson, see pp. 101-2.

[2]   In Chapter X of *Things Near and Far* Machen records his encounters with a remarkable unnamed lady who resembled 'Miss Lally', a character in *The Three Impostors* (the 'Novel of the Black Seal'). She was in fact the Bensonian actress Hilda Wauton (1880-1957), who later married Carl Leyel, Frank Benson's secretary, founded a chain of herbal shops and became a successful cookery writer.

High St.,
Old Amersham,
Bucks.
Jan. 18. '45

Dear Armstrong,

There is a letter looking for you somewhere in the world. It excuses a long silence; and it may never find you, so I will recapitulate. I never got really well after my pneumonia experience of a year ago. Late in last autumn, the Dr had to be summoned in a hurry. He said 'tired heart', rest, etc; and so I lounge about in a dressing gown, in a hopeless sort of way. I remember very well that cheerful meeting at the K[ing's] Arms; and I hope that we shall all meet again there, and I hope that there will be something to drink. Of course, all wine has long ago been drunk: but one can often get threepenn'orth of gin or whiskey for three shillings, and a threepenny bottle of bass for 1/-.

I am sorry to hear of your loss of two old friends, Hudson I don't think I ever heard of: Sturge Moore's name I have long known. I think I saw it in Elkin Mathews' and John Lane Lists, before the days of the Bodley Head. I do not really know Max B[eerbohm]. I met him for a few minutes — at Theodore Wratislaw's — in 1899: he kindly supported my application for a Civil List Pension: and he was very pleasant at the '43 lunch. I was pleased to hear gentle applause from him, when I spoke of *Little Women* as 'that delightful book'. I forgot: I have another complaint/excuse. I see very badly. So last night I read *Precious Balms*[1] — because the type is large, clear, with double leads; and I confess it did me some good to find that the *Lady's Pictorial*, in 1894, said *The G[reat] G[od] Pan* was an 'unmanly' book. Lately, I have been reading Maisie Ward's *G. K. Chesterton* — informing, even interesting here and there; but dullish as a whole. Norah Hoult[2] has written a very good novel, *There Were No Windows*, a tragic book, on the last years of Violet Hunt.

Our love and best wishes,

Arthur Machen

---

[1] *Precious Balms* (1924) was a curious compilation by Machen of his 'bad' notices.

[2] For Norah Hoult, see p. 134.

High St.,
Old Amersham,
Bucks.
April 16. '45

Dear Armstrong,

Imprimis: let me tell you that my sight has become very uncertain, and so let me beg you to make your address *splendidior vitro*[1] — clearer than glass. I am sorry to hear that Collins has proved an ingrate. Never mind: when I was about 9 years your senior, I had 4 neat MSS in a drawer, all turned down in various circumstances of disgrace. For example, Allen & Unwin (t. Fisher Unwin) told me that 'Hieroglyphics' seemed to be 'super journalism' — a phrase not intended as a compliment. I think I must have told you that 'Penguin Books' asked me to make a selection of short stories[2] 4 or 5 years ago. The scheme was held up by Hutchinson demanding a fee of £20 for two stories. Now, I understand, Hutch has relented, and the book may go forward. Or it may not. You know the Doctor's couplet: 'Alas, what ills the scholar's life assail'. I often feel it is a great pity that 'publisher' won't scan as a substitute for 'patron' in the second verse.[3]

I saw a very commendatory allusion to your paper on 'The Dowson Legend'[4] in the *Sunday Times* or *Observer* yesterday. I used to hear of him now and again from Jepson[5] — who thought drink had been his ruin.

T'otherday Cyril Clemens (Intern. Mark Twain Society) wrote asking if I had known [Arthur] Symons 'very well'. I told him that I was remarkable for hardly knowing any of the Nineties men at all.

I hope you will be back in October; I hope I shall be here to see; I hope there will be something to drink at the King's Arms.

Our best wishes,
Yours,

Arthur Machen

[1]   Horace, *Odes*, Book III, xiii.

[2]   *Holy Terrors* (1946).

[3]   Samuel Johnson, *The Vanity of Human Wishes* (revised version 1755).

[4]   Gawsworth wrote *The Dowson Legend* (1939) to refute exaggerated slurs on Ernest Dowson's reputation; certain writers had claimed the poet revelled in drunkeness and drug-taking.

[5]   For Edgar Jepson, see p. 240.

High St.,
Old Amersham,
Bucks.
June 12. '45

Dear Armstrong,

Not so much your 'illegible scrawl' as my bad eyesight — a dreadful drawback to life, in all sorts of ways.

I am glad to say that all our long anxieties about Hilary are over. He is returned, somewhat oddly — and very happily — looking better than we have ever seen him, and as cheerful as you please. You would think that tough fighting, his walk through Italy, Italian and German prison camps made up into a famous holiday. He is not sure when he will be out of the army; but since he enlisted in the early summer of '39, I suppose he may hope for an early exit.

Can they give you some apparatus to contain and restrain that sad ankle of yours? The very knowledge that one must walk with great care is apt to lead to nervous and unsteady steps. Do remember us to your brother and his wife; I remember our very pleasant meeting at the King's Arms — how many years ago? Cyril Clemens! You put a note of exclamation. I fully assent. He seems to me to lead an absurd life; and I don't see that there can be much profit in it. And again the note of exclamation: Gerald Gould![1] I once read an article by him demonstrating that Keats was mistaken in supposing the nightingale to be immortal; and thence deducing that Keats had no imagination, but merely fancy.

There was a letter in the *Sunday Times* this week which almost made me snuff the battle from afar, and to remark 'Ha, ha' in the manner of Job's war horse. It was in a correspondence on the curious fact that, till quite lately, Cumberland shepherds counted their sheep by Welsh Numerals. This particular letter was from one Professor Gruffydd, M.P. (of whom I know nothing) relating that his grandmother, (*ob.* 1912) used to recite certain words — Hôn, Thôn, Fedar, Fen — which she called 'Fairy Counting'. The Prof. said absurdly, as I think, that they were of Germanic origin: I reflected that they might have fitted very well into the 'Novel of the Black Seal'. But that was finished 50 years ago.

I have heard no more from 'Penguin Books' about their proposed selection from my tales; but I can wait without much impatience.

I don't think I told you that poor Ben, who used to bring our drinks at the King's Arms, was lost on a bomber in the Mediterranean. He was an excellent fellow.

With all good wishes,
Yours sincerely,

Arthur Machen

---

[1] Gerald Gould (1885–1936), the poet, essayist and critic; assistant editor of the *Daily Herald* 1919–22.

High St.,
Old Amersham,
Bucks.
July 31. '45

Dear Armstrong,

I don't think I know the Goodens: I may have met them some time ago at the King's Arms. I think Mrs G. is right about The Griffin; it is a very pleasant pub: but a long walk for me in these days. There is always something to drink there, and it is always open. whereas the K[ing's] A[rms] is often shut, and when open, it is apt to say: 'no whiskey', 'no bottled beer', and so forth.

It is against such infamies and many others like them, that Britain has risen in its might, and swears it will Nationalize the Bank of England.

I have always wanted to know where Shakespeare got his 'Jack Cade' stuff for *Henry VI, Pt 2*. From *Chronicles*? Or Tradition? There are some very moving appeals put into Jack Cade's mouth:-

'You shall all be free, and I will rule over you.'

'The five-hooped pot shall have ten hoops, and I will make it felony to brew small beer.'

— I quote from a long memory.

Journalists and friends have been working hard to portray Countess Margot.[1] It is odd how all the stuff I have read is a failure. They say 'scintillating', 'sparkling', individual', 'wonderful hostess', 'what wit', etc etc: but nothing comes over. It is an extremely difficult art, this of portrait painting. I often think of odd personalities that I have known — and know that I could not transfer them to the page.

I know a little of the man on whom you are lecturing, Jones,[2] from occasional references in Boswell. He is styled in one piece of contemporary verse, 'Harmonious Jones!' He had what I consider the sensible habit of always propounding to himself a classic model, when he projected a new book. If, for instance, Jones thought of writing on the Governance of India, he would propose as a model, Aristotle on Politics.

Do give our cordial regards to your brother and his wife and may your release come soon. This is what the Lama said to the Cobra: but don't say I called you one.

All the best,
Yours sincerely,

Arthur Machen

[1]   Margot Asquith (1864–1945), the socialite and hostess; wife of Herbert Asquith, Prime Minister 1908–1916. Machen was often mistaken for Asquith, whom he resembled.

[2]   Sir William Jones, the founder of the Royal Asiatic Society of Bengal, Calcutta, where Gawsworth was lecturing on Indian poets writing in English.

High St.,
Old Amersham,
Bucks.
May 3. '46

Dear Armstrong,

I am very glad to hear you are back; and I suppose you are not sorry. And if you have not a roof you have a job,[1] and the latter will provide the former in due time. Tell Aneurin[2] to hurry up.

Will you lunch with us at the Kings Arms on Satdy, May 18 as soon after 12 as you can manage? Go into the little old room which we always frequented: you will find us there, or we will suddenly appear.

I have saved up for you a proof copy in wrapper of the little Penguin book, *Holy Terrors*. I will bring it along.

> All the best,
> Yours sincerely,
>
> Arthur Machen

Let me prepare you, for what the few years have done for me: imperfect copy, many leaves missing, poor condition, binding damaged![3]

[1]   Editing *The Literary Digest*.

[2]   Aneurin Bevan MP, Minister of Housing.

[3]   Machen was now in his eighty-fourth year.

> High St.,
> Old Amersham,
> Bucks.
> Jan. 10. '47

Dear Armstrong,

I am extremely sorry to hear of that pleurisy. It is not dangerous, but I believe extremely painful and distressing, and tiresome in a very high degree. I do hope you will be soon rid of it.

Now for apology. Believe me I am profoundly grateful for all the trouble you have taken on my behalf for these many years past; but I am totally incapable of doing what you wish. I have 'gone off' badly since we met. That was my last visit to the Griffin. About a month ago, I went as far as the K. Arms — and I am only just recovering. I cannot read or write, to any purpose: I am in fact a helpless invalid. But: when you are quite recovered and the airs are milder, if you and your wife will come to tea, you and I will sit in a corner and mutter for a while, and I will try to answer any questions[1] you may put, your voice being directed to my practical ear.

Good luck to your projected edition of your poetry.[2]

> Yours sincerely,
>
> Arthur Machen

1   Gawsworth's biography of Machen was never completed. The manuscript is held by the University of Southern California, Los Angeles.

2   Gawsworth's *Collected Poems* (1948).

John Gawsworth and Arthur Machen (centre) from Thomas Burke's *Will Someone Lead Me to a Pub?* (1936 – drawing by Frederick Carter).

MISCELLANEOUS
CORRESPONDENCE
1887 – 1946

To our trusty and well beloved, Harry Spurr, [1]
Greeting:

We arrived in these delicious solitudes on Saturday last, with minds and bodies somewhat shattered by the horrors of the excursion train; but the mountain air did soon refresh us. On Monday we went for a good long walk to a place called Wentwood Chase and ate our lunch under the greenwood tree. Tomorrow we hope to go to a place called Uske;[2] and propose to undertake several small excursions of the same kind till the time is up. I am devoting to a large extent to the consumption of tobacco and find that amusement more profitable than ever, since the scents of cavendish are mingled with those of meadowsweet and roses and honeysuckle . . . Yesterday I went to the ancient and honourable city of Caerleon-on-Uske, which is, in fact, my birthplace. They had some foolery called a bazaar, into which I allowed myself to be entrapped, and where I was most hideously bored, fussed, and worried. I am going to write to Mr Ruskin to ask his opinion of bazaars.

Well, as you may imagine, there is no news *here* to tell: and I lack wit to invent *matter*. So do remain,

Yours very faithfully
and infernally,

Arthur Machen

---

[1]   Harry Spurr, the publisher and close friend of Machen.

[2]   In *The Chronicle of Clemendy*, published the following year, Machen marvellously describes Usk (pp. 16-17): 'This town lies beside the fair river of the same name, and is sheltered on every side by wooded hills and sweet, greeny slopes; and to the east you can see the enchanted forest of Wentwood . . . But, if you once cross the bridge and get into Uske, you will have plenty to look at without thinking of Wentwood, that is, if you are fond of quaint houses, wild old-fashioned gardens, and odd nooks and corners of every sort. And, better than all, there are old tales and legends still lingering about the sunny streets, and sleeping on the settles next to the fire; but it is getting rather difficult to wake them up now, because you see they are very old.'

[22 July 1887]

Dear Spurr,

   . . . I have certainly had splendid weather, and we have tramped about hill and dale, by mountains and river through this delicious land to our heart's content. We have tasted of the native beverage *cwrw dda*,[1] as also of *seidr*: we have drunk from holy wells and the mountain torrents, we have laughed, sung and joked in a thoroughly Silurian[2] manner. I have read out your letters to Miss Hogg,[3] who approves of them altogether and sends you her kind regards. My pipe is still going at high pressure, and as you say, the local vendors of the lusty cavendish and the bland honeydew begin to look out for investments and adopt conservative views . . . I cordially agree with Mr Ruskin, concerning bazaars. They are as you say, damnable institutions, altogether devilish and filthy, and cannot be regarded except as a preparation for the infernal torments of the Bottomless Pit . . . during my short holiday . . . things have been settled in the pleasantest way possible;[4] the manner of which I will expound to you when we meet . . .

   Well! here's luck and to our merry meeting.

Yours very sincerely,

Arthur Machen
Silurist

---

[1] i.e. 'good beer'.

[2] Gwent was the land of the Silures.

[3] Amelia (Amy) Hogg, Machen's first wife. They married on 31 August 1887. After a long struggle against cancer she died in 1899. Machen exercised an extraordinary silence about her, mentioning her only in the occasional letter and briefly and obliquely in *Things Near and Far*.

[4] Probably a reference to their forthcoming marriage at Broadwater Parish Church, Worthing.

98 Great Russell Street,
London.
[7 October 1887]

My dear Zingaro,[1]

Or wanderer over the Realm of England both on this side sea and beyond seas; your epistle received this morning with much joy. It caused, however, several of those roars which you seem to deprecate. We have been going on pretty well at York Street,[2] and have taken, one way or another, a good deal of money. The new *Lucifer* is just out, and with it an important leaf of mine of *Works of Theosophy and Occult Science*,[3] skilfully faked by hand of the Phoenix. I forget whether the Doom of the Obscure Thing[4] was pronounced before you left; I meant that sudden, terrible and final pronouncement of sentence, where no time is left for pleading, and all perceive the thing is bust.

After November no more Walford, praise the pigs. The High Class Gypsy[5] has been in once or twice; I believe he spends most of his time in that Resort of the Learned Vagabonds, the British Museum, slogging away at his Lives of the Alchemists;[6] to be published by us. I fancy it will be rather a good thing.

Now this is as long a letter as I can write you between breakfast and 10 o'clock, so farewell, and may fair winds waft you to the enchanted Region of York Street. Vale.

Yours very faithfully,

Arthur Machen, Silurist

[1] Harry Spurr. *Zingaro* is the Italian for 'gipsy'.

[2] Machen at this time was cataloguing for the publisher George Redway of York Street, Covent Garden, who was also a second-hand bookseller specializing in works of the occult.

[3] *George Redway's Literary Circular*, a list of books compiled jointly by Machen and A. E. Waite.

[4] A reference to the demise of the literary journal *Walford's Antiquarian*.

[5] A. E. Waite.

[6] *Lives of Alchemystical Philosophers* (George Redway, 1888).

12 Melina Place,
NW8.
July 17th 1923

My dear Spurr,

Many thanks: I am sorry you can't come tomorrow; but that shall be for another near day.

I have been to a doctor at last. His prescription is simple:

Eat nothing that you like.

Drink nothing that you like.

Take an earthquake — in powder form —

twice a week.

Still, it is beginning to do me good.

Yours,

Arthur Machen

12 Melina Place,
NW8.
[24 March 1924]

My dear Spurr,

There are some funny folks in N. Y. City. I will insert your explanation as you suggest. My real emotions were: 'How this rumour would hurt the feelings of the Governors of Pentonville, Wormwood Scrubs, Broadmoor and other excellent and well-managed institutions.'[1]

When do you return? I am awaiting the *Precious Balms* matter from the typist, and have just reminded her about it.

A 'friend' of mine in Chicago, Vincent Starrett,[2] is issuing another private volume[3] of my stuff with Covici-McGee. I just grin; there is nothing else to do.

I hope all prospers well with you.

Yours very sincerely,

Arthur Machen

[1]   In the prospectus for *Precious Balms* Machen compared working for the *Evening News* to prison life.

[2]   Charles Vincent Emerson Starrett (1886-1974), the Chicago journalist and writer, was the first to champion Machen in America with his booklet *Arthur Machen: A Novelist of Ecstasy and Sin* (Chicago: Walter M. Hill, 1918). A leading figure on Chicago's literary scene, Starrett exhumed the reputations of several neglected writers, notably Ambrose Bierce, Stephen Crane and Haldane Macfall, and became a foremost authority on Sherlock Holmes. His pastiche, *The Unique Hamlet* (1920), is one of the most keenly sought Sherlockian titles.

[3]   Starrett's second Machen collection was *The Glorious Mystery* (Chicago: Covici-McGee, 1924). See pp. 231-2.

---

12 Melina Place,
NW8.
Aug. 14. '24

My dear Spurr,

Thank you very much. I hope my business man did not in any way pester you. I told him that I did not want any money now: what I asked him was — how much was due to me on account of P.B. [*Precious Balms*]. I supposed he would find out that by reference to his own memoranda. However, no harm done.

I have told you the terms on which I will sign etc. the 'Arméd Man'.[1] I never change my terms.

With regard to *Eleusinia*: it is for you to consider whether this reprint can be made to pay, say, £100 for each of us. Literary merit, I suppose has little to do with an affair of this kind; but 'E.' is certainly boyish balderdash. I can manage the Introduction all right. I should think a facsimile of the original title would make a more suitable frontispiece than the caricature.

Yours very sincerely,

Arthur Machen

[1]   Machen's 'An Excellent Ballad of the Arméd Man' (1889) was published by John Gawsworth in *The Poetry Review*, January-February 1950.

---

12 Melina Place,
NW8.
[14 December 1927]

Moving, God help! tomorrow, to 28 Loudoun Road, N.W.8.
    My dear Spurr,
    1. Do you happen to know the address of one Keating (I think 'T.F.')[1] of
New York? He is a great Conrad collector. I am doing a job for him, and in the
horror and confusion of this move, his letter has gone astray. If you can send me
the address, it would help me out of a horrid mess.
    2. Will you give me £20 for *The Chronicle of Clemendy* 1st edition?
    You will infer, and rightly, that things are not too well.
                                Yours,

                            Arthur Machen

---

[1]   Actually George T. Keating. Machen wrote a commentary on Conrad's *Victory* for
    A Conrad Memorial Library: The Collection of George T. Keating (New York:
    Doubleday, Doran & Co., 1929).

Northend House,
Northend,
Nr Henley on
Thames.
November 2nd. 1893

Messrs Elkin Mathews & Lane[1]
Dear Sirs,
    I herewith send for your consideration a m.s. story called *The Great God
Pan.*[2]
    If unsuitable, would you be so kind as to return it to me?
                        I remain
                    Yours faithfully,

                    Arthur Machen

36 Great Russell St.,
W.C.
Jan. 20. '94

Messrs Elkin Mathews & John Lane
Dear Sirs,
   About 2 months ago I sent you a m.s., called *The Great God Pan*, which you acknowledged at the time.
   Could you give me any idea as to whether it is likely to prove suitable?
                    I remain
                 Yours faithfully,

                 Arthur Machen

[1]   John Lane (1854–1925) established The Bodley Head with his partner Elkin Mathews in 1887.

[2]   *The Great God Pan and The Inmost Light* was published as Volume V of John Lane's Keynotes Series in December 1894.

36 Great Russell
Street, WC.
February 3rd. 1894

John Lane, Esq.
My dear Sir,
   I am sending you the pieces I mentioned in my last letter.
   They are all pasted into a scrap-book, and I have ticked with red pencil the stories and articles which seem to me most appropriate for the purpose.
   As a possible alternative to some of them, I also send a MS tale (10,000 words) called 'The Inmost Light'.
   I send in the scrap-book a proof of the etching I shewed you the other night. It seems to me a very good one, and I think we should have no difficulty in coming to terms with the artist. Don't you think an etched frontispiece adds

very much to a book: a genuine etching is now a perfect rarity. In the print-shops I see nothing but process work.

I remain
Yours faithfully,

Arthur Machen

P.S. Mrs Machen has hunted in the back numbers of the *Ladies Pictorial* for 'Penelope' but without success. She also consulted the pseudonyms in Hazell, but 'Penelope' is not there!

---

36 Great Russell
Street, WC.
March 8. 1894

John Lane, Esq.
My dear Sir,

I herewith return you the MS of *The Great God Pan*, and *The Inmost Light*.

I have done my utmost to meet the suggestions of your reader, as you will see by the paper enclosed with MS, giving particulars of what I have been able to effect, and of what I have been obliged to leave undone.

Suggestions II and I, which I could not carry out are really cases of 'can't'; I have tried and failed.

The only case of 'won't' is the suggestion to cut out the 1st chapter 'The Experiment' and with it the motive, from *The Great God Pan*. The 'credibility', the whole effect of the story rest on this. If I were writing in the Middle Ages I should need no scientific basis for the reason that in those days the supernatural *per se* was entirely credible. In these days the supernatural *per se* is entirely *in*credible; to believe, we must link our wonders to some scientific or pseudo-scientific fact, or basis, or method. Thus we do not believe in 'ghosts', but in *telepathy*, not in 'witchcraft', but in *hypnotism*. If Mr Stevenson had written his great masterpiece about 1590–1650, Dr Jekyll would have made a compact with the devil; in 1886 Dr Jekyll sends to the Bond Street chemists for some rare drugs.

I trouble you with all this explanation in order that you may see that my refusal to make this demanded change is not a case of common author's irritability, but a question of principle and artistic method.

I remain

Yours faithfully,

Arthur Machen

---

36 Great Russell St.,
W.C.
August 28. 1894

John Lane, Esq.
Dear Mr Lane,

We are leaving town on Friday next. I suppose the m.s. of *The Great God Pan* is all right; I wrote to your firm in the sense you indicated.

May I ask you if in the re-arrangement of your business you are likely to have any vacancy in the editorial department? I should very much like to undertake editorial work, of which I have had a good deal of experience.

I remain

Yours sincerely,

Arthur Machen

---

4 Verulam Buildings,
Gray's Inn, WC.
July 18. 1896

Dear Sir [Paul England],[1]

Thank you very much for your letter of appreciation. The instrument of language is such a delicate thing and is so usually ignored that a man who tries to use it to some purpose has in a general way to be content with his own applause, even if he can get that. It is a pleasure therefore to be assured from outside that something a little curious has been done. I always compare literature to Alchemy; the gold, the ideal book, is never found, but on the way one sometimes discovers rarities.

I should be very glad to see you; we are at home (nearly) every afternoon but would you come on Monday or Tuesday at 4? Let me have a line to say which day would suit you. You need have no scruples as to taking my time; a good talk is never an interruption.

I remain
Yours very truly,

Arthur Machen

[1] For Paul England, see pp. 44–5.

---

5 Cosway Street,
London: N.W.
Feb. 12. 1906

My dear England,

   I think our last letters 'crossed': I wrote you an answer to your last but one, addressing it to the 'School of Expression': I hope you got it. I am glad you have come into your Johnson; it has always been a great favourite of mine. But, like Johnson, I have always been much fond of the Biographical side of literature: I had much rather read gossip about Pope than his verses: And there is something enchanting to me about the black darkness and barbarism that overshadowed the eighteenth century. Think of the life of an obscure man of letters in London over 1725–1750: There is something almost mystic in its dread obscurity and peril and 'unknown-ness'; coupled as these qualities are with the utter spiritual obscurity that had settled on most minds at that time. Read even Smollett (a very clever fellow) on Gothic Architecture *apud Humphry Clinker*[1] — 'tis a curious feast to the philosophic mind. I love in Johnson to come across the scrappy references to unknown poets — Hamilton of Bangour, for instance — of whom I want to learn no more, certainly not to read their poems — calf 12mo probably.

   There is no news of any interest over here that I am aware of. The 'Dream' is coming off in a month or so; and is to be succeeded by 'Measure for Measure'. Some anonymous humorist sent Stuart a bundle of blue pencils! We hear rumours that Garnet[2] is returning with you; is there any truth in these? Leslie Faber[3] is going to read *Omar Khayyam*!, to the accompaniment of a string quartet. Xtopher[4] played over some of the music he has written for this festival:

it struck me as beastly; and I believe I do not differ from Xtopher in this opinion. But what a horrible idea altogether. Leslie, I believe, says that he is to have a theatre of his own in two years time. I have been amusing myself lately by going to the B[ritish] M[useum] where I make researches into the origin of the Holy Grail Legend to gratify a curiosity excited by Waite's ingenious but (I think) mistaken theory on the subject. He is inclined to believe the Legend the cryptic manifesto of the 'Interior Church'; he would love to connect it with Cabalism, the Templars, the Albigenses. Now I am always telling him that nothing good ever comes out of heresy, but he won't believe me. There is one circumstance that puzzles me; I wonder whether you can throw any light on it: the early Celtic writers make the epithet 'glassy' = holy or blessed or 'magic'. Glastonbury is *ynys* written = the glassy isle: a certain book belonging to St Columba is *liber vitreus*: the monastic house on Bardsey Island is *Ty gwitrin* = the glass house, and Merlin in one legend vanishes in a glass boat. What is the idea, I wonder? Is it the *shining brightness* of glass, or its greenish (fairy?) colour, or what? On the general question of the Grail, I am happy to say that I do not think it will be possible to come to any cut or dried conclusion. Nutt[5] and the folklorists have done their worst with it in the worst spirit, but it has eluded them. And I believe our Neo-Buddhists have spoken too!

Were you not amused with our general election? There is going to be fun in the House; not at first, perhaps, but later. As for the clergy and the schools, I cannot pity them. They have had the chance of teaching the Faith — instead of which they have taught Moses in the Lion's den, Daniel in the Bullrushes, and (to the advanced) the one assurements of the Temple and the kings of Israel and Judah!

If you have not read 'The Light Invisible' by Robert Benson: do so quickly — *liber vere mysticus*.

I drink all good things to Garnet in 'Garnet'.

Yours,

Arthur Machen

[1]   Machen wrote an Introduction for an American reprint of *The Expedition of Humphry Clinker* in 1929.

[2]   Garnet Holme was a member of the Benson company from 1896 and a founder member of the 'Rabelaisian Order of Tosspots'; see p. 31.

[3]   Leslie Faber was another Bensonian.

[4]   For Christopher Wilson, see p. 33.

Alfred T. Nutt wrote two studies expounding his theories on the Grail legend. Machen took issue with him and their differences were aired as correspondence in *The Academy* in 1907. The debate was reprinted in *The Glorious Mystery*.

---

6 Cosway Street,
N.W.
Feb. 7. 1910

My dear England,

We were very much grieved to hear from Williams this morning that you have got an attack of appendicitis. W. tells us that yesterday's news was good, and that you will escape an operation; so I hope that they will let you out of hospital before long. But one has so many troubles that it is a little hard to be bothered with the body. I have such excellent health myself, that I am sure I should regard appendicitis as a great impertinence.

I don't know that our news is much. We are so constantly occupied in wondering where next week's income is to come from, that ennui is perpetually banished. I had an interview the other day with old Brammall, the manager of the Britannia, Hoxton. He told me with an air of triumph, that he only got his pantomime past the censor on the day that it was produced. He seemed to think this a notable achievement: it made my liver glow with difficult bile (Horace) as I saw a long perspective of similar follies, leading, I should think, to a tour round Hanwell, Colney Hatch, Bethlehem, Earlswood and Broadmoor.

Did you hear the last of the Belle Kennedy? It is just creeping into the papers. Last Wednesday she called at the D.M. [*Daily Mail*] office, and sent up a note to the Editor to the intent that she was at that moment poisoning herself in the waiting-room. The editor rushed down and found that she had done it — *à la* Mantaline. She is now doing well in hospital. The odd thing is that all this tale got into the American press, and was kept out of the English papers, till this morning.

We are anxious to learn news of Frank.[1] You know, I think, that his neglect of his teeth brought him into a sad state of sickness — milk for ten days — and now I believe he is going to stay with the aunts at Milford and then with the Warners at Harrow. We have just signed the lease of our new flat, and Tom the Cat has been solemnly written into the Deed, so that 'other animal' is legally defined as 'not including a cat'. This is very gratifying.

Other items: a gentleman named Klingender wrote to me to say that he was going to commence publishing and to resurrect 'Hieroglyphics': what would I like to write for him? I told him what I would write, and he told me what he would pay — and on that we parted company. His nature was profoundly Klingenderish.

I have been asked to write for the *English Review* now under the editorship of Austin Harrison (dramatic critic of the *D. Mail*, and literary editor of the *Observer*). I get so many liberal offers that I can hardly believe that my boots are in holes. We were down at Warburton's[2] the other Sunday. He told me that he was playing the Bull in the 'Blue Bird', and shortly after, that one of his lines was, 'You have now exactly 1395 seconds before you in which to choose.' This struck me as most inconsistent in a Bull; and it turned out that he doubled *Time* with the *Bull*.

Well, I hope that you may soon obtain a good deliverance out of hospital and out of the pains of appendicitis.

With all our best wishes
Yours,

Arthur Machen

[1] Frank Hudleston (d. 1927), Machen's brother-in-law.

[2] E. A. Warburton, a Benson actor who toured with the company in America in 1913. After being taken seriously ill there, he returned to England and died the following year.

Edward House,
Lisson Grove,
N.W.
June 20. 1910

My dear England,
Many thanks for your letter; I hope you are making great strides towards a perfect recovery.

I know Exmouth, that is, I know it as a 'Blue Myth' knows it. I have been there twice with Garnet [Holme] and Billy. The first time, I remember, there were great revelries on a place 'the island'; the second time it rained furiously and we had to play in a hall. We were followed by no less a person than Courtice Pounds! Going to Exmouth as a 'myth' I have but vague impressions of the place; it struck me, I think, as a charming and delightful country, but lacking in that touch of wonder and mystery which the Welsh country seems to possess. But this may be the mere prejudice of a Welshman; or if not prejudice, that odd link between the man and his native soil, which certainly exists in some cases.

I think there are reasons why vagrant actors *should* be better than other people in that they are earning their living by doing work which they like. So few people are able to unite work and liking. So it is that very few actors are *accidiosi*; they are free, at all events, from that weary and lethargic boredom which — according to Dante — is a sure passport to hell. But when actors get on well, and get a 'London engagement', I am afraid that they become, very often, ordinary world's people, declining into a sad state of pomposity and respectability, which is dismal to witness.

The *Academy* case[1] gave me one of the most amusing days that I have ever spent. Of course the case should never have been brought into court at all; if I had been on the paper when Horton wrote his famous letter to the *Daily News*, I would have taken the skin off his back in the next week's issue, under some such heading as 'O Thou False Tongue'.

Still, it was great fun: to see how Carson[2] set out to bully and found himself the bullied was as entertaining as can be, and the *obiter dicta* of Darling, J. were excellent. Darling, by the way, in his summing up made a much better speech for the *Academy* than that made by their own counsel, the amiable and feeble Cecil.[3] Of course, a good many of the quips were spoilt in the reporting. Thus:

> *The Judge*: Now Mr Machen, what would you say of John Knox?
> *Mr M*: My lord, I am quite unable to say what I think of John Knox —
> *in this place!*

This was quite mangled.

As for the *Academy* article; it was atrocious in taste and unspeakably silly in argument; its offence was worse than anything of Dr Horton's. But I do not regard Crosland[4] as a responsible human being. Douglas ought to know better.

I would not call *Barnaby Rudge* tedious. It has such excellent things: The Maypole, Dennis, Tappertit, Miggs, Chester, the locksmith, and those scenes in Newgate. Dicken's hatred of Protestantism is, as you say, very singular. It was quite unreasoning, I should think, and may represent a Catholic tradition and sentiment in their last stages. Ruskin, I believe, said of D. that he had the same sort of love for old churches and buildings as has a jackdaw! And this, I should suppose, was a judgement pretty near the mark.

I am going to the Pageant tomorrow for the *Evening News*. I do not dislike this sort of work, though I do not like it. The mischief is that there is not nearly enough of it! I am not at all good at smelling out what is going to happen and then 'suggesting a story'.

I would advise the old mixture of a little gin with that lime juice. Gin does a world of good in the sick room.

Williams was around the other night: Pigeon I have not seen.

Yours,

Arthur Machen

[1] Lord Alfred Douglas brought an action against the Methodist lay-preacher Dr R. F. Horton. Machen had unfavourably reviewed a book by Horton for *The Academy*. Horton, writing in the *Daily News*, accused the periodical of becoming 'an organ of Catholic propaganda'. Douglas, the proprietor and editor of *The Academy*, sued, but lost the case and was forced to sell his paper to meet the costs.

[2] Edward Carson, K.C.

[3] Robert Cecil, K.C.

[4] For T. W. H. Crosland, see pp. 44-5.

Edward House,
Lisson Grove,
N.W.
Monday

My dear England,

'Helen' is not very interesting.

Ruskin is utterly wrong about architecture, because ar[chitecture] is the art of building, not of providing spaces for ornament and sculpture. To judge of a cathedral, I would say one should stand half-a-mile away. Its art is seen in its great proportions, in the relations of choir to nave, both to transepts, these to spire or tower, all to pitch of roof. Judge it as you would a mountain seen from afar, judge it with regard to its bases and foundations and its high peaks. Afterwards, you may view the ornaments and sculptures, as you may esteem flowers and grasses and mosses on the mountain side.

Wretched old fool! He reminds me of 'John Halifax' and 'The Three Musketeers'. I used to ask myself why I had not read those books. Finally, I found them both in theatrical lodgings — and read them. I perceived how right I had been in neglecting them.

See the enclosed. How true it is that a filthy tongue is the index and prophet of a filthy people.[1] The nation that is capable of the beastly word that I have marked, is easily capable of the beastly action in question; I'd 'blasser' them.

Yours,

Arthur Machen

---

[1]   The enclosure has not survived, but it is likely that Machen is indulging his contempt for all things German.

Edward House,
Lisson Grove,
N.W.
Sunday

My dear England,

The poet who loved a gross, gay tale was Tennyson. He did not demand wit; but that quality which is called Rabelaisian. I do think that there is genius in the fabric of 'Charles Auch',[1] but there is folly also to an extent almost miraculous. The author's father was a John's man, and yet she could speak of Cambridge as 'an academe celestial'!

I quite agree with you as to Crabbe, speaking from a very slight acquaintance. He was a luminous man, though his light fell on mean places. I was brought up on Sala's 'Twice Round the Clock', and re-reading after 35 years or so, was astonished to find how good it still tasted. Of course there are terrible phrases. 'Piscatorial Bourse', I think, for Billingsgate, a terrible fount of speech from which the dialect once called 'Telegraphese' flowed; but there was a real core in Sala. He was not a Roman in those days, and in fact, I believe, only became a Roman *in articulo* or pretty near it. He was received by Cardinal Vaughan. 'Silence' I have not read; 'Transformation' I looked into and disliked when I was a boy; but 'The Scarlet Letter': there, in the idiom of that great and friendly people, you have the goods!

Did you see that I have been down to Torquay to watch 'the pictures' being made? I enjoyed myself enormously; I do not know which I liked more; the pine trees in the sunlight on the cliff, looking Italy, or the company of the actors and the 'shop' of the stage. *Canis Reversus*; and I came back to the office feeling homesick. We had a lot of sailing and rowing to do, and when a picture was about to be taken the leading man suddenly said he was very sick, and would have to go ashore. Whereupon the management angrily declared that nothing could be done without 'loyal co-operation'. But how can you rescue a drowning woman, if you are in the pangs of sea sickness? It would not look well.

Drink your absinthe as long as you can at Brighton; London is accursed.

Yours,

Arthur Machen

[1]   Elizabeth Sara Sheppard, *Charles Auchester* (1853)

---

12 Melina Place,
NW8.
Wednesday

My dear England,

Many thanks for your letter. The 'Fragments of Life' certainly cost me the most horrible pains, after the first chapter. I do not know how I ever got it finished. There is a version with a false ending in *Horlick's Magazine*. I remember one oddity which accompanied the writing of the latter portion: my feet felt cold as ice, with a kind of non-natural chill. Which, indeed, I perceived to be the case; for, writing in the kitchen in Cosway Street, I opened the gas oven and lit the gas, proposing to put my feet inside! But on taking off my stockings, I found that by the test of feeling with my hands, the feet were *not* cold at all. This was very odd; it did not seem to me to promise a blessing on the work.

As for the 'Chronicle':[1] the stories, *qua* stories are — really, Mrs Todgers — so very, very bad. But I began the book when I was 22½ and ended it when I was 23½.

On Whitsunday morning I was rolling to St Clement Danes Church, on my way to the North Gallery. I will be with you next Saturday at 1.30.

Yours,

Arthur Machen

[1]   *The Chronicle of Clemendy*.

Lynwood,
Amersham, Bucks.
February 18. 1931

My dear England,

I think that Moore[1] can write very beautiful and delicate English: he is undoubtedly *ingeniosus*. But the *nebulo* is continually spoiling the ingenious one's work, reminding him that fleecy clouds are exactly like the lace on ladies' underclothing; that, owing to the hopeless degradation and vulgarization of the English tongue, the literature of the future must be written in Welsh and Irish; that Anne Brontë was the genius of the family: reminding him, in fine, of a thousand imbecilities. His early second-rate Zola was quite good in its way: 'The Mummer's Wife' is, no doubt, almost a photograph of some particular *Cloches de Corneville* company. I cordially agree with 'Mummer Worship'. I like actors very much indeed: when they are content to be actors. I judge from that amazing Garvin notice, that G. is trying to do his very best for a man he likes, who has written a bad book.

Did you see the 'advance' note about Sylvia's[2] new poem in last Sunday's *Observer*? A good send off.

Tell Marques[3] to buy his 5,8 and dark liver — quite enough to begin with.

Yours,

Arthur Machen

You were saying that I once saw a good deal of Moore: that was as the *Evening News* interviewer.

---

[1] For George Moore, see pp. 136-7. His works were frequently castigated by Machen, who reviewed Moore's *The Brook Kerith* (1916) as 'the pseudo-biblical gibberish of a half-baked Wesleyan'.

[2] For Sylvia Townsend Warner, see p. 124.

[3] Luiz Marques was a Portuguese friend who loved the oddities of the English language. He edited the *Anglo-Portuguese News* in Lisbon, which he sent to Machen. The weekly carried his article about Machen, entitled 'Heaven and Notting Hill', in 1952.

4 Verulam Buildings,
Grays Inn, W.C.
May 21. 1897

Grant Richards,[1] Esq.

Dear Mr Richards,

Thanks very much for your kind letter of the 20th inst.

Now as to your criticism of *Phantasmagoria*:[2] I can only say that very possibly you are right, but I hope not! The MS is 'going the rounds', and I daresay will not find a publisher, or certainly, not for some time. The *Pan* was written at the beginning of '91, and was published at the end of '94! Looking as clearly as I can at this present book, I think there are undoubtedly many and grievous faults in it, but I believe that as a whole it is on a higher level than the former novels, that there are things in it which beat anything I have done (see the comedy of *The Critic!*).

You object to the environment of the beginning; but it is the environment which largely shapes the character: it is these *bacilli* of the village which are largely responsible for the pathological condition of the patient.

The episode you mention is undoubtedly morbid, but it is meant to be morbid, and is, I think, good art. Good policy I am sure, with you, it is not, and I was not in the least surprised when you declined the MS. I should have been much surprised, though very glad, if you had accepted it. You will remember that almost my first remark was that you would probably find it 'impossible'.

I wish you would come and see us here. We are at home nearly every day from 4 p.m. We shall be away for a week from next Monday, but after that you will always find us.

I remain
Yours very truly,

Arthur Machen

---

[1] Grant Richards was the publisher of future Machen works such as *Hieroglyphics* (1902), *The House of Souls* (1906) and *The Hill of Dreams* (1907).

[2] Machen's original title for *The Hill of Dreams*.

Edward House,
Lisson Grove,
N.W.
June 18. 1910

Martin Secker,[1] Esq.

Dear Mr Secker,

I am sorry, but as I told you, *The Secret Glory*, if published at all, will have to fetch that £100 minimum.[2]

But I am not in a hurry! *The Hill of Dreams* was written in 1897, published in 1907.

Please accept my best wishes for a prosperous beginning of your publishing career.

Yours very truly,

Arthur Machen

P.S. I have always been of the opinion that my books have not been properly handled. They should not be put on the market as ordinary 6/- novels, but rather in the style adopted — I think — for *Marius the Epicurean*: blue boards, white backs and a price like 10/6 net.

---

[1]   Martin Secker (1882–1978) became one of the foremost publishers of his day. An admirer of the literature of the 1890s, he entered publishing in the offices of Eveleigh Nash in 1908.

[2]   After a quarter-of-a-century as a writer Machen was evidently determined to reap some benefits from his labours. As he wrote to Colin Summerford on 21 July 1926: 'I was dismally cheated over "The Hill of Dreams", and I never received, and never will receive a single penny for "Hieroglyphics".' Secker did not publish *The Secret Glory* until 1922.

Edward House,
Lisson Grove,
N.W.
Nov. 2. 1915

Dear Mr Secker,

I should be very glad for you to publish *The Secret Glory* on these terms:
£100 in advance of 25% royalty; this £100 to be paid now, on delivery of the manuscript.

The copyright to be leased to you for a period of seven years.

American rights on usual terms.

I will write to Savage;[1] the proprietor of *The Gypsy* on hearing from you. I gave Savage the story for his quarterly; but as the August number is not yet announced, I hardly think that *The Gypsy* need be considered.

Yours,

Arthur Machen

[1]   For Henry Savage, see p. 233. Parts of *The Secret Glory* appeared in *The Gypsy* in 1915 and 1916.

From a letter to an American correspondent: 5 May 1924

As to Starrett, I am sorry, but I am having nothing to do with him. He has turned pirate; both *The Shining Pyramid* and *The Glorious Mystery* are impudent piracies done without my knowledge, approval or consent.[1] I passed over the former of the two offences because Starrett had done a lot for me, but the second crime has tipped up the scales. These affairs are causing me very serious embarrassment in your country. My publisher in New York blames me for not refusing the cheque for *The Shining Pyramid*. I laughed and told him that was an impossibility. I could not refuse the cheque since there was no cheque, and never has been a cheque. If those two books had been brought out by a smart bookseller under the Black Flag, I should have accepted the fact as perfectly natural. But I fail to understand the sort of friend who picks your pocket as he tells you what a fine fellow you are.

Arthur Machen

[1] In defence of Vincent Starrett, it should be noted that Machen had given him *carte blanche* to reprint his old articles and stories in gratitude for Starrett's petitioning of American publishers over *The Secret Glory*. 'Lift whatever you like from the "Academy" and "T.P.'s Weekly",' he wrote to Starrett in January 1918 (*Starrett vs Machen: A Record of Discovery and Correspondence*, Autolycus Press, 1977, p. 40). But Machen was clearly embittered at not receiving a share of the profits from *The Shining Pyramid*, and felt convinced that once again publishers had swindled him; although Michael Murphy, Starrett's literary executor, has stated that neither of the two American collections made money (*op. cit.*, p. 13). In addition, the Starrett titles made unwelcome rivals to Alfred A. Knopf's and Martin Secker's publications. When Starrett visited London in October 1924 a reconciliation between the two writers took place, with Machen commenting: 'About this affair of ours, Starrett. There are three remarks to be made, I think, and I shall make them and then, if you agree, we'll ring down the curtain on that episode. First, it was foolish of me to give you permission to reprint my early things. Second, having done so, it was wrong of me to forget. Third, it was wrong of you to print those things of mine in a book without first submitting to me a table of contents' (*op. cit.*, pp. 17-18). This acknowledgement of faults on both sides is perhaps the most judicious summary of the unhappy conflict.

---

12 Melina Place,
London, N.W.8.
March 23. 1925

Dear Mr Carter,[1]

Very good. I await communication from Elkin Mathews, and will discuss the matter with him.

There are morsels of this quarter, once so delicious, still left. But peculiarly evil flats are rising on every side, and will no doubt continue to rise, till there is nothing left of the old grace of St John's Wood. And where an old house and garden still remain the owners in most cases lop their trees into revolting forms, suggestive of gout!

This is a very bad age in most things, and amongst its evils I reckon the 'garden cities' as the worst.

Yours sincerely,

Arthur Machen

[1] For Frederick Carter, see p. 111. Carter's book of symbolic drawings, *The Dragon of the Alchemists* for which Machen wrote a slightly bewildered Introduction, was published by Elkin Mathews in 1926.

28 Loudoun Road,
London, N.W.8.
Dec. 26. 1927

My dear Savage,[1]

Your letter came on the very Christmas morning: many thanks for your old-fashioned and good wishes. *Blwddyn newydd dda y chwi* - which is to say, a Happy New Year to you.

Indeed; may it be better than the last. '27 has been to us a year of sorrows and fears. Poor Hudleston[2] is dead — a few days after you left England. He had a tremendous liking for you. We miss him most bitterly. I have written a brief biographical note as an Introduction to the English edition of his new book: *Gentleman Johnny Burgoyne*.[3]

Our new house is a minor grief. It is much larger and more 'convenient' in every way than the old; and we loathe it, since it has no mystery in it.

Let your American friend send his book to: Victor Gollancz, 14 Henrietta Street, W.C.2.

I envy you both away down there: beyond the rates and taxes. Here, as it seems to me, there is nothing but trouble.

Remember me to Flanagan.[4] With all good wishes.

Yours,

Arthur Machen

[1] Henry Savage, the poet and author. After the early death of his friend Richard Middleton, Savage persuaded T. Fisher Unwin to publish a series of his works and wrote Middleton's biography. With Middleton and Machen, Savage was a member of the New Bohemians tavern society. He wrote the Introduction to *Arthur Machen: A Bibliography* (Henry Danielson, 1923).

[2] Frank Hudleston. He died in November 1927.

[3] *Gentleman Johnny Burgoyne* was published by Jonathan Cape in 1928.

John Flanagan, an artist friend of Savage. His portrait of Machen hangs in the Reference Library at Newport, Gwent.

---

28 Loudoun Road,
London, N.W.8.
Jan. 26. '28

My dear Savage,

Thank you so much for the Broadway House introduction. I have been waiting to write to you till the matter was concluded, and it is now settled; that I shall do them a treatise to be called 'Sabazius' — the name of the mystic Bacchus. Of course it will be nothing; I have been dead for some time, but I cannot afford to say so. You are alive, and I hope you get on tremendously with your novel.

No news, I think. The usual few at Henekeys on Jan. 7; the usual vain attempts to convince Gow[1] that the ghost neither walks nor talks: Garland[2] calm, watching the case on behalf of the Holy Father. I forget whether I told you that owing to the changes at the *Princess Royal*, we have moved down the road to the *Duke of York*, where the landlord has got in our customary drinks and does his best to oblige.

I hope Flanagan is all right now.

I have been doing one or two articles for the cheerful and engaging Hayter Preston, of the *Referee*.

Yours,

Arthur Machen

P.S. I hear the Life of Crosland is out: price One Guinea.

[1] For David Gow, see p. 48.

[2] Herbert Garland, essayist and one-time secretary of the New Bohemians.

---

28 Loudoun Road,
London, N.W.8.
April 25. 1928

My dear Savage,

We have been away, recovering from a minor influenza, for the last fortnight. I am writing this day to Gollancz, injecting a hint.

I am sorry, indeed, that you have no better news to report. I had a saddish note a few weeks ago from old Waite. I wrote back, miserable enough myself, to the effect that it seemed rather hard; that I thought each of us, in his own way, had tried to do his best for a good many years, that we deserved a happier ending, and so forth. Let me include you in our little list.

As for Caradoc:[1] I passed on your notion, as I told you; but I did not hope for any good result. I have not heard from him for about 4 months.

Yet in spite of all, as I ended to old Waite: 'Yet His Name is the Merciful, the Compassionate.'

Yours,

Arthur Machen

[1]   For Caradoc Evans, see pp. 91-2.

28 Loudoun Road,
London, N.W.8.
Nov. 5. '28

Dear Mr Wilson,[1]

In the first place, please let me say that I thoroughly appreciate the position with respect to the Lectures.

As to the question, whether Philosophy can be of any service to working-men, I think a ruling which covers this question was given on Saturday, July 30th, 1763, by that Chief Justice of Human Intelligence, Samuel Johnson. Johnson and Boswell had taken oars at the Temple Stairs for Greenwich. The question arose whether a knowledge of Greek and Latin was an essential requisite to a good education. Johnson said, 'Most certainly', adding that it was wonderful what a difference learning made even in the common intercourse of life. Boswell said that many people got through the common business of life very well, without any learning.

'*Johnson* "Why, Sir, that may be true in cases where learning cannot possibly be of any use; for instance, this boy rows us as well without learning, as if he could sing the song of Orpheus to the Argonauts, who were the first sailors." He then called to the boy, "What would you give, my lad, to know about the Argonauts?" "Sir" (said the boy) "I would give what I have!" Johnson was very much pleased with his answer, and we gave him double fare.'

And the Doctor added that any man of uncorrupted mind would give what he had for knowledge.

This I take it, is the theoretical truth of the matter. In practice, there must be limitations. For instance, it would be a good thing — in theory — if a Durham miner were able to read *Omar Khayyam* in Persian and the *Mabinogion* in Welsh; but in practice he has no time for the studies involved. There is one study, I think, in which *every one* who has anything to do with the things should engage; and that is Logic, Scholastic Logic. By far the best manual is *Elements of Logic* by Richard Whately. I would have every man in your class go through this book: I think it of the very first consequence.

With all good wishes
Yours sincerely,

Arthur Machen

[1]   Charles Wilson was a schoolteacher in Northumberland.

Lynwood,
Amersham, Bucks.
July 24. 1930

Dear Mr Morrissey,[1]

Pray accept my most grateful thanks for your thesis. Naturally, I have read it with great interest, since every man is interested in his own works & days. And — so far as a man can be a judge in his own cause — it strikes me as fair & judicious. You are quite right, for example, about the ending of 'The Terror': it is muddled and bad. It would have been much better to leave the mystery without explanation. And, as you say, I am no novelist. I do not like to see 'The Hill of Dreams' and 'The Secret Glory' discussed as novels. They are, or they are meant to be, Romances: tales of adventure of the spirit.

By the way: 'Clemendy' derives in no way from the 'Mabinogion'.

I am afraid that the publication of your admirable thesis would not be a profitable adventure. Seven or eight years ago; I think there might have been money in it; but not now. Your country men 'discovered' me at that date or a little earlier; but since then they have firmly replaced the earth on my remains, and trodden it down hard. I judge by the Royalties my American publisher sends me. Over here nobody knows any thing about me. Still, I have found, on the whole, a very great deal of enjoyment in the writing of books.

If you can be troubled, I wish you would send a few photographs of Nashville and Vanderbilt University. And — here is a point of local learning — is there any old English origin discoverable for the Tennessee mountain idiom 'we uns' and 'you uns'? It often happens that what we call *Americanisms* turn out to be ancient English words and phrases, long forgotten in England.

With renewed thanks for your most valued present

I remain

Yours very sincerely,

Arthur Machen

---

[1]   Ralph Grainger Morrissey. His thesis, 'Arthur Machen: A Study' (1930), is in the Vanderbilt University Library.

Lynwood,
High St.,
Amersham, Bucks.
Feb. 24. 1931

Dear Mr Morrissey,

In the first place, please accept my apologies for this long delay. Extenuating circumstances are; poor health, old age, and idleness.

No, I am not contemplating a new book. To the best of my (sorrowful) belief, I have said my say. It is a pity, since I always found writing a book made an excellent burrow: it keeps one warm.

If you had your thesis on hand, say, nine or ten years ago, I would advise publication. But now, to use an inelegant English idiom, I am 'dead mutton' in your country — and in mine. But I have had very good sport in literature. It was the whimsicality inherent in the constitution of the universe that arranged for 'The Bowmen'[1] — not exactly a masterpiece — to be my one popular success.

I see you complain of the torrid summer of 1930. Here, it rained every day from July 15 to August 25. Then, for a week, the thermometer went up to 89°, 90°, 92°, 94°. And then it rained, roughly speaking, for the rest of the year. Now, we are having fine, sunny mornings and night frosts. You, I suppose, are beginning to feel the warmth of spring.

I hope the antique shop is turning out well.

With all good wishes
Yours sincerely,

Arthur Machen

---

[1]   'The Bowmen', Machen's wartime tale which had given rise to the Angels of Mons legend, was published in the *Evening News* on 29 September 1914. Published in book form in August 1915 it became a best-seller. See p. 245.

Lynwood,
High Street,
Amersham, Bucks.
Oct. 14. 1930

Dear Mr Owlett,[1]

Please give Lady Watson[2] my warmest thanks, and tell her that I should be proud indeed to possess the MS of one of his lyrics.

It is dreadful to think that a great English poet should be brought in his old age to such a pass; but this is the age of Greta Garbo and all guttersnipes: not of Poets.

It has been for some time my impression that we are entering on a period of barbarism quite as destructive of God and all goodness as that which followed the ruin of the Roman Empire.

Yours sincerely,

Arthur Machen

1   Frederick Charles Owlett, the author and critic.

2   The wife of Sir William Watson, the poet (1858-1935). Machen and Owlett set up a fund to relieve Watson's poverty.

Lynwood,
Amersham, Bucks.
Jan. 29. '31

Dear Mr Owlett,

I hope my delay in writing may have caused no inconvenience. I am sorry to say I mislaid your address.

To summarize our conversation of last Saturday: I think we agreed that the best way lies between two extremes. To invest the money and dole out miserable quarterly sums by way of relieving a man who may not live to receive more than two instalments is, clearly, out of court. It is a scheme which would only occur to a barbarian — or a man of business. On the other hand, I gathered from you that there were objections against handing over the entire sum forthwith. The middle course suggested was, I think, to pay out, say, £50 or £60 a month for the next six months.

Of course, should any special need or emergency arise, the Committee would have a free hand to meet it. Suppose, for example, that the doctors thought that a stay in Madeira — or anywhere — was advisable: then the Committee should make a special grant forthwith.

That, I believe, was the general trend of our discussion.

Yours sincerely,

Arthur Machen

---

6 Cosway Street,
London, NW.
February 24th 1910

My dear Jepson, [1]

Thanks very much for *No. 19*. I am saying a word in season about it in the *Nation*. I have *not* pointed out that Marks is not a Welsh name, since I know that you harbour an obstinate superstitition on this point.

Scene: Fotheringay Castle

Queen Elizabeth: I will give my virrrgin body to a mann —

Stage Manager: Gaze at *Leicester* on that line: he's the man you mean, you know.

Queen Elizabeth: Maikes it seem a bit warm, don't it? — and begett a race of
(confidentially)   kings etc. etc.

But I have grave fears that on his noble piece the curtain will never rise. The management is a compound of bad record and present imbecility that is in itself a rich entertainment. I would not have it altered, but I am afraid that it is not good for business.

I once met a Colonel years ago. He was Colonel Trotter, I think of the 93rd. His manner was highly offensive and his wife was Evangelical. I trust that both have now come safe to Purgatory fire.

Every night and all as the old Lyke-Wake Dirge says; and that the gross, leaden, and peccant parts of Colonel Trotter (of the 93rd) and of his wife are now being refined away in the Immortal Athanor.

I know nothing of Astrology. I understand that it involves mathematical calculation; therefore I knew that it was not for me. As to my sign: I once heard the Young Man in Spectacles and a person known as Sephariel discussing in my presence whether I was under Libra or Aries:[2] I do not know. Such of their arguments as I understood, struck me as childish and nonsensical in the extremist degree.

I think it quite well that Keep is gone to his own place, both phenomenally and noumenally. Mahatmas have (practically) ceased; but mediums abide for ever . . .

With kindest regards to you both,

Yours,

Arthur Machen

---

[1]   Edgar Jepson (1863–1938), the one-time editor of *Vanity Fair*, was a successful writer of detective and fantasy fiction. He became a close associate of John Gawsworth and was a welcome member of the Machen literary circle. His most enduring works are likely to be his autobiographies, *Memories of a Victorian* (1933) and *Memories of an Edwardian* (1937)

[2]   i.e. W. B. Yeats (the Young Man in Spectacles) and the astrologer W. Gorn Old (Sephariel). Machen was born under Pisces.

Edward House,
Lisson Grove,
London NW.
July 28th. 1910

My dear Jepson,

I am sorry to say that my memory for dates is so scandalous that I doubt whether I can supply the required date.

However, I know when I was born — March 3rd, 1863. I was married to A.H.[1] in 1887; she died in 1899. I married D.P.H.[2] on June 25th, 1903. I fear that this is not precise enough, but I can do no better.

I suppose you are on the point of going out of town. We leave on Tuesday for three weeks; two in Pembrokeshire and one near Esher.

I wish you had a few more editorships at £10 a week to hand on. At the present, affairs are in such a state that the mere English stoicism, however imaginary, is too weak for the occasion. I can only say . . . that the other day I read in the paper that some costermongers can make £1 a day in good times and rarely fall below 10/- a day in bad!

What price sour milk?

England will never be Merry England more till we return to the Catholic Faith, Beef Steaks (with an Onion, if you will), and the Strongest Ale: this last to be consumed in enormous quantities.

Yours,

Arthur Machen

[1]   Amy Hogg.

[2]   Dorothie Purefoy Hudleston.

Lynwood,
High Street,
Amersham, Bucks.
September 15th 1933

My dear Mr Ireland,[1]

I have wondered, now and again, whether I should issue another summons; but I concluded, to use your own phrase, that life was complex; that you had your reasons for silence.

But, let us try anew. Next Tuesday is Amersham Fair; an ancient, noisy, and gaudy business, stretching the whole length of this old street — which has altered little in the last hundred years. Will you come down and look at it, and listen to it? If so, we should be very glad to see you between 6 & 7. There will be a sandwich and a glass of punch. If you come, remember that this house is in the Old Town at the bottom of the hill. Over the door, is the inscription, LYNWOOD, and it is best to knock, not ring.

It is, indeed, hard to deal with the mysteries. Hard, as you and I know, to express them in art; hard even to speak of them. It was St Paul, I think, who heard things which it was not lawful to utter. And, it is to be remembered, that only a hair's breadth divides the mysteries from the blasphemies. That may be seen only too clearly in the pitiable obscenities of *A Glastonbury Romance*.[2] And there is the other confusion: I have known Spiritualists to be styled mystics — wherein they are most vilely miscalled. I have seen a good deal of them in my day, and also of people of a somewhat higher order, who would call themselves occultists; but they are all in utter darkness.

I hope you will come on Tuesday. But if you are for quiet; then we will choose another day.

Yours sincerely,

Arthur Machen

---

[1] John Ireland (1879-1962), the composer, was influenced by Machen's writings. Although English, he possessed a strong affinity with the Celtic spirit. Machen's *The House of Souls* especially appealed to him, its themes mirroring his own intuitive feelings. His *Legend* for Piano and Orchestra, composed in 1933, was dedicated to Machen.

[2] John Cowper Powys, *A Glastonbury Romance* (1932).

High Street,
Old Amersham,
Bucks.   .
September 17th 1941

Dear Dr Ireland,

In the first place: let me congratulate you cordially on being for the present hard at work, and on being stuffed with ideas for the future. What better fortune can a creative artist desire? Even a good and great drink at a happy hour in the right place and in fit company is not so choice a gift as this. I shall await December 29th with most pleasurable anticipation.

To your questions: there is a uniform edition of my books, called the 'Caerleon' Edition,[1] nine volumes of it. I should think it might be had cheaply enough, since it was 'remaindered' years ago. As to separate vols: if these are out of print in the Adelphi edition, I believe they are all right in the original 7/6 editions. Anyhow; why not try for second hand copies at Foyles', Charing Cross Road, London, W.C.2.

As to the man whom you wish to dose with the Silurian Mysteries; I think your plan is right: 1. *Far Off Things* 2. *Things Near and Far* 3. *London Adventure* 4. *Hill of Dreams*. The notion is to interest the desired reader in the author, in the concrete; before you lead him to the author's imagined world. I should always recommend a reading of Mrs Gaskell's *Life of Charlotte Brontë* as a preface to the works of Charlotte Brontë.

All my thanks for your most benevolent and active interest in my books.

Write again soon
Yours,

Arthur Machen

PS. I don't think that any very illuminating survey of my writing has been done.

---

[1] *The Caerleon Edition of the Works of Arthur Machen* was published by Martin Secker in 1923.

Lynwood,
High Street,
Old Amersham,
Bucks.
May 28th 1946

My dear Dr Ireland,

Many thanks for the Rameau.[1] I am reading it with pleasure, though an ignoramus in the great art of music. The Fellows of All Souls at Oxford were formerly required to be *mediocriter musice docti*, to have a moderate skill in music. My standard is very much lower.

Could you get down here on Saturday, June 8th? Beat on our knocker at Noon; and we will go down to the King's Arms and try and get something to eat and drink. We have lived into evil days on both counts.

Yours sincerely,

Arthur Machen

[1] Jean Philippe Rameau (1683-1764) was the leading French composer of his day.

High St.,
Old Amersham,
Bucks.
Feb. 12. '37

Dear Mr Millar,[1]

In reply to your question: there is no biography of me, recent or otherwise. The true story in the *Western Mail* cutting derives ultimately from an extinct paper, *The Outlook*, in which it was inserted by a friend of mine many years ago.

Fytton Armstrong (otherwise John Gawsworth) wrote a life of me, which, for one reason or another, failed to please the publishers.

Thank you for the article on Caradoc; I agree with you that it is temperate and judicious. Caradoc was always a bit of a *farceur*, inclined to caricature. But I am very far from saying that his violent attack is void of foundation.

I should be very much honoured by an honorary degree from the University of Wales. But — a delicate point — I am a man of very narrow means, and I do not think I should be justified in spending my guineas on the cap, gown and hood of the degree.

Yours sincerely,

Arthur Machen

[1]   J. Leslie Millar, a local literary figure in Newport.

High St.,
Old Amersham,
Bucks.
April 19. 1937

Dear Mr Millar,

I am delighted to hear that you are now for all practical purposes fit, well and recovered. As you say, the mere slip of the foot kills the Australian; while you happily survive a mountain whirlwind.

It is extremely kind of you and Mrs Collins to busy yourselves in this matter of the degree; but let me beg of you not to bother and worry yourselves. Don't give the affair more trouble than it deserves.

Here is my sketchy pedigree. My aunt Maria (daughter of Daniel II) just remembered the Old Red Priest,[1] and used to say I was very much like him; especially in a big voice, and a trick of bellowing!

If I were in Australia; it would come upon me to arise, as the Highland song says, and get me back to Henllys!

I don't remember receiving any letters from Monmouthshire folk about my work; with the notable exception of the late Major Addams Williams, Llangibby.

Note: it was *The Great God Pan*, not *The Hill of Dreams* that was translated into French: by the late P. J. Toulet, a literary man of some distinction.

I *think* (I do not know) that *The Bowmen* sold about 80,000 copies. The 2nd edition had several additional tales, & new matter in the Preface: this, I believe, was reprinted till the demand was exhausted.

You have my full authority to make enquiries of the American publishers. I am very misty about these details of editions and so forth.

With our best regards to Mrs Millar and yourself.

Yours sincerely,

Arthur Machen

---

[1]   The Revd Hezekiah Jones. See pp. 180-1.

High St.,
Old Amersham,
Bucks.
Dec. 29. '37

Dear Mr Millar,

Many thanks for your kind letter and good wishes. Pray receive in return our wishes; to you, your wife, and your family for all good fortune and happiness in 1938.

I am sorry to say that poor Waite is not yet himself again. He gets up for a short time every day; but is advised to keep as quiet as possible. When we get into the seventies, injuries do not heal readily; and I think he must be 78.[1]

We are having but sorry weather here, and I suppose it is not much better at Newport. I have a vivid recollection of January 18th, 1881, when there began a snowstorm that went on for 36 hours.

Pray commend us to our Newport friends: Mr Collins, Mr Fletcher, Mr Hando.[2]

I remain
Yours sincerely,

Arthur Machen

---

[1]   Waite reached his eightieth birthday on 2 October 1937.

[2]   W. J. Townsend Collins (1868-1952), the journalist and author; Kyrle Fletcher (1905-69), the bookseller; and Fred J. Hando (1888-1970), the local artist and historian. Machen's Introduction to Hando's *The Pleasant Land of Gwent* (1944) was one of his last literary efforts.

High St.,
Old Amersham,
Bucks.
Dec. 21. '43

Dear Mr Millar,

In the first place; let me wish you and Mrs Millar and all your house a very happy Christmas. Will your sons be at home? I hope they are well.

I think you are all a little harsh to the B.B.C. people responsible for 'The Shining Land'.

Don Quixote is one of the greatest books in the world: but Don Quixote without Sancho Panza would be nothing or next to nothing. And Sancho was a very gross, illiterate, guzzling, swilling and knavish fellow. Compliment poor Davies[1] & myself by calling us a composite Don Quixote: then, that Monmouthshire poacher, who called as a witness 'my sister Blodwen's eldest daughter's young man' may take Sancho's place.

Look at it that way.

Next year, if we live, may we keep Christmas with open lights.

Yours very sincerely,

Arthur Machen — Leolinus Siluriensis[2]

---

[1] W. H. Davies (1871-1940), the 'tramp' poet who was a native of Newport.

[2] This was Machen's pseudonym adopted for *The Anatomy of Tobacco*. Leolinus, the poor scholar, reappears in the Epilogue to *The Chronicle of Clemendy*.

High St.,
Old Amersham,
Bucks.
July 3. '39

Dear Mr Michael,[1]

That cautionary, 'if I can', of mine was lucky. I don't know anything about my own bibliography in any exact sense.

But here are one or two things I think I can correct in the enclosed:

β   Was the 'Fragment of Life' (and 'The White People') published as a separate book in 1906? If so,. I have forgotten. Both tales are included in the collection: *The House of Souls*.

γ   'Confessions of a Literary Man'.[2] This, with a very few very minor alterations, was published under the title of *Far Off Things*.

δ   'The Way to Attain'. A few sheets of my complete translation of *Le Moyen de Parvenir* were printed. Danielson, I believe, had a few sets. The grossness of Béroalde, Canon of Tours (1610) sickened the printers. I rewrote, cut out here, added there; and the result was *Fantastic Tales*.

But if you want to resolve questions of Machen Bibliography, go to the Doctor of that Science, John Gawsworth, 33 Great James Street, London, WC1. If he is not too busy, I am sure he will help you.

I am likely to be more useful over literary questions:

'What did you mean precisely by that?'

'What is the allusion in this?'

And, largely in mere irrelevance, for example; that photograph was taken at Perth, in 1907, when I was playing Sir Daniel Ridgeley in Pinero's, 'His House in Order'.

And again: the Review that gratified me extremely. It was in the old *Westminster*: I forget what book of mine was under notice, but the reviewer said: 'Mr Machen, whom some may remember as an impressive actor,' etc., etc.

I have to break off. I have got your MS list of Additional Titles, and will refer to them when I answer your next letter.

Yours sincerely,

Arthur Machen

---

[1]   David Parry Martin Michael (1910–86), later the headmaster of Newport High School, was collecting material for a Ph.D thesis on Machen; the typescript is held in the Machen archive at Newport Central Library. His study, *Arthur Machen*, was published by the University of Wales Press in the 'Writers of Wales' series in 1971.

[2]   *The Confessions of a Literary Man* was serialized in the *Evening News* from March–July 1915.

High St.,
Old Amersham,
Bucks.
July 23. '39

Dear Mr Michael,

I have annotated the List to the best of my ability. As to *The House of Souls*: this was an 'Omnibus'. It contains: 'A Fragment of Life', 'The White People', 'The Great God Pan', 'The Inmost Light', 'The Three Impostors', 'The Red Hand'.

And as to the stage:

Joined F. R. Benson in 1901 — about a fortnight before the death of Queen Victoria.

Left Benson in June 1901. Was engaged by George Alexander to play a small part in *Paolo & Francesca*. In the meantime: Played in *Pastorals* run by Harcourt Williams and Garnet Holme: the company almost wholly Bensonians. This for 3 weeks.

Played then Comic Irishman in music-hall sketch called *The Just Punishment*, at the 'Hoxton Varieties' and another East End Hall, called, I think, the 'Cambridge'. This for a fortnight.

Then in *The Silent Vengeance*, a melodrama written by Harry Grattan of the Gaiety, run by Charles Terry, a brother of Ellen. This for 6 weeks, on tour.

Then in *The Varsity Belle*, a farcical comedy run by a Mr Parrington. This for 6 weeks, on tour.

Then in an old comedy tour in the West, run by Garnet Holme and a Mr Frost, a business manager for Forbes Robertson and others. This for a fortnight: at the end of which I began rehearsing *Paolo & Francesca* at the St James's Theatre.

Such was my first year on the stage. An outline of later years may follow in a short while.

All my books have appeared in book-form.[1]

Salutations to Mynydd Maen & Twyn Barlwm.

Yours sincerely,

Arthur Machen

---

[1] This is not quite correct. Machen has forgotten about his book *Fleet Street Recollections*, also titled *Fleet Street Diversions and Digressions*, commissioned but not published by Eyre & Spottiswoode in 1927. See p. 176.

High St.,
Old Amersham,
Bucks.
Oct. 13. '39

Dear Mr Michael,

I hope, anyhow, that you and your wife enjoyed your holiday, in spite of the shadows on it, and the troublesome ending. We are in dark days; but the odd thing is that everybody says it is a fine season for books. The theory is that, it being disagreeable and dangerous to go abroad, people are sitting at home and reading hard.

You addressed Armstrong quite correctly. I am sending on one of your Lists to him, by way of reminder, with your address in case he has mislaid it. He really is a busy and distracted man. He edits some 'Digest' or other , and has to glance through One Thousand Books and Papers in One Thousand Minutes every month.

Now to our queries.

A Few Letters[1] were privately printed in Cleveland, Ohio, U.S.A. — I think for some club there.

The Glorious Mystery — a collection of odds and ends of articles and stories, made in America.

Tom O'Bedlam[2] — an essay on the old song, printed in America. I have never seen a copy. The slump of '30, '31 came down on the U.S.A. and the man who commissioned the essay. It was printed, I believe, but nobody sent me a copy.

La Grande Trouvaille was issued by the Ingenious Mr Searle — somewhere about the same date as *Collector's Craft*. I am inclined to think there was a third leaflet from the same source; but my memory of these transitory things is at its vaguest.

Stage Calendar

Spring – Summer, 1902: *Paolo & Francesca* at the St James's.

Autumn 1902 – Spring 1903: *If I Were King* at the St James's.

Spring 1903: Not in production of *Old Heidelberg* at St J's:

Went on Tour with Alexander in that piece & in *If I Were King* in autumn, 1903, and played in *Old Heidelberg* at the St James's till spring of 1904.

April – June 1904. With F. R. Benson at Stratford-on-Avon, and in Public School Tour of an English version of *Agamemnon, Libation Bearers*, and *Furies*.

Autumn, 1904. With Tree Company on Shakespearian Tour.

Autumn, 1905. *Mice and Men* Tour: Smalls & Fit-ups.

Autumn, 1907. *His House in Order* Tour: Smalls & Fit-ups.

Spring, 1909. Farewell — to all intents and purposes — to Stage[3] with the part of the Enchanter in *Henry VI, Part II*. With Benson, at The Coronet, Notting Hill Gate, and at Stratford-on-Avon. Remarkable only for this: — that Shakespeare gives the magician's part simply as: *Conjuro te* etc,. I wrote up 'etc'. to two or three pages of res. So far as I know, I am the only actor who ever wrote his own part in Shakespeare.[4]

It was exactly the farewell to the beloved stage that I should have chosen; especially since, as the theatrical heaven darkened & the stage thunder began to mutter and my cue got near, Lady Benson came behind me and murmured in my ear — after her wholly charming and delightful fashion — a story very remote from the business of the approaching scene.[5]

To conclude all fitly, I sent in my bill for this final performance at Stratford thus:

To summoning Foul Fiend, Aschmoddai (Hebrew Characters); jjs.

To discharging same: jjs.

The business manager told me later that the Auditor of Accounts was a good deal puzzled.

I have told you a long tale.

Yours sincerely,

Arthur Machen

[1]   *A Few Letters from Arthur Machen* (The Rowfant Club, 1932).

[2]   *Tom O'Bedlam and His Song* (Westport, Conn.: The Apellicon Press, 1930).

[3]   Machen's final stage appearance took place in 1928. See p. 117.

[4]   In 1901 Waite had provided him with an incantation for the role which was passed on to his fellow Bensonian Matheson Lang.

[5]   See Aidan Reynolds and William Charlton, *Arthur Machen: A Short Account of His Life and Work* (The Richards Press, 1963), p. 93.

SELECT BIBLIOGRAPHY
The principal works of Arthur Machen

This select bibliography lists the first editions of Arthur Machen's books together with some of his more important pamphlets. London is the place of publication unless otherwise stated. *A Bibliography of Arthur Machen* by Adrian Goldstone and Wesley D. Sweetser (Austin, Texas: University of Texas Press, 1965) provides a comprehensive guide to the various editions of Machen's works and his contributions to periodicals and books by other writers.

Eleusinia. Privately printed: Hereford, 1881

The Anatomy of Tobacco: or Smoking Methodized, Divided, and Considered After a New Fashion. George Redway, 1884

The Literature of Occultism and Archaeology. George Redway, 1885

The Heptameron or Tales and Novels of Marguerite Queen of Navarre [tr.]. Privately printed: The Dryden Press, 1886

A Chapter from the Book called The Ingenious Gentleman Don Quijote de la Mancha which by some mischance has not till now been printed. George Redway, 1887

The Fortunate Lovers: Twenty-Seven Novels of the Queen of Navarre [tr.]. George Redway, 1887

The Chronicle of Clemendy; or, The History of the IX Joyous Journeys. Privately printed: Carbonnek, 1888

Thesaurus Incantatus. The Enchanted Treasure; or, The Spagyric Quest of Beroaldus Cosmopolita, in which is sophically and mystagorically declared The First Matter of the Stone. Privately printed, 1888

The Way to Attain, by François Béroalde de Verville [tr.]. The Dryden Press, 1889

Fantastic Tales or The Way to Attain: A Book full of Pantagruelism [tr.]. Privately printed: Carbonnek, 1890

The Memoirs of Jacques Casanova [tr., 12 vols]. Privately printed, 1894

The Great God Pan and The Inmost Light. John Lane, 1894

The Three Impostors or The Transmutations. John Lane, 1895

Hieroglyphics. Grant Richards, 1902

The House of the Hidden Light, Manifested and Set Forth in Certain Letters Communicated from a Lodge of the Adepts by The High Fratres Filius Aquarum [Arthur Machen] *and Elias Artista* [A. E. Waite]. Privately printed, 1904

The House of Souls. E. Grant Richards, 1906

Dr Stiggins: His Views and Principles. Francis Griffiths, 1906

The Hill of Dreams. E. Grant Richards, 1907

The Bowmen and Other Legends of the War. Simpkin, Marshall, Hamilton, Kent & Co., 1915

The Great Return. The Faith Press, 1915

The Terror: A Fantasy. Duckworth & Co., 1917

War and the Christian Faith. Skeffington & Son, 1918

The Secret Glory. Martin Secker, 1922

Far Off Things. Martin Secker, 1922

Things Near and Far. Martin Secker, 1923

The Caerleon Edition of the Works of Arthur Machen [9 vols]. Martin Secker, 1923

The Grande Trouvaille: A Legend of Pentonville. Privately printed: The First Edition Bookshop, 1923

The Shining Pyramid. Chicago: Covici-McGee, 1923

The Collector's Craft. Privately printed: The First Edition Bookshop, 1923

Strange Roads [includes 'With the Gods in Spring']. The Classic Press, 1923

Dog and Duck. New York: Alfred A. Knopf, 1924. Jonathan Cape, 1924 [as *Dog and Duck: A London Calendar et caetera*]

The London Adventure or The Art of Wandering. Martin Secker, 1924

The Glorious Mystery. Chicago: Covici-McGee, 1924

Precious Balms. Spurr & Swift, 1924

Ornaments in Jade. New York: Alfred A. Knopf, 1924

The Shining Pyramid. Martin Secker, 1924 [trade edition, 1925]

A Preface to Casanova's Escape from the Leads [tr.]. The Casanova Society, 1925

The Canning Wonder. Chatto & Windus, 1925

Dreads and Drolls. Martin Secker, 1926

Notes and Queries. Spurr & Swift, 1926

Tom O'Bedlam and His Song. Westport, Connecticut: The Apellicon Press, 1930

Beneath the Barley: A Note on the Origins of Eleusinia. Privately printed [by John Gawsworth], 1931

In the 'Eighties: A Reminiscence of the Silurist put down by him. Privately printed [by John Gawsworth], 1931

An Introduction to John Gawsworth's 'Above the River'. Privately printed [by John Gawsworth], 1931

A Few Letters from Arthur Machen. Cleveland, Ohio: The Rowfant Club, 1932

The Glitter of the Brook. Dalton, Georgia: Postprandial Press, 1932

The Green Round. Ernest Benn, 1933

Remarks upon Hermodactylus, by Lady Hester Lucy Stanhope [tr.]. Privately
    printed [by John Gawsworth], 1933

The Cosy Room and Other Stories. Rich & Cowan, 1936

The Children of the Pool and Other Stories. Hutchinson & Co., 1936

A Handy Dickens [ed.]. Constable & Co., 1941

Holy Terrors. Penguin, 1946

Tales of Horror and the Supernatural. New York: Alfred A. Knopf, 1948. The
    Richards Press, 1949

Bridles and Spurs. Cleveland, Ohio: The Rowfant Club, 1951

*A.L.S.: An Unimportant Exchange of Letters Between Arthur Machen and
    J. H. Stewart, Jr*. Wichita, Kansas: The Printing House at the Sign of the
    Four Ducks, 1956

A Note on Poetry. Wichita, Kansas: The Four Ducks Press, 1959

From The London Evening News. Wichita, Kansas: The Four Ducks Press, 1959

Starrett vs Machen: A Record of Discovery and Correspondence [ed. by Michael
    Murphy]. St Louis, Missouri: Autolycus Press, 1977

Guinevere and Lancelot and Others. Newport News, Virginia: The Purple Mouth
    Press, 1986

The Collected Arthur Machen. Duckworth & Co., 1988

For further reading

A wealth of published material concerning Arthur Machen exists. A list of titles
containing references to Machen or his works exceeds twelve pages in the
Goldstone and Sweetser *Bibliography*, while a further six pages are devoted to
articles in periodicals. The books cited on the following page include the
principal biographical and critical studies published to date.

Danielson, Henry, *Arthur Machen: A Bibliography*, with Notes, Biographical
    and Critical, by Arthur Machen. London: Henry Danielson, 1923. New
    York: Haskell House Publishers, 1970

Gekle, William Francis, *Arthur Machen: Weaver of Fantasy*. Millbrook, New
    York: Round Table Press, 1949

Gilbert, R. A., *A. E. Waite: Magician of Many Parts*. Wellingborough, Northants: Crucible, 1987

Goldstone, Adrian and Wesley D. Sweetser, *A Bibliography of Arthur Machen*. Humanities Research Center Bibliographical series, No. 2. Austin, Texas: University of Texas Press, 1965. New York: Haskell House Publishers, 1973

Michael, D. P. M., *Arthur Machen*. Writers of Wales series. Cardiff: University of Wales Press, 1971

Reynolds, Aidan and William Charlton, *Arthur Machen: A Short Account of His Life and Work*. London: The Richards Press, 1963. London: Caermaen Books, 1988

Sewell, Father Brocard [ed.], *Arthur Machen: Memories and Impressions*. Llandeilo: St Albert's Press, 1960. Articles reprinted from the *Aylesford Review*, Vol. II, No. 8, Winter 1959–60

Starrett, Vincent, *Arthur Machen: A Novelist of Ecstasy and Sin*. Chicago: Walter M. Hill, 1918. Reprinted in *Buried Caesars: Essays in Literary Appreciation*. Chicago: Covici-McGee, 1923

Sweetser, Wesley D., *Arthur Machen*. Twayne's English Authors Series, No. 8. New York: Twayne Publishers, 1964

Waite, A. E., *Shadows of Life and Thought: A Retrospective Review in the Form of Memoirs*. London: Selwyn and Blount, 1938